# The Future of Britain and Europe

The Policy Studies Institute (PSI) is one of Europe's leading independent research organisations undertaking studies of economic, industrial and social policy, and the workings of political institutions.

PSI is a registered charity, run on a non-profit basis, and is not associated with any political party, pressure group or commercial interest.

PSI attaches great importance to covering a wide range of subject areas with its multi-disciplinary approach. The Institute's researchers are organised in groups which currently cover the following programmes:

*Crime, Justice and Youth Studies – Employment and Society – Ethnic Equality and Diversity – European Industrial Development – Family Finances – Information and Citizenship – Information and Cultural Studies – Social Care and Health Studies – Work, Benefits and Social Participation*

Information about the work of PSI and a catalogue of available books can be obtained from:

External Relations Department, PSI
100 Park Village East, London NW1 3SR

# The Future of
# Britain and Europe

*Jim Northcott*

POLICY STUDIES INSTITUTE, LONDON

PUBLISHING

The publishing imprint of the independent
POLICY STUDIES INSTITUTE
100 Park Village East, London NW1 3SR
Telephone: 0171-468 0468; Fax: 0171-388 0914

ISBN 0 85374 645 1

PSI Research Report 776

A CIP catalogue record of this book is available from the British Library.

1 2 3 4 5 6 7 8 9

PSI publications are available from
BEBC Distribution Ltd.
P O Box 1496, Poole Dorset, BH12 3YD

Books will normally be despatched within 24 hours. Cheques should be made payable to BEBC Distribution Ltd.

Credit card and telephone/fax orders may be placed on the following freephone numbers:

FREEPHONE: 0800 262260

FREEFAX: 0800 262266

Booktrade Representation (UK & Eire):
Broadcast Books
24 De Montfort Road, London SW16 1LZ
Telephone: 0181 677 5129

PSI subscriptions are available from PSI's subscription agent
Carfax Publishing Company Ltd.
P O Box 25, Abingdon, Oxford OX14 3UE.

Printed and bound by Bourne Press Limited, Bournemouth.

# Contents

## Charts and Maps

# Acknowledgements

This book was written by one person, but it is based on the work and ideas of many.

It has followed from PSI's *Britain in 2010* project, and accordingly owes much to all those who contributed to that exercise: to the multidisciplinary PSI team who worked on the project, to the many people outside PSI who also took part, and to the organisations which provided the funding and served on the *Participants' Committee*.

It has also benefited from the work of the Forward Studies Unit of the Commission of the European Communities and its 12-nation `shaping factors' project; from the statistical material provided by *Eurostat*; from help with demographic projections by David Berdy of *Marti Oliver Associates*; and from the macroeconomic projections prepared for *Britain in 2010* by Terry Barker of *Cambridge Econometrics*.

While much of the report has been based on PSI's own research, extensive use has also been made of the reports, papers and articles of many other individuals and organisations in Britain and abroad, which are listed in the references section at the back. Their contribution has been indispensible.

Many people at PSI have given useful help, and a special debt of gratitude is owed to Ian Christie who has drawn freely on his exceptional range of knowledge and interests to provide ideas and suggestions at the beginning, numerous specific comments for improving the drafts, and invaluable encouragement and support throughout.

Finally, it is a pleasure to put on record the contribution of the three sponsors - *GEC, IBM* and *Unilever* - whose funding enabled the project to be undertaken, and also the support from *Pilkington*.

While the help from all these quarters has been most valuable and is much apreciated, it should not be supposed that the selection of the information reported or the inferences or conclusions drawn from it reflect their views.

Sponsors
      The General Electric Company plc
      IBM United Kingdom
      Unilever

# 1 Introduction

How is Europe likely to develop in the decades ahead? And what part is Britain likely to play in the evolution and expansion of the European Union?

In Britain much of the recent discussion of the future of Europe has been in terms of day-to-day events: decisions at European summit meetings, votes in national referenda, majorities in the House of Commons. These events can be important, and can sometimes abruptly upset previous expectations. They can also give a misleading impression of the way Europe is likely to evolve in the decades ahead. An alternative approach is to examine likely *longer-term* developments in Britain, other European countries, and the world beyond, and consider how these may produce underlying pressures which influence the future shape of Europe.

In 1991 PSI published *Britain in 2010*[1], the result of a major project in which the Institute's researchers in a range of different subject areas joined together to provide a systematic, overall forward view of likely developments in Britain and the rest of the world over the coming two decades. This report was the catalyst which led to the Commission of the European Communities setting up projects in each of the countries of the European Union to undertake similar exercises from their differing national perspectives. The results were published in 1993 in *The European Challenges Post-1992: Shaping Factors, Shaping Actors*[2]. There were also separate reports setting out future-shaping factors as seen from the national perspective of each of the twelve member countries of the European Union[3,4,5,6,7,8,9,10,11,12,13,14].

This book goes on from there, re-examining the findings of the PSI study on longer-term factors likely to be important in shaping the future of Britain, and comparing them with the factors likely to be important in other European countries - from the perspective of whether they will tend to bring the countries of Europe closer together, or the reverse. It

1

then goes on to consider the possible implications of these factors on the future shape of the European Union and on whether Britain's place will be central, peripheral or outside altogether.

The six chapters of Part I examine likely longer-term developments in Britain and other EU countries. The five chapters of Part II bring together the findings of Part I, show how these will affect the future shape of the European Union, and outline the options open to Britain in the light of this.

Chapter 2 looks at the longer-term security issues for Europe in the post-Cold War world: new kinds of nuclear risks, the remaining threat of external attack, the new problem of active conflicts within Europe, the future peace-keeping role in the wider world, and the possibility of a substantial 'peace dividend' - and their implications for closer European defence co-operation and for the enlargement of the Union.

Chapter 3 considers the continuing gap between the countries of the North and those of the South, future food and resource problems arising out of population growth, aid and other needs of the developing countries, and the prospect of increasing immigration pressures - and the European response to these issues.

Chapter 4 looks at expected future demographic and social changes in Britain and other European countries: of the impact of fewer young people and more elderly and very old people, of rising divorce rates and more one-parent families, of changes in income distribution and the growth of an underclass - and the responses being made in different European countries to these developments.

Chapter 5 examines environmental developments: changes in towns and countryside, problems of transport and waste management and of air and water pollution, and also the global issues of biodiversity, ozone depletion and global climate change - and the joint European initiatives taken in response to these challenges.

Chapter 6 considers future changes in numbers and types of jobs and the implications for education and training, changes in the size and characteristics of the future labour force, and the factors likely to influence future levels of unemployment - and the national and European policies for dealing with these issues.

Chapter 7 examines the past performance and future prospects of the economy in Britain and other European countries, in the context of the emerging global market system. It considers the development of the Single European Market and other European economic policy developments.

Chapter 8 brings together the key findings from the six broad subject areas covered by the previous chapters to weigh up the implications for the future of Europe of the main long-term shaping factors identified.

Chapter 9 examines further the far-reaching implications of European Monetary Union; chapter 10 reviews the no less far-reaching implications of enlargement; and chapter 11 outlines the likely future shape of Europe in the light of these longer-term underlying forces.

Finally, chapter 12 considers the future of Britain in relation to the European Union. Given the way that Europe seems likely to develop, is Britain likely to be at the heart of it, on the periphery, or outside it altogether? There are a number of important ways in which Britain is different from most of the other member countries of the European Union. Will these differences prove sufficiently vital for Britain to feel unable to go along with the developments favoured by other members, and feel forced to keep apart? Or will Britain, despite these differences, conclude that the balance of advantage lies with joining in these developments and becoming an integral part of the new Europe that is emerging?

This book is in a sense a supplement to PSI's *Britain in 2010* report, reviewing the longer-term issues from a European perspective so as to provide a context for the European choices which will need to be made by Britain in 1996 and after.

In order to keep the book to a readable length, much of the material has had to be compressed. It is rather like the 'tip of the iceberg', showing only a small part of the material involved. However, a list of references (identified by index numbers in the text) is given at the back to provide further information on many of the issues discussed.

# Part I

# Forces for Change in Britain and Europe

What are the longer-term developments which will have most impact on the future of Britain? How far are similar forces at work in the other countries of the European Union? What will be their impact on the future shape of the Union? In particular, are the longer-term forces at work likely to draw the members together in a closer kind of union - or will they point towards some looser kind of association? And are they likely to favour a wider union, with more new members - or to make it difficult to expand beyond the present membership?

The following six chapters examine six areas identified as likely to be of particular importance in the longer-term future of Britain: security after the end of the Cold War, the repercussions of developments in the Third World, population and social changes, environmental issues, employment, and the economy. In each area they consider likely developments in Britain and the extent to which similar developments are likely in other EU countries; and the policy issues which will arise, and whether they will best be dealt with by each country separately, or will need measures undertaken jointly by the European Union as a whole.

# 2 Security

The ending of the Cold War has fundamentally changed the security situation facing the countries of Europe. The emphasis will shift away from the threat of invasion from the East towards the need for capabilities for peace-keeping within Europe and farther afield, and for controlling the spread of nuclear and conventional weapons. Reduced American involvement in Europe, the rising cost of high-tech weapons systems, the need for effective response to conflicts in Eastern Europe, and the advantage of a joint position in arms-control negotiations will all generate pressures tending to bring the countries of Western Europe closer together. At the same time, the security concerns of countries in Eastern Europe will add to pressures from them to be allowed to join the European Union.

## End of the Cold War

In less than half a decade from 1985, Mikhael Gorbachev's policies of *glasnost* and *perestroika* led to:

- the ending of the Warsaw Pact;

- the independence of the former 'satellite' countries in Eastern Europe and the reunification of Germany;

- the break-up of the Soviet Union;

- the collapse of Communism in Russia itself and in most of the other countries in the former Soviet bloc; and

- substantial immediate reductions in both nuclear and conventional forces, with further large reductions agreed in the future.

Thus the threat of a massive invasion which hung over Western Europe for four decades has finally been removed. The ideological drive behind the Cold War is dead, and the present Russian Government is not hostile to the West. But how secure are the changes? Could Russia again become a threat in the future?

Russia's shift towards a market-based economy has been undertaken in the absence of a suitable managerial or institutional infrastructure, or of Western aid, trade or investment on the scale expected, and has resulted in much disruption and a fall in total output of 43 per cent between 1990 and 1994[15]. This has been associated with increasing corruption and organised crime, rising unemployment, widening inequalities and, for most people, real income falling further from an already low base. In consequence there has been much hardship and increasing disillusion with the changes.

In 1991 and 1993 there were attempted coups aiming to overthrow reformist governments and in the parliamentary elections in 1993 there was considerable support for conservative communists, extreme nationalists and others opposed to the changes. The military, the KGB, and other conservative institutions have recovered some of their former influence, and a consensus is growing around the ideas that internally the pace of change should be moderated, and externally Russia, as a `great power', should be more assertive in pursuit of its national interests [16].

The new Russian nationalism is concerned to preserve the integrity of the Russian Federation itself, but also assumes that Russia should have a `special role' in the `near abroad' - the other republics of the former Soviet Union. There is particular concern - right across the spectrum of political factions - to uphold the interests of the Russian minorities in these neighbouring countries. Altogether there are estimated to be about 25 million ethnic Russians in the `near abroad', and they comprise more than 20 per cent of the population in Ukraine and Kyrgyzstan and more than 30 per cent in Latvia, Estonia and Kazakhstan[17]. Already the Russians have undertaken military operations in Chechenya within Russia and in a number of the other republics, and the need to protect the rights of Russian minorities may well be given as grounds for further interventions in the future.

It seems likely that in the future Russia and some of the CIS republics will see mutual advantage in coming closer together again in an economic union - much as countries in Western Europe have done.

# Cold War
# 1985

| | |
|---|---|
| NATO Countries | Warsaw Pact Countries |

*Powerful Soviet forces confront NATO face to face in Germany. Soviet and Warsaw Pact armies outnumber and outgun NATO in Europe.*
*Red Army tanks and bombers within 200 km of Bonn, within 600 km of Paris.*
*Iron Curtain, confrontation, tensions, capability for sudden massive attack on Western Europe.*

# Post Cold War
# 1995

| | NATO | | Russia |
| --- | --- | --- | --- |
| | Countries | | |

*Major Russian and NATO force reductions in Europe, Warsaw Pact disbanded, Soviet Union broken up.*
*Former satellites now democracies, forming neutral block separating Russia from Western Europe, with armies likely to resist, not assist, any Russian attack.*
*Red Army now 1,000 km further east.*
*Open borders, friendly relations, economic assistance, no possibility for invasion of Western Europe.*

And it also seems likely that Russian political influence will remain strong in most of the CIS republics, and may on occasion involve military intervention - anywhere on the spectrum from commendable peace-keeping to deplorable imperialism.

But worrying as some developments in Russia may be - not least to the Russians themselves - they do not add up to the likelihood of Russia becoming again a military threat to Western Europe. The strong balance of probability remains that the Russian economy will improve, the new democratic institutions will be preserved and strengthened, and external policy, even if more assertive, will not become fundamentally hostile to the West.

But be this as it may, defence policies have to take account of worst-case scenarios. Suppose at some stage the military or an extreme nationalist, such as Zhirinovsky, came to power, could Russia once again pose a mortal threat to Western Europe? The key consideration is that the balance of military power has shifted fundamentally and irreversibly:

- The Warsaw Pact no longer exists, and Russia's former allies are now pro-Western and seeking to join NATO;

- The Soviet Union itself no longer exists, and many of the break-away republics have unresolved disputes with Russia;

- The Russian Federation itself, representing less than half of the former Soviet bloc, faces separatist problems in some regions and has to guard against further break-up;

- The Russian economy is weak, particularly in key new technologies, and the defence industries have been drastically run down - in 1992 more than 600,000 industrial workers and 200,000 R&D workers left the sector, and defence industry output fell to a quarter of the 1988 level[18];

- The Red Army is less than half the size it was in 1988, and is being cut further to less than a third of its 1988 size[16].

- Any attempted invasion would be faced by insurmountable logistical problems - a few years ago the Red Army in East Germany was more than 300,000 strong and was only 200 km from Bonn and 600 km from Paris; now it is 1,000 km farther away, and separated from Western Europe by Ukraine, Belarus, the Baltic states and a belt of pro-Western former satellite countries.

Thus the 1990 NATO summit agreed that the Soviet Union should no longer be seen as an adversary[19] and the 1993 defence white paper[20] acknowledged:

> The effectiveness of the former Soviet armed forces has declined dramatically ... offensive capability has dramatically reduced ... A major external threat - that is, one of Cold War dimensions - is therefore ... unlikely to re-emerge in the foreseeable future.

## New threats to security

However, the removal of the main threat to Western Europe does not mean that no security problems remain. The collapse of the Soviet empire has brought liberation to the nations of Eastern Europe and advances in human rights and democratic institutions to the people of Russia. However, it has also brought a dangerous instability to parts of Eastern Europe and some of the republics of the former Soviet Union. The ending of Soviet domination and the constraints of the Cold War have released an upsurge of nationalism giving rise to repression of minorities and disputes with neighbours which have led to serious tensions in many areas and the outbreak of armed conflicts in Croatia, Bosnia, Moldova, Georgia, Armenia, Azerbaijan and Tajikistan. And within the Russian Federation itself the conflict between Russian nationalism and the aspirations of the many ethnic minorities has brought tensions and, in Chechenya, actual war.

Also, there remain various other causes of potential conflict around the world, some previously accentuated by the two superpowers' preoccupation with the Cold War, others suppressed by it - nationalism, religion, dictatorships and disputes over territory and resources. Since the end of the Second World War there have been more than 150 wars around the world, resulting in more than 23 million deaths[21], many of them arising from causes not primarily associated with the Cold War. There has also been an upsurge in international terrorism by extremist political and religious groups, which could claim far more than the present thousand casualties a year if they get access to weapons of mass destruction.

In the new world situation over the coming decades the countries of Europe are likely to have four main security needs:

1. Avoidance of nuclear conflicts as a result of misjudgement or proliferation;

2. Defence against external attack;

3. Containment of conflicts within Europe; and

4. Contribution to resolution of conflicts in the rest of the world.

## Nuclear risks

The ending of the Cold War has removed the threat of all-out nuclear war between the two superpowers leading, perhaps, to the extermination of humanity; and it has also made possible considerable progress in nuclear disarmament. The START (Strategic Arms Reduction Treaties) have involved the Russians accepting a 95 per cent reduction in the number of warheads in land-based intercontinental missiles, and smaller reductions in the number of submarine and bomber-based strategic weapons. The treaties provide for the reductions to be completed by 2003, but at a summit meeting in 1994 it was agreed to start the dismantling as soon as the START II treaty is ratified[22].

Intermediate-range missiles have been withdrawn under previous agreements, and there has also been a general withdrawal of tactical nuclear weapons. Finally, there have also been agreements to ban chemical and biological weapons.

However, the previous `overkill factor' was so great that, even when the planned cuts are completed, the remaining stockpile of 3,500 nuclear warheads in Russian hands will represent more than a hundred times

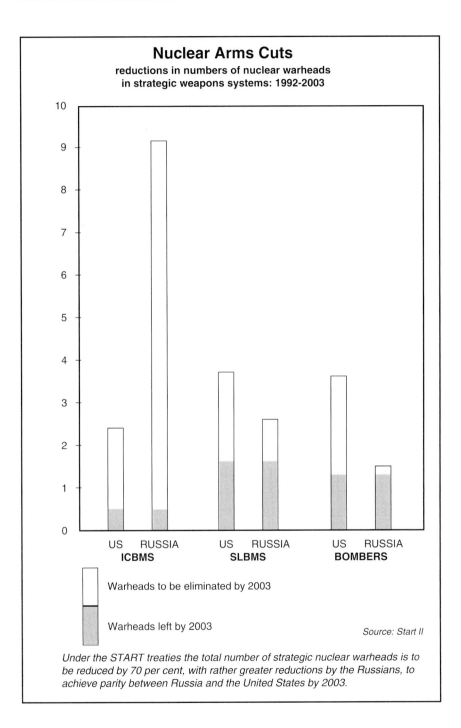

# Nuclear Arms Cuts
**reductions in numbers of nuclear warheads
in strategic weapons systems: 1992-2003**

Warheads to be eliminated by 2003

Warheads left by 2003

Source: Start II

*Under the START treaties the total number of strategic nuclear warheads is to
be reduced by 70 per cent, with rather greater reductions by the Russians, to
achieve parity between Russia and the United States by 2003.*

the total explosive power of all the munitions used in the Second World War[21,23]. The continued existence of nuclear capability on this scale in an unstable Russian Federation poses a number of risks.

First, there is the risk of 'catastrophe by accident'. Great efforts have been made to devise systems to avoid risk of nuclear weapons being discharged by accident, but there are formidable difficulties in providing foolproof safety while still preserving capacity for rapid response to attack. Already during the Cold War, it is now becoming clear, that there were a number of occasions when disaster nearly occurred due to errors of judgement (as in the Cuba missiles crisis), misinterpretation of intentions (as in a NATO exercise in 1993) aircraft crashes, computer malfunctions and other systems errors[24,25]. With greatly reduced East-West tensions the risk of this in the future should be less; but with greatly reduced efficiency and stability in Russia the risk may in the future be *greater*.

Second, there remain serious unresolved disputes between Russia and some of its neighbours, which could end in war; and the major political divisions within the Russian Federation could end in civil war. Either kind of conflict could bring the possibility of the nuclear weapons in the remaining stockpile being used.

Third, the break-up of the Soviet Union produced 'instant proliferation' in the sense that Ukraine, Belorus and Khazakhstan overnight became additional nuclear powers. At the time of the break-up it is estimated that there were more than 2,800 Soviet strategic warheads and more than 5,000 tactical warheads outside Russia[26]. However, it is believed that all tactical nuclear weapons have already been returned to Russia and, after a succession of delays, it appears that all the strategic missile systems have been returned or dismantled also.

However, the fourth risk arising from Soviet instability - that weapons material and delivery systems will find their way into the hands of other countries seeking a nuclear capability - is serious and growing. The presence of hundreds-of-tons of surplus plutonium, thousands of surplus nuclear warheads, and thousands of unemployed weapons specialists in a country with incomplete control over any of them, and organised crime taking an interest in all of them, poses a global security problem. Already a number of illicit shipments of weapons-grade plutonium have been intercepted in Germany[27] and a clandestine market has grown up also in `red mercury' which it is claimed can be used to make much more compact nuclear weapons[28].

The risk of a general spread of nuclear weapons to additional countries is a less immediate problem than the huge existing stockpiles of the nuclear superpowers, but in the longer term it could bring disaster - if a nuclear capability is acquired by more and more powers, some of them with autocratic and erratic régimes and bitter disputes with neighbours, it will be only a matter of time before the weapons are used.

The risk of proliferation is more than hypothetical. In addition to the secondary nuclear powers, Britain, France and China, it is believed that Israel, India and Pakistan have already developed nuclear weapons systems, North Korea may have done so[29], and Iraq would have succeeded in doing so within two or three years[30] - bringing a very different sort of Gulf War if the invasion of Kuwait had been deferred until they were ready for use.

While South Africa has dismantled its nuclear weapons and Brazil and Argentina have given up their weapons programmes, most industrialised countries have the potential to develop nuclear weapons, but have not so far had the inclination to do so, while several developing countries have had the intention to do so, but not yet the means; and the CIA has estimated that 15 developing countries may be producing ballistic missiles by the end of the century[31].

The solution to the Russian stockpile risk is widely seen to lie in further rounds of major nuclear disarmament, concluding, perhaps, in a programme leading to complete nuclear disarmament over a 15-year period, as proposed originally by Gorbachev in 1986[25]. The solution to the proliferation risk is widely seen to lie in the tightening of existing anti-proliferation arrangements, with stronger inspection rights for the International Atomic Energy Authority, a comprehensive nuclear test ban, and a stop to the reprocessing of nuclear waste to produce plutonium for a new generation of 'fast-breeder' nuclear reactors [32,33].

These issues came together in the negotiations for the renewal of the 1970 Nuclear Non-Proliferation treaty in 1995. During several weeks of argument, the non-nuclear states expressed dissatisfaction at the incomplete progress in nuclear disarmament by the nuclear powers over the previous 25 years. The treaty was eventually renewed, for an indefinite period, but with provision for a comprehensive ban on nuclear testing from 1996 and for a commitment by the nuclear powers to a `programme of action' for `determined pursuit' of further disarmament leading to the `complete elimination of nuclear weapons'. The treaty further provided for frequent reviews of progress in this.

Although the agreement on a permanent ban on nuclear testing was followed, within days, by another test by China and, within weeks, by the announcement of a further `final' series of tests by France, it is still hoped that, once the treaty is in operation in 1996, the ban on tests thereafter will be respected.

The effect of the frequent reviews will be to increase pressure on the United States and Russia to carry on the process of nuclear disarmament through a START III treaty, as has already been proposed by Mr Yeltsin. In the previous START treaties the British and French nuclear forces were not included in the negotiations because they were insignificant in scale compared with those of the two superpowers. However, if further major cuts in the superpower arsenals are in prospect, this will no longer be so - particularly after the British capacity is at least doubled by the replacement of the Polaris system by the Trident one.

In these circumstances the Russians have already suggested that a new treaty should include some scaling down of British and French nuclear forces as a condition for further reductions in their own. And other countries may be increasingly inclined to press for complete abolition of the British and French nuclear capability as part of the drive to prevent additional countries going nuclear - the reason countries most commonly advance for seeking a nuclear capability is that others have it already: 'if it is necessary and justifiable for them, why not for us too?'

Thus it seems likely that over the coming decades the British and French nuclear status will come under increasing pressure. This may give rise to serious conflicts of policy and interest between Britain and France and their European partners, putting an obstacle in the way of closer defence collaboration, and souring the atmosphere for closer union in other areas. The question will increasingly be asked: what is the purpose of a British, a French, or even a European, nuclear capability in a world where the main requirement has shifted from deterring Soviet aggression to preventing proliferation?

Another aspect with European implications is the proposed ban on reprocessing. Britain has recently opened the Thorp plant intended to take nuclear waste (mainly from German power stations) and reprocess it to produce plutonium (mainly for Japanese power stations.) The project has been attacked on economic grounds (the fall in price of uranium, the development of cheaper dry-storage techniques for nuclear waste, the cancellation of orders for waste processing from Germany[34], and doubts over future demand for plutonium for Japan); and also on the grounds that it may lead to the accumulation of large stocks of plutonium which would constitute an environmental hazard and a potential target for countries seeking to break the non-proliferation controls or for international terrorists. This venture is therefore likely to come under continuing attack in the years ahead and may give rise to friction with some of Britain's partners in Europe and with the United States, which has made the restriction of plutonium production a major element in its anti-proliferation policy.

## Defence against external attack

The CFE (Conventional Forces in Europe) agreement provided for a rough parity in Europe by November 1955 between the forces of NATO and those of the Warsaw Pact; but since the Warsaw Pact forces were much greater than those of NATO, the effect was to require greater cuts from their side than from NATO; and since the Warsaw Pact is defunct, but NATO is not, Russia alone is allowed only a part of the Warsaw Pact total and the effective reductions are even greater. Altogether Russia is allowed only about one-third of the previous Warsaw Pact number of tanks, and about half the previous numbers of combat vehicles, artillery pieces and combat aircraft, while the reductions required in NATO forces are much smaller.

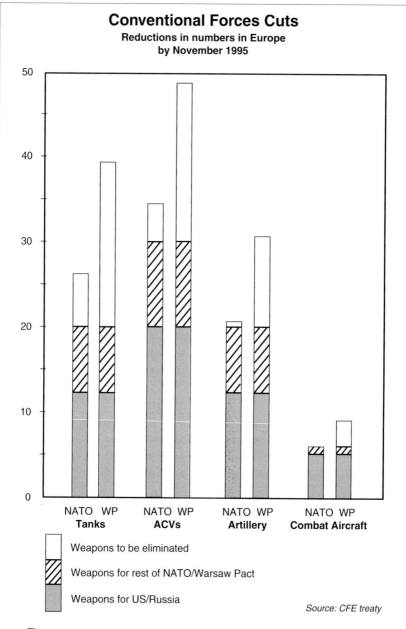

## Conventional Forces Cuts
### Reductions in numbers in Europe by November 1995

Weapons to be eliminated

Weapons for rest of NATO/Warsaw Pact

Weapons for US/Russia

*Source: CFE treaty*

*The agreement on conventional forces cuts will bring parity in heavy weapons between the United States and Russia; and also between other members of NATO (which still exists) and other members of the Warsaw Pact (which does not). Hence the previous Warsaw Pact superiority in conventional forces is being converted into a Russian inferiority.*

Thus the conventional forces balance in Europe have been reversed. Where previously the combined Warsaw Pact forces had a strong superiority in conventional forces, poised menacingly in Central Europe, now the forces of Russia alone are *weaker* than those of the NATO countries, and stationed much farther away from the heart of Europe. Accordingly, they are in no position to launch a sudden decisive attack. Moreover, it is likely that continuing unilateral cuts will make the Russian forces weaker still; and it is probable that their attention will be focused less on Western Europe than on internal security and problems in the 'near abroad'. Indeed, the Russians have already a need for an increase in the proportion of their forces allowed in the southern theatre under the CFE because of the problems in Chechenya and the independent Caucasus republics.

Thus the threat from Russia is no longer a very serious one; and the threat of external attack from other quarters is even more remote. Nevertheless, it will still be prudent to make *some* provision for the defence of Western Europe against external attack, particularly as the Americans have already indicated that they intend to reduce their forces in Europe to one-third of the previous level[35], and it may well be that at some future time they will wish to pull out altogether.

The emphasis is likely to be, increasingly, on the countries of Western Europe making provision for their own defence. There will still be a need for an American commitment to Europe, not least as protection against the remaining Russian nuclear capability, and hence a continuing role for NATO, although over time this is likely to become more of a last-resort standby one. But increasingly the main weight of European defence is likely to be placed on the Western European Union (WEU), the European pillar of NATO. This used to be opposed in Britain on the grounds that building up the WEU would be seen by the Americans as being in competition with NATO and would weaken American commitment to European defence. Recently, however, Robert Hunter, the US ambassador to NATO has explained that the reverse is the case[36]:

> We support the WEU as a means of preventing the re-nationalisation of defence . . . the more the European allies help themselves, the more Congress is likely to pay for transatlantic defence.

The staffing of the WEU has been increased and, with a view to making limited forces from different countries as effective as possible, a start has been made on setting up internationally-integrated military formations: the Eurocorps consisting initially of a French and a German armoured division, and later joined by units from Spain and Belgium; the Multinational Division consisting of Belgian, British, Dutch and German air-mobile forces, and the UK/Netherlands Amphibious Force of marines[23]. These are seen as but the start of a process of increasing integration, although there is clearly a very long way to go before there are enough units sufficiently integrated to comprise a 'European Army' which, if it comes, may be expected to co-exist alongside continuing national armies which it will complement rather than replace.

Another area where increasing European integration is likely is in arms procurement. It is anomalous that in 1992 Britain, France and Germany together bought only 48 combat aircraft and 15 tanks, compared with 183 and 216 respectively bought by the United States [37], yet the European countries are currently producing three different advanced fighter aircraft and three types of main battle tank, while the United States manages with only one of each[19].

Modern high-technology weapons systems are increasingly expensive to develop and, faced with a drop of two-thirds in US defence purchases between 1985 and 1995, the American defence industry has been undergoing a radical restructuring to ensure that it will be able to operate on a viable basis in the smaller markets in the decades to come. In Europe, with a defence market that is much smaller, and also shrinking rapidly, there is no possibility of providing a viable industrial base on the basis of each country supplying its own needs from its own resources; the choice is between becoming increasingly dependent on non-European suppliers, or going much further down the road of defence-industry integration, in the form of joint procurement, joint projects, company mergers and probably the extension of the Single Market to defence equipment.

It is proposed to establish a joint Franco-German-British arms procurement agency and already there are 19 major European arms co-operation programmes, there have been more than 30 international take-overs in the European arms industry, and a number of major new transnational arms production companies have been set up[38]; but for a sustainable defence industry base to be established it is likely that far more will be needed in the way of standardising national requirements, as well as government initiatives to smooth the difficulties involved in drastic industrial rationalisations.

If the end of the Cold War has brought major changes to the defence needs of Western Europe, it has brought even greater changes to *Eastern* Europe, from a formal acceptance of defence *by* Russia to an active concern for defence *from* Russia. With experiences of Russian domination in both recent and earlier history, and with greater proximity to any remaining threat arising out of instability within Russia, most of the countries of Eastern Europe are anxious to have their security guaranteed through inclusion in Western defence arrangements - preferably through membership of NATO or, failing that, indirectly through joining the European Union.

NATO, while sympathetic in principle, has been understandably reluctant to rush into commitments to countries which have different military systems, insecure democratic institutions and, in some cases are following policies provocative to Russia, such as in Estonia where the large Russian minority has been required to pass Estonian language tests as a condition of citizenship.

Insensitive incorporation of Eastern European countries into Western defence systems could be perceived as a threat by the Russians and might help bring about the very eventuality it was designed to avoid.

In view of this asymmetry of perceptions it is likely that links will be built up slowly and cautiously, via the Partnership for Peace scheme, which has been joined by Russia itself. However, as the Eastern European countries demonstrate their stability, and join the European Union, and as Western European defence becomes more of a European and less of an Atlantic matter, it may be expected that the former satellite countries will become increasingly part of a wider European defence system - as will also the former neutral countries of Finland, Sweden and Austria.

## Conflicts within Europe

Whereas for decades it has been unthinkable that any of the democratic countries of Western Europe should ever wage war on one another, since the end of the Cold War the same is not true of Eastern Europe. There are a number of factors which make for instability in some of these countries:

- ex-Communist leaders determined to cling to power at any cost;

- ex-Communist institutions, officials and attitudes of mind still holding influence;

- unemployment, poverty, inequity and crime in the course of change to a different economic system;

- fragile foundations to new democratic institutions, including lack of tolerance for oppositions and minorities;

- large minorities with different cultures, languages and religions; and

- ancient enmities expressed again after decades of suppression.

The tensions arising from these factors have already brought war to Croatia and Bosnia, and conflict could easily spread to other parts of former Yugoslavia and to other countries. Disunity and unpreparedness have resulted in failure to reverse the aggression or halt the suffering. There is a French saying that 'history doesn't provide second helpings'[39], and it is important to learn the right lessons from the Yugoslav tragedy. These have been summed up by the late Manfred Wörner, Secretary General of NATO, as follows [40]:

> Political solutions and diplomatic efforts will work only if they are backed by the necessary military power and the credible resolve to use it against an aggressor.

> We need limited military options to use for limited political or diplomatic objectives.

The most important lesson is that no international organisation can work efficiently without the political will and unity of its member states.

A capability for quick and decisive crisis intervention in Eastern Europe will need to be based on units trained and equipped for rapid deployment and operation as a single force - reinforcing the desirability of closer military co-operation between different countries and implying a shift in the balance of equipment procurement needs.

It also implies the setting of clear objectives for military operations and the establishment of effective methods of control over their execution. Thus the need for early and successful intervention in conflicts in Eastern Europe will not only add to pressure for greater integration of military units and training; it will also bring pressure for joint policies and action in security and foreign affairs - something which is likely to be much more difficult to achieve. However, Mr Volker Rühe, the German Defence Minister has already proposed, as a long-term goal, the full merger of the Western European Union with the European Union; and meanwhile has proposed the ending of the unanimity rule in WEU decisions, although, for the time being perhaps allowing individual countries to opt out of particular military missions[41].

## Conflicts outside Europe

Long-term defence commitments to distant places by Britain and other European countries have for decades been diminishing, and in the next century it is likely that few if any will remain. In recent years, however, changing public attitudes and increasingly vivid television coverage of disturbing distant events, have resulted in greater willingness to contemplate international intervention under the auspices of the United Nations, not only to monitor peace arrangements between countries previously at war, but also to carry out operations to *make* peace between countries and to intervene *within* countries when there is extreme abuse of human rights, repression of minorities or breakdown of administration. As the UN Secretary-General Perez de Cuellar said in a speech in 1991[42]:

We are clearly witnessing what is probably an irresistible shift in public attitudes towards the belief that the defence of the oppressed in the name of morality should prevail over frontiers and legal documents.

In consequence, between 1987 and 1993 the number of UN missions quadrupled, the number of troops involved increased eight-fold, and the total cost of the operations increased fifteen-fold - and the arrears in financial contributions to pay for them rose to more than $600m[43]. And although some of the missions have been far from fully successful, it seems likely that UN interventions will be even more frequent and ambitious in the future - with demands for ever greater contributions to them from countries like those of Western Europe which can deploy well- trained, well-equipped and well-disciplined forces.

If UN peace-keeping operations come to represent an increasingly important part of total defence efforts, it will have a number of implications for the future evolution of European security arrangements. The need for highly mobile, instantly ready, well-trained and closely-integrated units will put a further premium on the creation of international formations and the closer integration of European military structures generally. The need for quick firm response to crises and a bigger say in decisions will add to the pressure for closer integration of European security and foreign policies. And the emphasis on lightly-equipped units will be a further blow to defence industries geared to production of heavy equipment for set-piece battles in Central Europe.

The defence industries may also be at risk in another way. Faced with sharply falling home demand, defence contractors, in Russia, the United States and Western Europe, have sought to offset this by expanding sales to other markets in the developing world. In this they have had support from governments concerned to increase export earnings - particularly Russia where arms are one of the areas in which the country is most competitive and arms are estimated to account for about 20 per cent of total exports[44].

However, it is likely that at some stage the point will be recognised that the supply of large quantities of modern weaponry to unstable

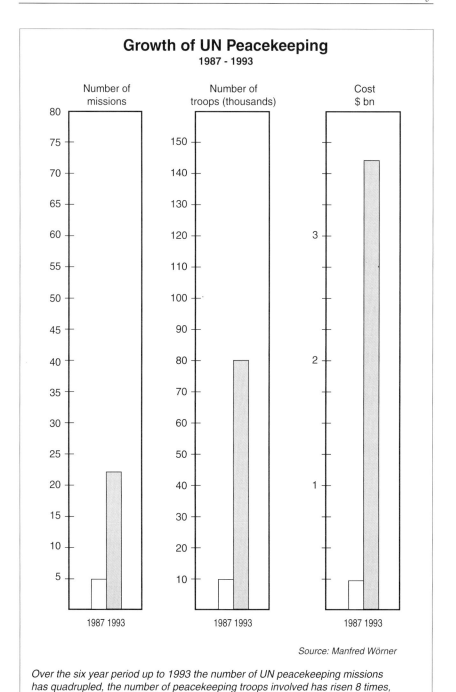

# Growth of UN Peacekeeping
## 1987 - 1993

Source: Manfred Wörner

*Over the six year period up to 1993 the number of UN peacekeeping missions has quadrupled, the number of peacekeeping troops involved has risen 8 times, and the total cost of the missions has risen 15 times.*

countries not only increases the likelihood of local conflicts and the extent of the damage resulting from them - it also increases the scale, costs and risks of any international actions to contain or end them. (The Gulf War would have been a very minor affair if Saddam Hussein had not been supplied with such large quantities of modern arms from abroad.) Hence, if fewer arms were sold abroad, potential future adversaries would be less well equipped, the threats posed by them would be less serious, the forces to contain them could be less powerful, and defence budgets could be less burdensome.

With the ending of the Cold War, military assistance has fallen by three- quarters[45] and conventional arms exports by a half [44], but in 1994 arms exports still amounted to more than $21bn [46], and in some regions have been increasing again in subsequent years. Countries in the European Union account for six of the top ten arms exporters, supplying about a quarter of the total, and together with the United States and Russia account for about 90 per cent of the total [45]. While any single country acting on its own to restrict arms exports faces the likelihood that another country will move in to supply the market, this would not apply if the major supplying countries acted *jointly* to reduce the trade. If the EU countries came together on this to negotiate with the Americans and Russians, there would be only three parties involved and the chances of securing agreement would be greatly increased. Getting agreement also from China, the other major supplier, will still be difficult, but this too could be helped by reducing competition between western suppliers - it appears that the competition to supply Taiwan with arms was a major factor in China's negative reaction to past proposals for restriction of arms exports[44].

Thus at some point the time is likely to come when it is perceived to be in the common interest to adopt a joint EU position on arms exports so as to facilitate agreement on worldwide reductions and give scope for greater reductions in defence expenditure. However, with defence spending reduced even more than it would have been otherwise, and with arms exports cut as well, the problems for European defence industries will be further accentuated - giving extra urgency to the need for a Europe-wide approach to arms procurement so as to make possible a viable future for them.

## Peace dividend

The various future security concerns cannot be met without the commitment of substantial resources of manpower, equipment and finance. However, together they do not amount to a threat on anything remotely approaching the scale presented by the Red Army in East Germany at the height of the Cold War. There is therefore clearly scope, after review of the new needs, for very considerable reductions in total defence spending over a period of years.

In Russia and the countries of Eastern Europe the cuts already made have been drastic. In Western Europe, the reductions, although substantial, have so far been much smaller. And the countries with the highest spending on defence, Britain and France, have made smaller reductions between 1988 and 1993 (from 4.2 per cent of GDP to 3.8 per cent, and from 3.8 per cent to 3.4 per cent, respectively) than some of the countries with lower spending on defence, such as Germany and the Netherlands (from 2.9 per cent to 2.0 per cent and from 3.0 per cent to 2.3 per cent, respectively)[47]. If future defence needs are broadly comparable, it may be expected that Britain and France will have scope for greater savings than other EU countries. This should help improve their competitiveness relative to countries with smaller peace dividends, not least by releasing scarce scientists, engineers and research resources from defence applications to civil uses.

The exact amount of the prospective peace dividend cannot be known in advance with precision, but it is likely to be large. It can be calculated, for example, that if by 2010 defence expenditure in Britain falls to about half the peak 1991/2 level in real terms, instead of rising broadly in line with economic growth, the saving by 2010 will amount to more than £20bn a year - equivalent to about double total central government expenditure on education[48,49]

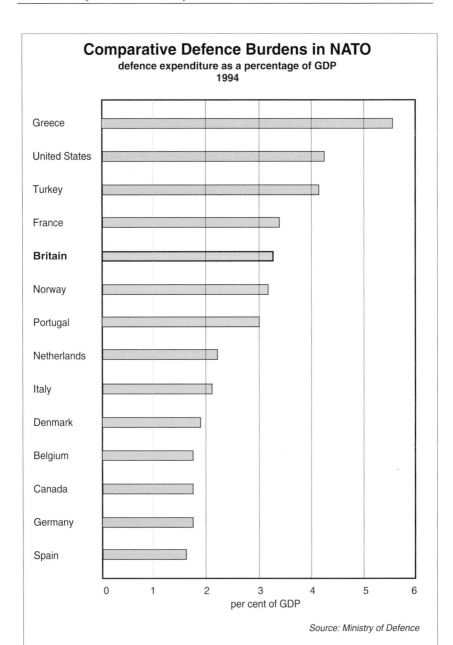

**Comparative Defence Burdens in NATO**
defence expenditure as a percentage of GDP
1994

Greece

United States

Turkey

France

**Britain**

Norway

Portugal

Netherlands

Italy

Denmark

Belgium

Canada

Germany

Spain

0    1    2    3    4    5    6
per cent of GDP

*Source: Ministry of Defence*

*France's spending on defence (as a percentage of GDP) is about the same as Britain's; the United States' is higher; and that of Greece and Turkey higher still (largely out of distrust of each other). Most of the other members of the European Union spend far less on defence than Britain.*

# Key Points for Europe                                Security

The end of the Cold War has greatly reduced the scale and changed the form of future European defence needs.

The threat of a Russian invasion has declined dramatically and is unlikely to re-emerge in the foreseeable future.

Reduced American involvement in Europe will mean that EU countries will have to take more responsibility for their own defence against any remaining external threat and will need to integrate their force structures to increase their effectiveness.

High-tech weapons systems are becoming increasingly costly and EU countries will only be able to keep up by pooling their procurement arrangements.

The desire for further nuclear disarmament and for prevention of nuclear proliferation will bring increasing pressure on Britain and France to reduce or give up their nuclear deterrents.

Effective response to crises in Eastern Europe will require further development of joint rapid-reaction forces and joint decision-taking in defence and foreign policy.

The reduced likelihood of major set-piece battles in Central Europe and the increasing importance of peace-keeping and peace-making operations outside Europe will imply reorientation of emphasis from heavy armour to light mobile forces.

Six of the top ten arms exporters are EU members. Joint EU initiatives will improve the chances of controlling international arms trade competition and reducing the scale of conflicts and of the forces needed for containing them.

The end of the Cold War should make possible a large `peace dividend' in all EU countries, particularly in Britain and France where defence expenditure has in the past been higher than in most of the other countries.

# 3 The Developing World

There is every likelihood that the ending of the Cold War between East and West will be followed by growing tensions between North and South. The gap between the industrialised countries (the `North') and the developing countries (the `South') is very large and is not narrowing. And within many of the countries of the South there are extreme social inequalities with explosive potential which, in recent years, have been mirrored by increasing inequalities in some of the countries of the North.

Growing populations and rising aspirations in the countries of the South are likely to have an impact on Europe in terms of resource depletion, political instability and increasing migration pressures. This will bring a need for co-ordination of Europe's immigration policies and for joint initiatives on trade, aid and investment to help solve the Third World's development problems.

## The North-South gap

Statisticians of the United Nations Development Programme (UNDP) have calculated that in 1991 real gross domestic product per head (GDP) in the South as a whole was only 18 per cent of that in the North [50]. (These calculations were on a 'purchasing power parity' basis; in terms of US dollars, average income per head was only 6 per cent of the North.) Food consumption was one-fifth lower, infant mortality five times as high and maternal mortality 17 times as high [50]. Average number of years in school was only one-third of that in the North, electricity consumption 11 per cent, ownership of television sets 10 per cent, and of telephones and of cars 6 per cent [50].

The South is far from monolithic. It includes some countries which have become rich from oil, and others which are becoming prosperous through efficient new manufacturing industries. But it also includes other countries which remain very poor and deprived. In the least developed third of the developing countries, GDP per head in 1991 (on

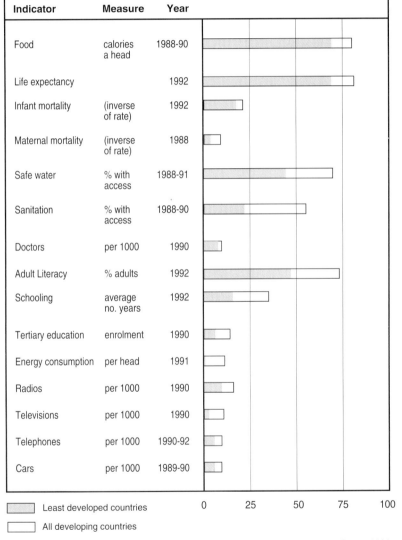

# The North - South Gap
**developing countries as a percentage of industrialised countries**

| Indicator | Measure | Year |
|---|---|---|
| Food | calories a head | 1988-90 |
| Life expectancy | | 1992 |
| Infant mortality | (inverse of rate) | 1992 |
| Maternal mortality | (inverse of rate) | 1988 |
| Safe water | % with access | 1988-91 |
| Sanitation | % with access | 1988-90 |
| Doctors | per 1000 | 1990 |
| Adult Literacy | % adults | 1992 |
| Schooling | average no. years | 1992 |
| Tertiary education | enrolment | 1990 |
| Energy consumption | per head | 1991 |
| Radios | per 1000 | 1990 |
| Televisions | per 1000 | 1990 |
| Telephones | per 1000 | 1990-92 |
| Cars | per 1000 | 1989-90 |

Least developed countries

All developing countries

0    25    50    75    100

*Source: UNDP Human Development Report 1994*

*The gap between the industrial countries and the developing countries is still very large, particularly in health, education, energy consumption and possession of consumer durables.*

the purchasing power parity basis) was only 6 per cent of the average in the North [50]. It is estimated that about one-quarter of the world's population lack safe water, one-third lack safe sanitation and more than one-fifth are without health services [50].

In some ways even more important than the existence of the gaps is whether they are getting narrower or wider. In some ways, such as life-expectancy, food supply and access to safe water, the gap has been narrowing [50]; but in others, such as educational opportunity and GDP per head, they have not [50]. It has been calculated by the UNDP that between 1960 and 1989 the developing countries as a whole nearly doubled their real GDP per head (on the purchasing power parity basis), but fell slightly further behind the industrialised countries which more than doubled theirs [51]. The least developed countries achieved a percentage increase less than one-third as great in their very low

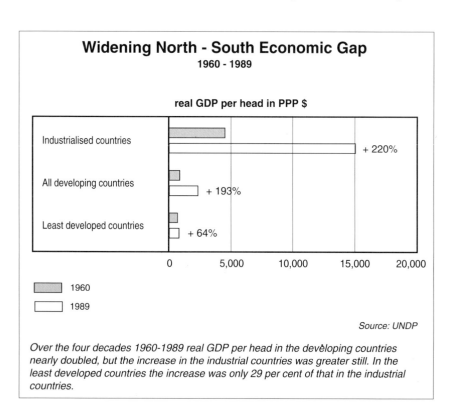

**Widening North - South Economic Gap**
1960 - 1989

real GDP per head in PPP $

Industrialised countries         + 220%

All developing countries       + 193%

Least developed countries     + 64%

0        5,000      10,000      15,000      20,000

1960
1989

*Source: UNDP*

*Over the four decades 1960-1989 real GDP per head in the developing countries nearly doubled, but the increase in the industrial countries was greater still. In the least developed countries the increase was only 29 per cent of that in the industrial countries.*

average GDP per head, and the gap between them and the industrial countries *widened* considerably [51].

In the early 1990s the economies of the developing countries have been growing faster than those of the recession-hit industrial countries, and the World Bank forecasts that in the decade 1993-2004, GDP in the developing countries will grow nearly twice as fast as in the industrial countries [52]. However, any narrowing in the gap in GDP *per head* will be far less because of the continuing rapid growth in population in many Third World countries. A special study of 82 developing countries for the UN Population Fund [53] found that in the 41 countries with slower population growth, incomes grew in the 1980s by an average of 1.23 per cent a year; but in the 41 countries with faster population growth, incomes *fell* by 1.25 per cent a year.

## Population growth

Between 1950 and 1990 the world's population doubled, to reach a total of 5.3 billion, and it is currently increasing by about 90 million people (another Britain and a half) *each year* - the fastest rate of increase in human history (504). The implications of further massive increases are serious.

UN demographers have calculated that if present fertility rates were continued indefinitely, world population would, in theory, rise to 21 billion in 2050 and 109 billion in 2100 - more than 20 times the 1990 level [54]. Fortunately, average world-fertility rates have been falling and are expected to fall further. The crucial questions are: by how much? and how soon?

The UN demographers have prepared long-term population projections [54] on the basis of three alternative sets of assumptions about future changes in fertility rates. The high projection gives an increase in world population to 12.5 billion in 2050; and the low projection gives an increase to a peak of 7.8 billion in 2050.

On the medium projection (based on the assumption that fertility rates will fall by one-third over the next three decades, and will subsequently fall further to replacement level) world population continues to rise rapidly to about 8.5 billion in 2025, due to the momentum built into the present young-age structure, but subsequently rises less quickly to reach 10 billion in 2050. It eventually stabilises at about 11.5 billion (about double its present size) in the middle of the twenty-second century.

The medium projection includes an increase in population between 1990 and 2025 of only 3 per cent in Europe, but increases of 33 per cent

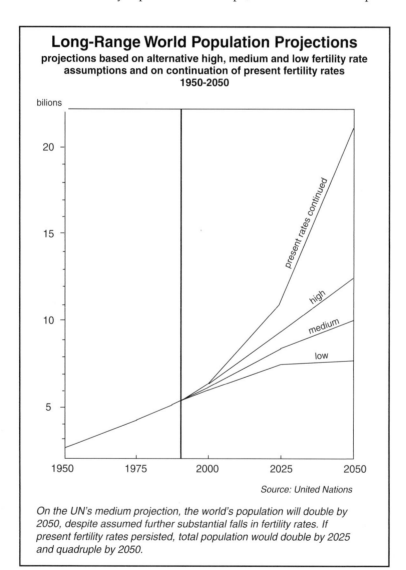

**Long-Range World Population Projections**
projections based on alternative high, medium and low fertility rate
assumptions and on continuation of present fertility rates
1950-2050

*Source: United Nations*

On the UN's medium projection, the world's population will double by
2050, despite assumed further substantial falls in fertility rates. If
present fertility rates persisted, total population would double by 2025
and quadruple by 2050.

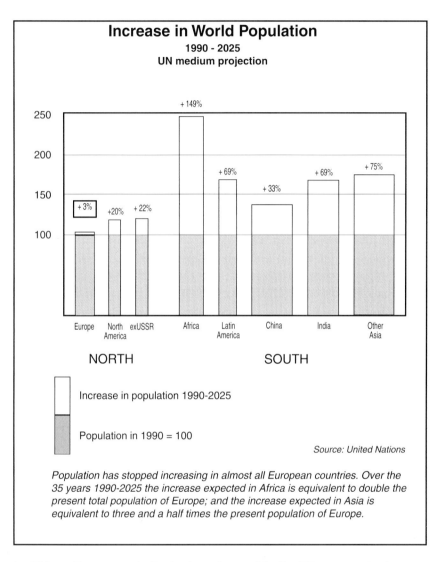

**Increase in World Population**
1990 - 2025
UN medium projection

| | |
|---|---|
| NORTH | SOUTH |

☐ Increase in population 1990-2025

▨ Population in 1990 = 100

*Source: United Nations*

*Population has stopped increasing in almost all European countries. Over the 35 years 1990-2025 the increase expected in Africa is equivalent to double the present total population of Europe; and the increase expected in Asia is equivalent to three and a half times the present population of Europe.*

in China, 69 per cent in Latin America and India, 75 per cent in the rest of Asia and 149 per cent in Africa.

On this projection Europe's share of world population will fall from 9 per cent of the total in 1990 to only 6 per cent in 2025, implying the possibility of a diminishing influence in the world unless the decline in population share is offset by greater cohesion between the various countries in the continent.

And the increase of 60 per cent in total world population over a period of only three-and-a-half decades may be expected to give rise to a number of serious problems, particularly in the least developed countries which are likely to be the ones with the fastest rates of population increase.

## Food

Two centuries ago Malthus predicted that rising population would be checked by the impossibility of feeding the extra people (55). Since then he has been proved wrong twice over - world population has doubled, and doubled again, and living standards, including nutrition standards, have improved. The increase in population in the nineteenth century was fed by Europeans exploiting previously under-used land in other continents; and the rise in population since the Second World War has been fed by increased agricultural yields through greater use of chemicals and machinery and by improved varieties of plants and livestock.

Further increases in food output should be possible in the coming decades, but it may be difficult to achieve increases on the considerable scale required. It is doubtful whether there is much new land which could be brought into use for food production, and much of the land already in use has suffered degradation due to deforestation, over-grazing, over-cropping and other unsuitable practices [56,57,58]. The area under grain has actually *fallen* since 1976 [59].

Much of the increase in world-grain production between 1950 and 1989 was due to more than ten-fold increases in world fertiliser consumption [60]. However, since 1989 world fertiliser consumption has been falling [60], and increases in the future are unlikely because more intensive use is bringing diminishing returns and running up against increasing problems in water pollution; and ultimately it will also come up against energy constraints - in modern high-tech grain production, for every calorie of solar energy used, there are several calories of fossil fuel energy in the form of fertiliser production, irrigation, machinery, vehicles and fuel[61].

The main scope for higher yields is therefore likely to lie in improved varieties of plants and livestock, particularly through the use of biotechnology. Past improvements have already resulted in plants with a greatly increased ratio of grain to roots, stalks and leaves, animals that use a higher proportion of their feed to produce meat, and species which mature faster, have greater disease resistance, and other useful qualities; but the scope for further gains will not be unlimited.

There may also be scope for getting more food from the sea but, while the total world fish-catch quadrupled between 1950 and 1989, it has not increased subsequently [62], and most of the main fishing grounds are now fully exploited with yields at or near the sustainable limits [63,64]. Indeed, several of the fishing grounds within reach of Europe have already been *over*-exploited, with the result that yields have been *falling*. Moreover, while fish can provide useful additional protein, they are a poor source of calories, most of which is likely to continue to come from grains.

Estimates vary greatly as to the limits of the size of potential further increases in food output in the long term. However, there seems little prospect of being able to feed the population increase postulated in the UN high projection. Even with the medium projection for population increase it may be very difficult to provide the huge increases in food production required.

Thus, while it is currently imperative to modify the European Union's Common Agricultural Policy to reduce surpluses in a period of world over-supply, it may well turn out that in the next century rising population will bring world food *shortages* and the need to re-expand agricultural output in Europe and other potential food-exporting regions.

## Other natural resources

At present only about one-third of all the practically accessible renewable water in the world is used [65], but average consumption per head has been rising about twice as fast as population, and the amount of water made unusable by pollution is growing rapidly and is now nearly as great as the amount of water actually used [66]. The global balance of fresh water is therefore likely to get much tighter as population continues to increase, and in some countries the limits are already being approached or even exceeded [56,67]. In countries facing water scarcities there will usually be scope for reducing the water used for irrigation in order to make more available for other purposes, but, since irrigation normally makes land two-to-four times more productive, this may accentuate any future world food shortages.

There are also liable to be problems in the longer-term future with some of the *non*-renewable resources. Proven world reserves of natural gas are equivalent to only about 60 years' use at current rates, and reserves of petroleum to about 40 years. With some important metals, reserves are even shorter: for copper 36 years, tin 27 years, mercury 22 years, lead 21 years and zinc 20 years [64]. These periods become shorter if allowance is made for increasing rates of consumption by the industrialised countries; shorter still if allowance is made for the developing countries wanting to raise their consumption levels to those of the industrialised countries; and even shorter still if allowance is made for major increases in world population.

However, it must be remembered that in the past the world market system has proved remarkably resilient in dealing with incipient shortages. As reserves run low and supplies become scarce, prices rise sharply and this encourages exploration for new sources, development of improved recovery technologies, and use of lower-grade or higher-cost sources hitherto regarded as uneconomic - and hence to an increase in effective reserves. At the same time the higher prices also lead to the development of substitutes, to greater economy in use and to managing without in some marginal uses - leading to a decline in demand. In the past these forces have repeatedly turned shortages into surpluses, and with an increasingly open global economy it may be expected that in the future the working of the market system will succeed again in keeping scarcity problems at bay - but not indefinitely. Where world resources are finite, and constantly being depleted, at increasing rates with rising population and consumption levels, it may be expected that at some point resource shortages will become a serious and intractable problem.

## Living Space

A further problem is living space. In many developing countries there is a combination of rising population, limited extra land in rural areas and a perception of better opportunities in the towns. As a result there has been a large-scale movement of population from the countryside to the towns whose share of total population has risen from 17 per cent in 1950 to 35 per cent in 1992 [50], and is projected to rise to 45 per cent in 2000. Altogether about 83 per cent of the total increase in population in the developing countries is in the towns - equivalent to about ten extra Londons each year [68] - and on the UN medium projection total, urban population in the developing countries is expected to increase 16-fold between 1950 and 2025 - more than three times as fast as the rate of urbanisation in the industrialised countries between 1840 and 1914[68].

It is expected that by the year 2000 there will be more than 300 cities in the developing world with populations of more than one-million people [68], some of them very large indeed. London and the other great cities of Europe, in 1950 among the world's largest, are now not even in the top 20 [68]. Many of these new cities will have very high population densities and very low standards of building, sanitation and public services, and will pose enormous social problems for the future.

## Migration

The impact of excessive increases in population will be felt primarily in the countries of the Third World, especially in some of the poorest ones which are likely to have the largest population increases and the least resources for accommodating them. There will also be an impact on Europe, in three main ways:

1. Depletion of resources will in time bring scarcities which push up prices of imported food and raw materials, undermining European living standards.

2. Competition for scarce resources and living space will bring conflicts in many parts of the world which will require higher European military expenditure for international peace-keeping operations and, ultimately, for the defence of Europe itself from external attack.

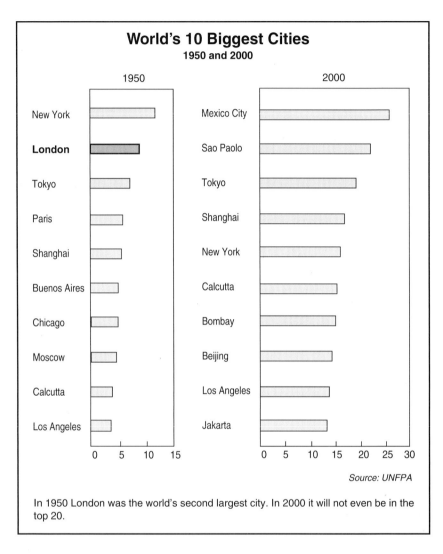

**World's 10 Biggest Cities**
1950 and 2000

Source: UNFPA

In 1950 London was the world's second largest city. In 2000 it will not even be in the top 20.

3. More conflicts will produce more refugees and poor job opportunities will produce more people seeking to migrate to parts of the world offering better prospects - such as Europe - leading to a steady growth in immigration pressures.

A World Bank study [69] estimates that there are already 100 million international migrants of all kinds around the world. It is estimated that by 1985 there were five-million migrant workers in the Gulf states; that during the 1980s seven-million migrants entered the United States legally, and possibly a further two-to-three million illegally; and that 15 million people entered Western Europe as migrants between 1980 and 1992 [68].

Remittances from migrants are estimated to total $70bn globally - second only to oil in value in international flows [68] - and in 1987 migrant workers' remittances were worth more than total development aid to Colombia, Morocco, Egypt, Jordan, Tunisia and India, and paid for more than one-fifth of imports in Jordan, Morocco, Pakistan and Bangladesh, and more than half of imports in Egypt [51].

Already some 36 million extra people join the labour force each year in the developing countries, in addition to the 700 million already unemployed or underemployed; already migration from South to North involves millions of people and is a significant item in the global economy; and each year increasingly more people in developing countries hear about life in the industrialised world through coverage in the media or from friends already there; and improvements in long-haul transport make it easier and cheaper to make the journey. So, if economic growth is slow and population growth is fast in developing countries, the pressures to move to Europe can be expected steadily to increase.

The three Maghreb countries of Morocco, Algeria and Tunisia form a region which has given rise to particular concern on account of its proximity to Europe, its substantial migration flows in the past, and its prospects of rapid population increase and slow economic growth in the future. In recent years fertility rates have been falling sharply in all three countries [70], bringing downward revisions of population-growth forecasts, and it is hoped that economic agreements planned with the European Union (see chapter 10) will speed up economic development. Even so, it is expected that the gap between EU and Maghreb average income levels will widen from about 10:1 in 1995 to about 14:1 in 2010 [70].

Another matter which has attracted attention is that immigration may come not only from the South but also from the East, where long

41

land frontiers are difficult to police. Here the possible enlargement of the European Union to include 10 countries in Central and Eastern Europe (see chapter 10) will in principle allow free movement of people from these countries to the existing 15 countries of the Union in Western Europe. It has been estimated that the accession of the four `Visegrad' countries (Hungary, Poland, the Czech Republic and Slovakia) could result in the migration of perhaps 3-6 million people from these countries alone [71]. It is not yet clear whether there may be some restrictions on the movement of people during a transition period; it is hoped that, partly as a result of EU membership, differences in living standards between East and West will be reduced; and anyway the opportunities for people in the countries of Central and Eastern Europe may be sufficiently good that not very many of them will be ready to contemplate the upheaval of a move. The problems will tend to come if those who do move choose to concentrate in just a few centres where the opportunities look particularly good.

Already there is growing concern about mounting immigration pressures and the need for an effective response to them in Belgium, where integration of migrants is seen as an increasing problem [3]; in the Netherlands, where migrants already account for more than 4 per cent of the population [11]; in Germany, where non-German immigration flows have been exceeding 700,000 a year[6]; in Greece, where illegal entry by sea is difficult to prevent [7]; and in Spain, where proximity and historical links have encouraged increasing numbers of migrants from North Africa [13].

One aspect which is giving particular concern is the way frictions arising from large migration in-flows are providing opportunities for extreme nationalist political parties to exploit them to win significant shares of the vote in elections in several EU countries, with the risk of future social conflict and political instability.

Most European countries have tightened their immigration controls, but unilateral action by national governments can no longer provide a solution. The Single European Market provides for free movement of people, so any migrant getting into any one of the member countries is free to proceed to any of the others - something which it is becoming increasingly easy to do following the Schengen agreement for the progressive dismantling of frontier controls between the EU countries (except, at least for the time being, for Britain, Ireland and Denmark.)

Accordingly, it has become essential, both for regulating legal immigration and for preventing illegal immigration, for all the EU countries to agree on *common procedures and policies* for people arriving at the Union's external points of entry, and for their treatment after arrival.

There is much uncertainty about how strong the immigration pressures will become, and about how difficult it will be to control them. There is concern that policing the external frontiers may prove increasingly difficult and that the removal of the old Iron Curtain intended to keep people *in* Eastern Europe may be followed by the erection of a new Iron Curtain intended to keep people *out* of Western Europe; and that the failure of even this may lead to increasingly rigorous internal police checks to detect illegal immigrants *after* they have arrived, with worrying consequences for civil liberties and community relations.

Neither prospect is appealing, so attention is likely to be directed increasingly to reducing migration pressures at source - by addressing issues of development and population in the countries which have problems.

## Development needs

There are three main ways in which the European Union may make a major impact on the problems of Third World development and population growth: trade, investment and assistance.

### Trade

Much of the development needed by developing countries can potentially be earned from export sales, but there have been a number of difficulties in the way. About half of the export earnings of the developing countries are from primary products, and prices for these have been subject to erratic fluctuations and are currently low - between

1980 and 1993 the prices of all groups of primary products except oil and timber fell by more than a half [52]. With food commodities there is the additional problem of restrictions, subsidies and price support systems estimated to be worth a total of $300bn a year [51] - to the detriment of exporters in the developing countries, and also of consumers in the industrialised countries.

The European Union's Common Agricultural Policy, which generates the production of large surpluses which are then expensively stored and later sold at a loss on world markets, is one of the most important examples of this. In the course of the GATT Uruguay Round negotiations the European Union was obliged to agree to reduce the size of export surpluses, and it is likely that in the future there will be pressure for the Union to further reduce subsidised exports and to allow more imports of food products from the developing countries - and also from Eastern Europe.

Earnings from exports of manufactures from the developing countries have increased greatly, from about 4 per cent of the world total in 1955 to 19 per cent in 1989. However, over half of these exports come from only five countries, all of them in East Asia [51], and here too price movements have been unfavourable.

Also tariff barriers against manufactures from the developing countries have been rising, costing them an estimated $40bn a year in lost exports and $75bn a year in GNP [51]. Non-tariff barriers are an even greater problem and currently affect nearly one-third of OECD imports from the developing countries. Of particular importance is the Multi-Fibre Agreement which affects about half of all developing countries' exports, costing them an estimated $24bn a year [51]. The phasing out of the Multi-Fibre Agreement and other changes agreed to in the GATT Uruguay Round negotiations, are expected to increase manufactured exports from the developing countries by around $35bn a year [51], equivalent to more than half the total of annual bilateral aid from all the OECD countries combined [72]. For some developing countries the removal of trade barriers should bring increases in the value of exports equivalent to several times the value of the aid they receive [73].

In Europe these changes will bring problems for the clothing industries and agriculture, but more than offsetting gains for consumers. Altogether it is estimated [52] that the EU and EFTA countries will between them get benefits from the Uruguay round amounting to $110bn, about 40 per cent of the world total. At the same time it is estimated that all the world's developing countries will between them get benefits amounting to rather less - $86bn - about 31 per cent of the total.

The Uruguay Round has also had the unintended effect of reducing the value of the help given by the European Union to the 70 developing African, Caribbean and Pacific countries under the Lom_ agreements. These agreements, in addition to providing development aid, allow entry to EU markets, free of duties or quotas, to all industrial products and most agricultural ones from the 70 countries - most of which are small and among the least developed. This change gave them a valuable advantage in, for example textiles and clothing, where imports from potential competitors were restricted by the Multi-Fibre agreement. With the phasing out of the Multi-Fibre agreement they will lose this advantage and face strong new competition from high-volume low-cost producers in countries such as Pakistan and China.

Since the Uruguay Round appears to have brought more benefit to the European Union than to the developing countries, and at the same time to have reduced the value of trade help under the Lomé agreement, it may be appropriate to review the Lomé arrangements with a view to seeing what additional help might be given in other forms.

*Investment*
Private inward investment should also play an important part in development. For most of the post-war period, foreign direct investment in the developing countries was not on a large scale. However, recently it has been increasing, from $10bn in 1986 to $40bn in 1992, about 70 per cent of it from the United States and Japan, but much of the remainder from Europe [52,53]. There has also been a marked increase in portfolio investment from $6bn in 1990 to $34bn in 1992, and a return of personal flight capital in some countries [73]. Further increases in private inward investment seem likely in the future.

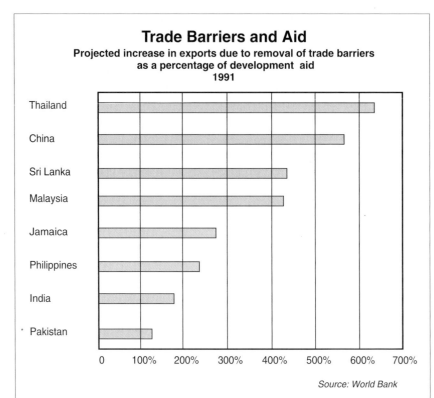

**Trade Barriers and Aid**
Projected increase in exports due to removal of trade barriers
as a percentage of development aid
1991

Thailand

China

Sri Lanka

Malaysia

Jamaica

Philippines

India

* Pakistan

0    100%   200%   300%   400%   500%   600%   700%

*Source: World Bank*

*Many developing countries find their exports impeded by barriers in the industrial countries. For some of them the removal of these barriers would bring increases in exports worth several times as much as the aid they receive.*

However, understandably, investment flows most strongly to the places where the prospective returns look best, which tend not to be the places where the need for investment is greatest. In 1992, for example, three- quarters of direct foreign investment in developing countries went to just six of the most rapidly growing ones and only very small amounts to most of the poorest ones[52].

*Other problems*
Many Third World countries also have other difficulties impeding their development. For some of them unfavourable terms of trade in services and technology transfer are a problem. Most of them have found high

interest rates a heavy burden. And for some of them the combined effects of high interest rates, unwise lending and unwise (or corrupt) borrowing has led to a build-up of massive debts and high servicing costs - in some countries mopping up a substantial proportion of export earnings and offsetting the benefits of development aid [51]. Reduced lending and increased debt-servicing costs turned net transfers from the richer countries to the poorer ones averaging $22bn a year between 1972

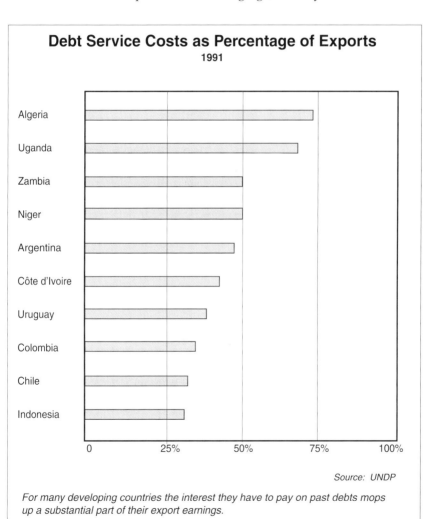

## Debt Service Costs as Percentage of Exports
### 1991

*Source: UNDP*

*For many developing countries the interest they have to pay on past debts mops up a substantial part of their export earnings.*

and 1983 into net transfers *from* the poorer countries *to* the richer ones averaging $18bn a year between 1984 and 1990 [74]. Subsequently overall net transfers have been positive again in 1991 and 1992, although net transfers from the World Bank, the leading development institution, were still negative [74].

Finally, the policies of some of the developing countries themselves have been prejudicial to development - mismanagement, corruption and, most notably, spending on defence which, in the developing

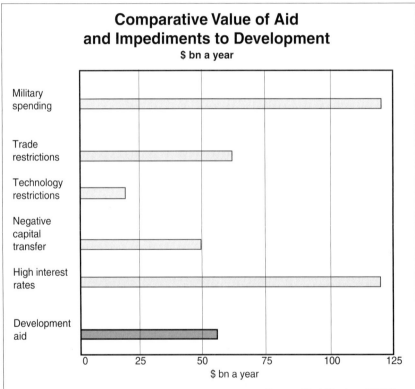

## Comparative Value of Aid and Impediments to Development
### $ bn a year

*Source: World Bank and UNDP*

*The cost to developing countries of trade and technology restrictions, adverse capital movements and high interest rates is equivalent to more than four times the total development aid they receive. Their own military spending amounts to more than twice the value of the aid they receive.*

countries as a whole in 1994, was more than double what they received in overseas aid [50,72].

## Development aid
The total value of overseas aid - about \$55bn in 1993 [72] - is far less than the combined value of other factors in development, such as trade restrictions, interest on debts and military spending, but it is still of great importance because it can be targeted to where it will promote the most needed kinds of development.

The two largest individual donors of overseas assistance are Japan and the United States, but the countries of the European Union together account for far more - in 1993 about half of the total [72]. The countries of the OECD, as a whole, provided development aid equivalent to 0.29 per cent of their combined GDP - less than half the UN target rate of 0.7 per cent. The United States's contribution, although the largest in absolute terms, was equivalent to only 0.14 per cent of GDP. Several European countries, in contrast, made contributions well above the UN target level[72].

The present pattern of overseas aid has less impact on development than it could do because:

- The total amount is too small - less than half the UN target level of 0.7 per cent of GDP [72].

- Less than one-third of bilateral aid goes to the least developed countries, and some of the countries with the lowest incomes per head get the least aid per head [51].

- Nearly half of bilateral aid is tied to the goods and services of the donor country, reducing its effective value by an average of about 15 per cent [73].

- Much aid is designed to secure political, military or trade advantages for the donor country, or is spent on prestige projects which are not the most cost-effective for securing development.

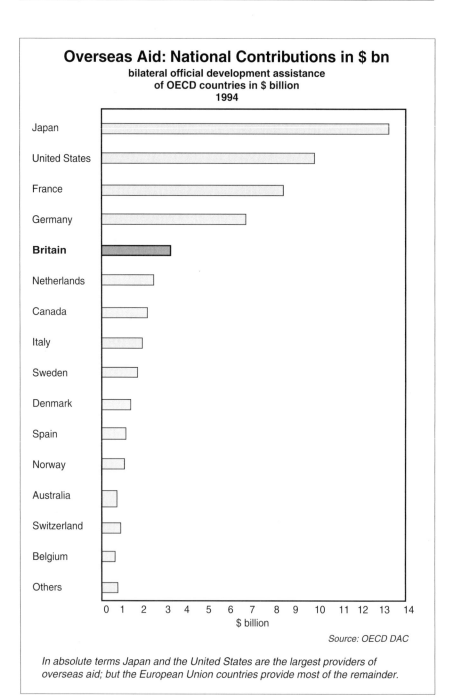

**Overseas Aid: National Contributions in $ bn**
bilateral official development assistance
of OECD countries in $ billion
1994

Japan
United States
France
Germany
**Britain**
Netherlands
Canada
Italy
Sweden
Denmark
Spain
Norway
Australia
Switzerland
Belgium
Others

0  1  2  3  4  5  6  7  8  9  10  11  12  13  14
$ billion

*Source: OECD DAC*

*In absolute terms Japan and the United States are the largest providers of overseas aid; but the European Union countries provide most of the remainder.*

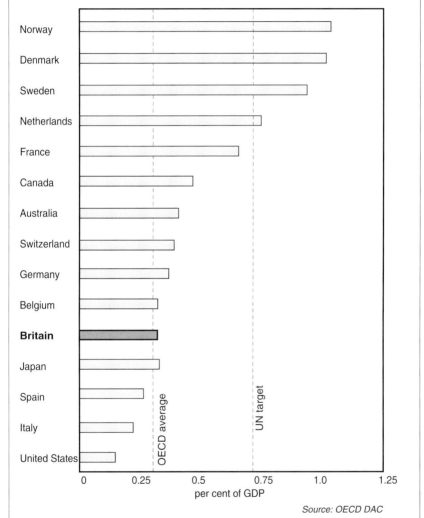

# Overseas Aid:
## National Contributions as percentage of GDP
bilateral official development assistance
of OECD countries as a percentage of gross domestic product
1994

*Source: OECD DAC*

In terms of percentage of GDP, Britain and Japan each contribute about the
OECD average of 0.3 per cent; the United States about half this; and Norway,
Denmark, Sweden and the Netherlands more than double this.

The World Bank, after a series of hard-headed studies in a wide variety of countries, has concluded that for quick improvements in human welfare, for securing sustainable economic development, and for arresting the rise in population, the needs are essentially the same: to target investment into four key priority areas of human development [74,75]:

- family planning

- education for girls

- safe water and sanitation

- primary health care

At present only about 12 per cent of overseas aid goes into these World Bank priority areas [51], and there is little doubt that if more of the aid were targeted in this direction the impact on economic and social development and on population growth would be considerable - even without any increase in the total amount of aid provided.

The European Union already has the world's biggest single aid programme through the Lomé arrangements, under which aid commitments have risen from ECU3.45bn in 1975-1980 to ECU12bn in 1990-1995, but which is anyway needing reconsideration in the changed circumstances following the GATT Uruguay round [76]; and EU countries already account for more than half of total overseas development assistance [72].

It is clear that the EU countries between them will be in a position to make a major impact on the forces driving immigration pressures if more of their aid can be effectively targeted at the key areas affecting development and population growth. However, this is more likely to be achieved if their efforts are combined in pursuit of a common European objective rather than in part dissipated through efforts to achieve national political, military and trade advantages.

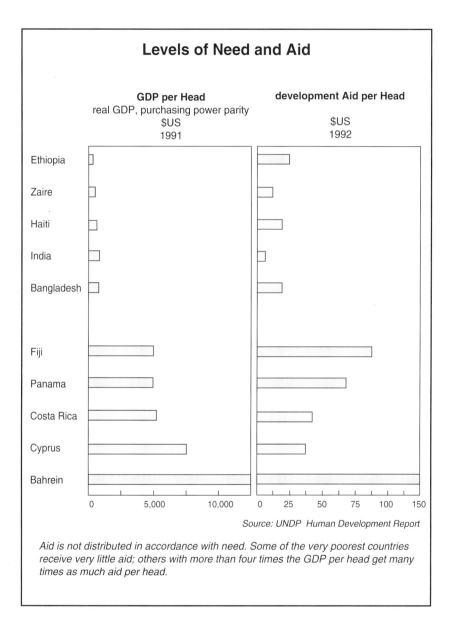

# Levels of Need and Aid

**GDP per Head**
real GDP, purchasing power parity
$US
1991

**development Aid per Head**

$US
1992

Ethiopia

Zaire

Haiti

India

Bangladesh

Fiji

Panama

Costa Rica

Cyprus

Bahrein

0          5,000          10,000          0          25          50          75          100          150

*Source: UNDP Human Development Report*

*Aid is not distributed in accordance with need. Some of the very poorest countries receive very little aid; others with more than four times the GDP per head get many times as much aid per head.*

## Key Points for Europe    The Developing World

The gap between living standards in the industrial countries of the 'North' and the developing countries of the 'South' is very large - and in many areas has not been narrowing.

Rapidly rising population in some countries threatens to outstrip supplies of food, water, mineral resources and living space.

The main impact will be felt in Third World countries, but Europe will be affected too in the form of resource scarcities, international conflicts and increasing immigration pressures - probably mainly from across the Mediterranean, but possibly from Eastern Europe also.

With the removal of frontier barriers within the European Union, immigration will need to be dealt with by joint EU policies and procedures at external points of entry and internally.

Ultimately immigration pressures on Europe will need to be dealt with at source - through the kinds of development which will provide better opportunities and slower population growth in the Third World.

Third World countries earn fifteen times as much from exports as they receive in aid, and the European Union, as the world's largest trading bloc, could help them earn more by reducing trade barriers.

Private investment is also important, and the European Union accounts for a third of all direct investment in developing countries.

Aid programmes are crucial because they can be focused directly on the areas where they will have most impact on human development and population growth. The World Bank has identified these areas, but at present only about 12 per cent of aid goes to them.

Control of immigration, reduction of trade barriers and focusing of aid on priority areas will all need concerted action by the European Union as a whole.

# 4 Population and social change

Population increases are levelling off in Britain and in almost all European countries, but an older age structure and changing social patterns will pose increasing problems for social security, health and social care services [4,5,6,9,11,13]. Governments in all European Union countries are reviewing how far they will be able to `afford' the welfare state in the future. Social protection arrangements vary greatly between different EU countries, and public opinion appears to favour trying to continue high levels of provision, but mainly through national, as opposed to Europe-wide, arrangements.

## Changes in total population

In Britain fertility rates fell sharply in the 1960s and have since remained slightly below replacement level; they are expected to remain at somewhere near present levels in the coming decades. With increasing prosperity and advances in medicine, death rates have been gradually falling. And, although inwards migration has been substantial in some years, it has been roughly matched by outwards migration, with the result that in the most recent period for which figures are available (1988-92) net inwards migration averaged only 7 per cent of the gross movements and amounted to only an insignificant 15,000 people a year. The combined effect of these changes in fertility, morbidity and migration was to bring a total increase of 11.4 per cent in population over the four decades 1951-91[77].

The central projection of the Office of Population Censuses and Surveys shows a diminishing rate of population increase over the coming four decades, with total population reaching a peak of 62.3 million in 2027, and then falling back a little to 62.2 million (7.7 per cent more than in 1991) in 2031[77].

Variant projections have also been made on alternative combinations of assumptions of future fertility and mortality rates. On the low-growth combination of assumptions, population rises only to

58.1 million (5.2 per cent above 1991) in 2031; and on the faster growth assumptions it rises to 66.0 million (14.2 per cent above 1991). Thus with the principal projection, the population increase is less than in the previous decades; and even on the high assumptions there is no suggestion of the very rapid population increases expected in some of the developing countries.

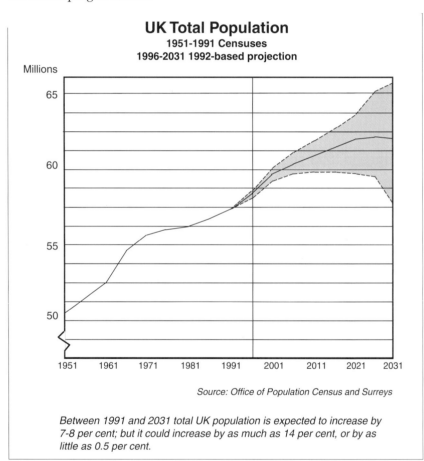

**UK Total Population**
**1951-1991 Censuses**
**1996-2031 1992-based projection**

*Source: Office of Population Census and Surreys*

*Between 1991 and 2031 total UK population is expected to increase by 7-8 per cent; but it could increase by as much as 14 per cent, or by as little as 0.5 per cent.*

All of the other countries of the European Union have experienced falls in fertility rates much greater than in Britain, with the result that, whereas in the 1950s they all had fertility rates higher than in Britain - some of them much higher - now they all (except Ireland) have fertility rates which are *lower* than in Britain, and also lower than the replacement level of 2.1 babies per mother.

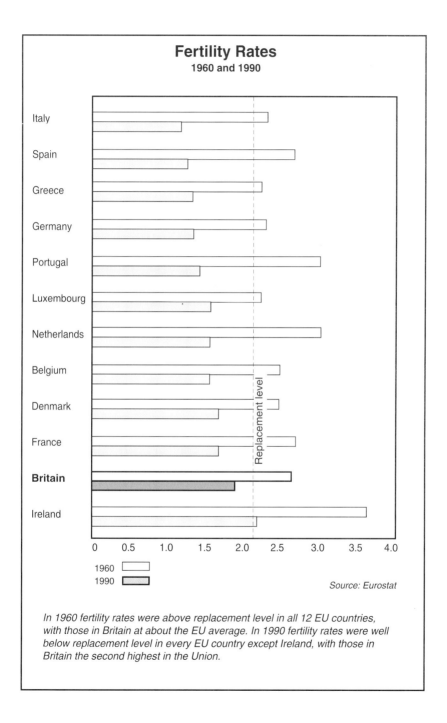

**Fertility Rates**
1960 and 1990

In 1960 fertility rates were above replacement level in all 12 EU countries, with those in Britain at about the EU average. In 1990 fertility rates were well below replacement level in every EU country except Ireland, with those in Britain the second highest in the Union.

Source: Eurostat

The reasons for this sharp decline, most of it in the past two decades, are not entirely clear. Among the possibilities suggested have been: a general undermining of confidence in the future due to slower economic growth and higher unemployment since the 1973 oil price shock; increasing shortages of housing, particularly at rents affordable by young people wanting to start families; diminishing influence of the churches and increasing use of family planning; and improved education and job opportunities for women, leading to greater weight being given to career aspirations and a later start being made on marriage and family. But whatever the reasons, there is widespread agreement that low fertility rates - below replacement level - are likely to continue in every country in the European Union, even including, probably, Ireland, where fertility rates have been much later to decline, but have recently been falling very sharply.

There have also been similar falls in fertility rates in the non-EU countries in Western Europe; also in most of the countries in Eastern Europe; also in the United States and Japan.

As a result of these low fertility rates the rise in population in all the countries of the European Union has been slowing down; and, in some of them, it is expected to be reversed, with the result that the population in 2020 is projected to be slightly lower than in 1990. There has been a similar slowing down in the increase in population in most of the countries in other parts of Europe, with the result that between 1990 and 2025 the United Nations forecasts a total increase in population of only 3 per cent in Europe as a whole - a far smaller increase than in most parts of the developing world.

## Changes in age distribution

Although Britain is one of the most densely populated countries in Europe, further increases in *total* population of the scale envisaged should not give rise to undue problems; substantially larger increases were successfully accommodated in the 1950s and 1960s and earlier periods. There may be more difficulty over the spatial and age *distributions* of the future population.

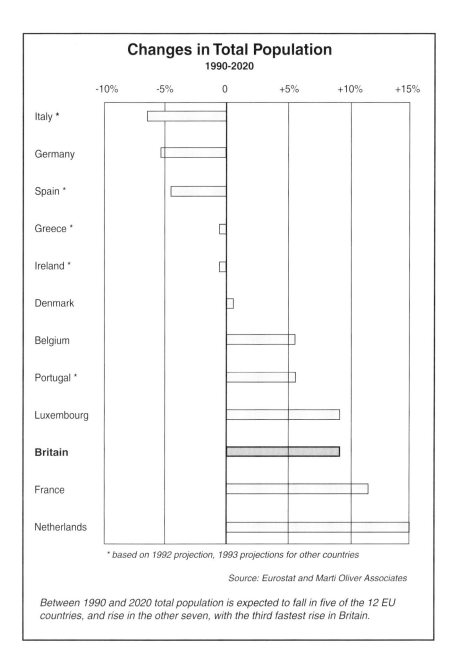

# Changes in Total Population
## 1990-2020

* based on 1992 projection, 1993 projections for other countries

*Source: Eurostat and Marti Oliver Associates*

*Between 1990 and 2020 total population is expected to fall in five of the 12 EU countries, and rise in the other seven, with the third fastest rise in Britain.*

The implications of changes in the *spatial* distribution are considered in chapter 5. The main features of the changes in the *age* distribution are reductions in the numbers of young people and of people in the most economically active age groups, and increases in the numbers of older people.

The proportion of young people under 16 years of age is projected to fall from 20.3 per cent in 1991 to 18.5 per cent in 2021 and 17.6 per cent in 2041. Over the same periods the proportion of people aged 65 and over is projected to rise from 15.7 per cent of the total to 19.4 per cent and 24.6 per cent; and the proportion of very old people aged 80 and over is projected to rise from 3.7 per cent of the total to 5.1 per cent and 9.2 per cent[77].

The expected fall of about one-tenth over three decades, and more subsequently, in the proportion of the population aged under 15 does not give rise to much concern; it may make possible some savings in expenditure on child care services and children's education, and thereby make it easier to find the resources that will be needed to increase the numbers staying on in further and higher education and to extend the provisions for vocational training.

Where there is more concern is over the increase of 22 per cent over three decades and 56 per cent over five decades in the proportion of people older than the `normal' retirement age of 65. This, combined with the reduction in the numbers in the more economically active age groups, has the effect of reducing the number of people likely to be at work to support each person above retirement age - with obvious implications of potential difficulties for pensions and for elderly care services generally.

And the projected increase of 41 per cent over three decades and 110 per cent over five decades in the proportion of very old people aged 80 and over has particularly serious implications for health care, because very old people make disproportionately heavy demands on the services available.

The projected increase in the number of old people over the three

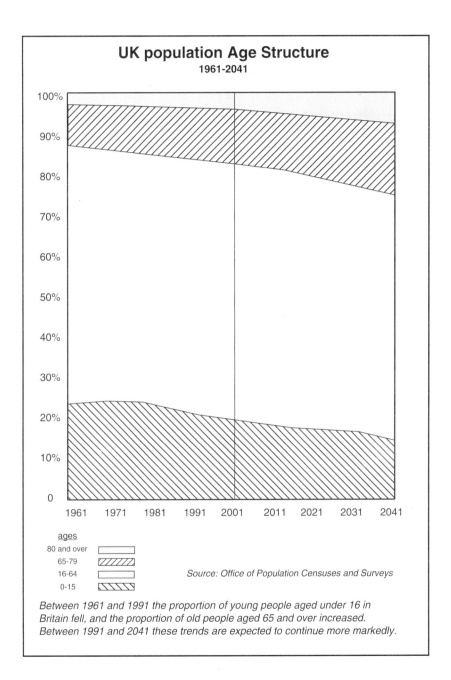

**UK population Age Structure**
1961-2041

100%

90%

80%

70%

60%

50%

40%

30%

20%

10%

0

1961   1971   1981   1991   2001   2011   2021   2031   2041

ages
80 and over
65-79
16-64                    *Source: Office of Population Censuses and Surveys*
0-15

*Between 1961 and 1991 the proportion of young people aged under 16 in Britain fell, and the proportion of old people aged 65 and over increased. Between 1991 and 2041 these trends are expected to continue more markedly.*

decades 1991-2021 is substantially less than occurred over the previous three decades, 1961-91, when the proportion of people over 65 increased by a third and the proportion of people over 80 nearly doubled. However, the further ageing of the population projected after 2021 will bring an age structure far older than any experienced in recent history.

Similar changes in population age structure are projected for other countries in Europe - but in most of them the changes are expected to be sharper than in Britain.

In all of the countries of the European Union there will be a decline in the proportion of the population which is under 15 years old, and also in the proportion aged 15-19. In all of them, except Ireland, the drop will be sharper than in Britain, with the proportion aged under 15 falling from 18.2 per cent in 1990 to a projected 14.9 per cent in 2020 in the European Union as a whole (compared with a fall from 19.0 per cent to 18.2 per cent in Britain), and the proportion aged 15-19 falling from 7.3 per cent to 5.5 per cent (compared with a fall from 7.0 per cent to 6.2 per cent in Britain.)

Thus in 1990 the proportion of young people in the population in Britain was about the same as in the European Union as a whole; but because the proportion is expected to fall on average about twice as quickly in the other countries, by 2020 the proportion of young people under 20 will be lower than in Britain in all of the other European Union countries except Ireland. This faster decline in the proportion of young people in the other countries will give them more scope than Britain to make economies in child care and children's education so as to be able to spend more on higher education and training or in other areas where rising population will imply increasing needs.

Also as in Britain, the proportion of older people in the population is rising in all of the countries in the European Union - in most of them at much faster rates than in Britain. Thus between 1990 and 2020 the proportion of people aged 65 or over in the European Union as a whole will rise from 14.5 per cent to 20.0 per cent - an increase more than twice as fast as in Britain. And the proportion in Britain which in 1990, at 15.6 per cent, was somewhat above the average for the European Union as a

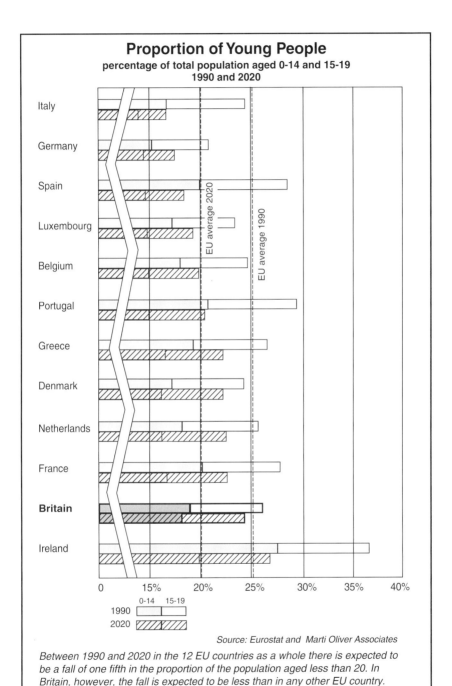

**Proportion of Young People**
percentage of total population aged 0-14 and 15-19
1990 and 2020

Source: Eurostat and Marti Oliver Associates

*Between 1990 and 2020 in the 12 EU countries as a whole there is expected to be a fall of one fifth in the proportion of the population aged less than 20. In Britain, however, the fall is expected to be less than in any other EU country.*

whole, by 2020, at 18.1 per cent, will be markedly *below* the average and lower than in any of the other countries except Ireland.

The most obvious problem arising from these demographic changes will be the provision of pensions for the increase of one-seventh in the expected number of people above 'normal' pension age in Britain, and for the increases of more than 40 per cent expected in Italy, Germany, France, Belgium, Luxembourg, Greece and Portugal.

To get a measure of the seriousness of the problem it is necessary to take account not only of changes in expected numbers of people of pensionable age, but also of changes in the numbers in the more economically active age groups (for this purpose taken to be 20-64). The ratio of the latter to the former is the 'elderly support ratio' - the number of people in the active age groups for each person of pensionable age. Between 1990 and 2020 the elderly support ratio in Britain is expected to deteriorate from 3.7 people per person of pensionable age to only 3.2 people. In all the other countries the deterioration is expected to be faster than in Britain, with the average for the European Union as a whole worsening twice as fast as in Britain, from 4.1 in 1990 to 3.0 in 2020. Thus, whereas in 1990 the ratio in Britain was the most unfavourable of any country in the European Union, the relatively slower rate of deterioration will mean that by 2020 the ratio in Britain is likely to be near the European average.

Demographic changes are not the only factors affecting the burden of pensions. In some countries the cost of pensions has been rising because of the granting of more generous levels of payment or terms of eligibility. In Britain, however, the reverse has been the case; future government commitments to pensioners have been reduced by encouraging opting out to company schemes and individual pension policies, and by limiting indexation of state pensions to increases in the retail price index, as opposed to average earnings, so that, as the economy grows, state pensions take a diminishing proportion of it.

Thus a worsening demographic position will present problems for pensions in Britain over the coming decades. However, these will be less difficult than for almost any other country in the European Union

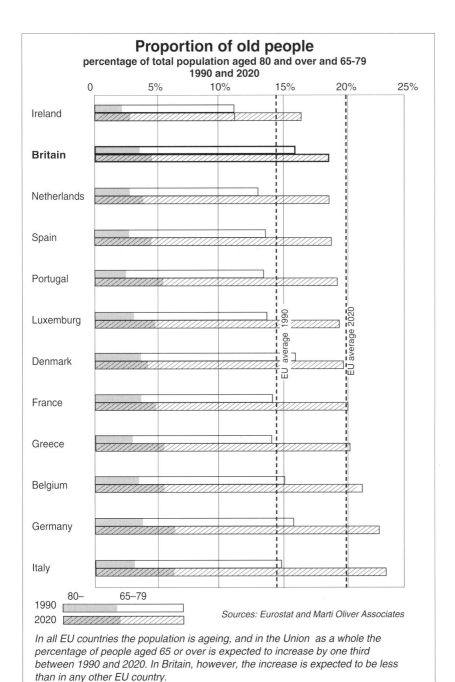

**Proportion of old people**
percentage of total population aged 80 and over and 65-79
1990 and 2020

In all EU countries the population is ageing, and in the Union as a whole the percentage of people aged 65 or over is expected to increase by one third between 1990 and 2020. In Britain, however, the increase is expected to be less than in any other EU country.

*Sources: Eurostat and Marti Oliver Associates*

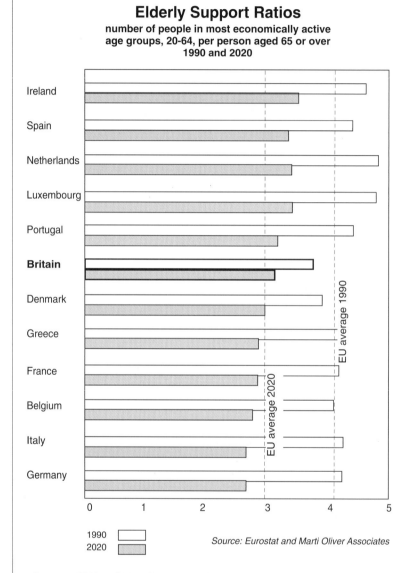

**Elderly Support Ratios**
number of people in most economically active
age groups, 20-64, per person aged 65 or over
1990 and 2020

Source: Eurostat and Marti Oliver Associates

*Between 1990 and 2020 the number of people in the most economically active age groups potentially available to support each person aged 65 or over is expected to fall in all EU countries. In Britain, however, the deterioration in the ratio is expected to be less than in any other EU country.*

because the demographic changes expected in Britain are much less severe than in other countries, and the institutional arrangements in Britain have a built-in tendency to dampen future increases in government spending on pensions.

(**Note**: *the above discussion is in terms of the three decades 1990-2020. It is likely that in the two decades following, 2020-40, the demographic position in Britain will worsen further. It may well be that the position in other European countries will also worsen further, but data for them on a comparable basis is not yet available. However, it is unlikely that the position of Britain, relative to the general European pattern, will change greatly.)*

One striking feature of the ageing population structure is the increase expected in all European countries in the number of very old people. Between 1990 and 2020 in Britain the percentage of people who are aged 80 or more is expected to rise by more than one quarter, from 3.6 per cent to 4.6 per cent; and in the European Community as a whole by more than one half, from 3.4 per cent to 5.2 per cent. The rise in Britain is important; but it is less than the rise expected in every other country and will leave Britain with a proportion of very old people much lower than in any other country in the European Union.

The importance of the increase in numbers of very old people lies mainly in their impact on health care costs. It is estimated that people aged 75-84 cost the National Health Service eight times as much per head as people aged 5-64; and people aged 84 or above cost 15 times as much[78]). They also cost more in personal care services; for example it has been estimated that in Britain between 1991 and 2011 the number of people aged 85 or more who will be unable to give themselves a bath will increase by 100,000, the number unable to walk down the road without help by 200,000, and the number unable to cut their toenails by 300,000[79].

Moreover, other demographic, labour market and attitudinal changes mean that family support, traditionally the main source of care for elderly people, may become scarcer as fewer women are willing to look after frail parents; and as more of the parents are in their eighties and nineties, more of their children will be in their sixties and not

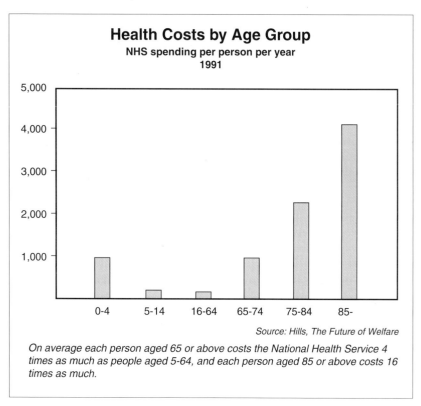

**Health Costs by Age Group**
NHS spending per person per year
1991

Source: Hills, The Future of Welfare

*On average each person aged 65 or above costs the National Health Service 4 times as much as people aged 5-64, and each person aged 85 or above costs 16 times as much.*

necessarily fit enough themselves to look after their parents. As a result social services may have to take a larger share of the burden of caring for the very old and infirm.

Also health care costs tend to go up independently of demographic changes. Some developments are likely to bring *lower* costs - for example, earlier diagnosis, less invasive diagnostic techniques, keyhole surgery and new technology alternatives to surgery, shorter hospital stays, increasing use of day surgery, and possibly the adoption of healthier life styles. However, in general, costs per person have tended to *rise* with more expensive drugs, more expensive surgical and diagnostic equipment, and the ever-widening range of treatments becoming available for conditions previously considered untreatable. For example, the cost of drugs nearly doubled between 1980-90[80], but is still much lower in Britain than in other European countries such as France, Italy, Switzerland, Germany and Belgium[81].

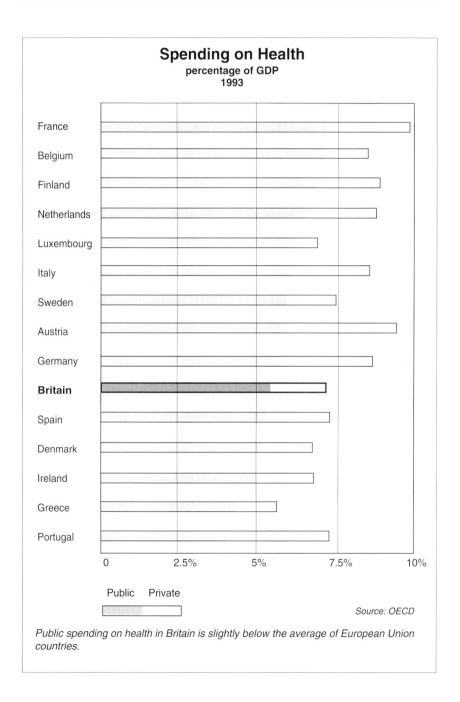

**Spending on Health**
percentage of GDP
1993

France
Belgium
Finland
Netherlands
Luxembourg
Italy
Sweden
Austria
Germany
**Britain**
Spain
Denmark
Ireland
Greece
Portugal

0    2.5%    5%    7.5%    10%

Public   Private

*Source: OECD*

*Public spending on health in Britain is slightly below the average of European Union countries.*

There is also the underlying factor that as people become better off they tend to want to take an increasing part of higher living standards in the form of improved health care. Consequently, health spending tends to rise faster than GDP. OECD studies have shown that in France, Germany, Italy, Japan and the United States spending on health as a percentage of GDP rose in all three decades from 1960 to 1990, with the percentage of GDP in 1990 twice as high as it had been in 1960[82]. In Britain also the percentage has risen, but less sharply.

It may be expected that increasing numbers of old people, rising costs of new treatments, and growing public expectations of improved standards in a more prosperous future, will combine to increase pressures for higher spending on health in the decades ahead in all European countries, including Britain where at present public spending on health, as a percentage of GDP, is below the EU average of other countries of the European Union, except Greece and Portugal; and total health spending is lower than in any country except Greece.

## Social changes

In addition to major demographic changes there have also been important social changes, some of which seem likely to continue in the decades ahead.

In Britain between 1971 and 1991 the marriage rate (for first marriages) halved[77]; the divorce rate (relative to new marriages) more than doubled; and the remarriage rate (as a proportion of all marriages) nearly doubled[77]). It is estimated that 40 per cent of the marriages started in 1987 will end in divorce[83], but many will remarry - in 1992 in 38 per cent of all marriages it was a second marriage for one or both partners[77].

Over the same two decades the proportion of unmarried people aged 20-40 cohabiting more than trebled to cover more than 20 per cent of the total, with about half the couples now married for five years or less having lived together before marriage[202]). Between 1971 and 1992 the proportion of live births outside marriage increased from 9 per cent to 31 per cent, and the proportion of families headed by lone parents increased from 8 per cent to 21 per cent[77]. Average household size has been falling and the proportion of one-person households has been increasing.

If these trends were to continue, it can be calculated that by 2010 the majority of couples would cohabit before getting married, and the majority of marriages would end in divorce, followed by remarriage; and *all* births would be outside marriage. It may safely be assumed that these trends will *not* all continue indefinitely; however, some of them seem likely to continue further before they level off, and it is already clear that they are indicative of major changes in family patterns.

It is not that marriage and the family are finished, but rather that they are taking new forms. Instead of marriage in the form of a single, stable, life-long union, people are tending to have a more varied series of relationships, with periods of cohabiting, periods of marriage, periods of separation and divorce, and periods of remarriage to new partners; with some children being born inside marriages, and some outside, but with three-quarters of the latter jointly registered by both parents; and with some children being brought up inside the original marriage, some by lone parents, in most cases the result of separation or divorce, and some by one original parent and a step-parent as a result of divorce and remarriage. At the same time the pattern common in the 1950s of close links between generations living near to each other has tended to be superseded by a more dispersed extended family pattern, with different generations living further apart, but keeping in touch by telephone and visits by car[84,85,86].

These changes are resulting in new and often complex family financial and child care arrangements; and new social welfare needs, which are not always very tidily met by social security and welfare services designed in an era when most families conformed to a single standard pattern. At the same time the five-fold increase in unemployment since 1973[87], the 35 per cent increase in homelessness since 1986, and the five-fold increase since 1982 in the number of households living in temporary accommodation[88], have placed further strains on the social services. Likewise the consequences of social problems, such as the rise in drug abuse and crime.

Similar changes are being experienced in other countries of the European Union, although not always in the same form or to the same degree.

Divorce rates have risen sharply in all the countries of the European Union (except Ireland where it is still not allowed) - but not as much in Britain where divorce rates are the highest in Europe and more than three times as high as in the countries of Southern Europe.

Births outside marriage have also risen sharply, more than doubling since 1970 in all the member countries of the European Union; in this the countries with the highest rates are Denmark and France, with Britain third, with a rate 50 per cent above the European Union as a whole. Comparative figures for cohabitation are not available, but figures for lone-parent families put Britain highest in Europe, with a rate 50 per cent higher than for the European Union as a whole[89]. And, as in Britain, other countries in Europe are also experiencing falls in average household size and increasing proportions of one-person households [90].

Unemployment rates have been higher than in previous periods in all European countries. Homelessness in Britain, France and Germany has recently been more than four times as high as in any of the other countries in the European Union[91]. The recorded crime rate has been rising in most European countries. In Britain the increase since 1980 has been higher than in most of the other countries and has become the highest in the European Union[92]; and the prison population has become the second largest in relation to size of total population[93].

In general, it would seem that the kinds of social changes which have been taking place in Britain have been happening also in most of the other countries of the European Union; but many of them appear to have gone further in Britain than in the other countries - bringing, perhaps, correspondingly greater need for changes in the social services.

## Social division

An area in which changes have been very marked in Britain over the past decade-and-a-half and which, if continued, would have major

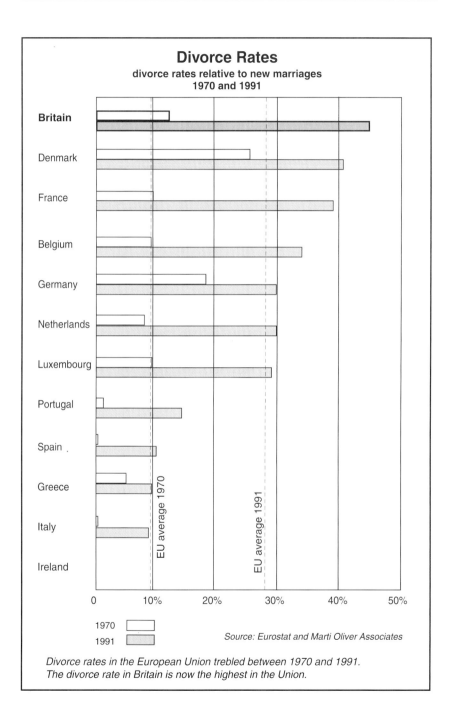

**Divorce Rates**
divorce rates relative to new marriages
1970 and 1991

Britain

Denmark

France

Belgium

Germany

Netherlands

Luxembourg

Portugal

Spain

Greece

Italy

Ireland

EU average 1970

EU average 1991

0    10%    20%    30%    40%    50%

1970

1991    *Source: Eurostat and Marti Oliver Associates*

*Divorce rates in the European Union trebled between 1970 and 1991.*
*The divorce rate in Britain is now the highest in the Union.*

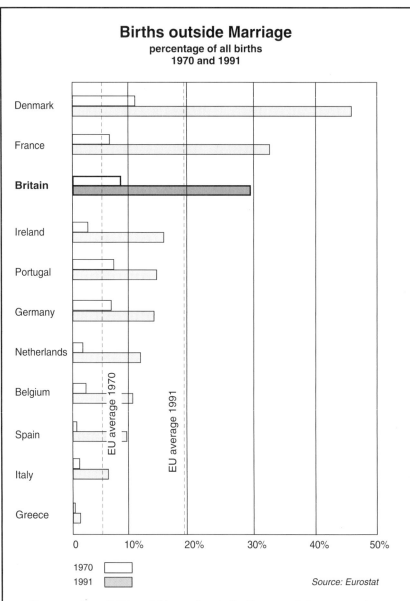

**Births outside Marriage**
percentage of all births
1970 and 1991

1970 □
1991 ▩

*Source: Eurostat*

*The proportion of births outside marriage in the European Union was nearly four times as high in 1991 as in 1970. The proportion in Britain was exceeded only in Denmark and France.*

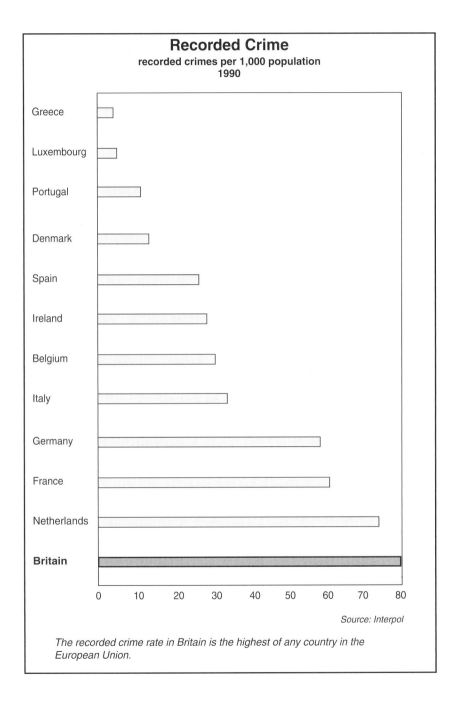

# Recorded Crime
## recorded crimes per 1,000 population
## 1990

Greece

Luxembourg

Portugal

Denmark

Spain

Ireland

Belgium

Italy

Germany

France

Netherlands

**Britain**

0   10   20   30   40   50   60   70   80

*Source: Interpol*

*The recorded crime rate in Britain is the highest of any country in the European Union.*

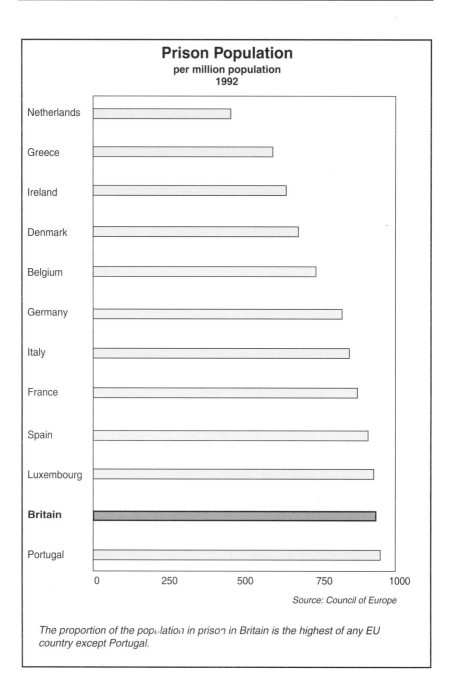

# Prison Population
### per million population
### 1992

| | |
|---|---|
| Netherlands | |
| Greece | |
| Ireland | |
| Denmark | |
| Belgium | |
| Germany | |
| Italy | |
| France | |
| Spain | |
| Luxembourg | |
| **Britain** | |
| Portugal | |

0    250    500    750    1000

*Source: Council of Europe*

*The proportion of the population in prison in Britain is the highest of any EU country except Portugal.*

repercussions on society in the future, is income distribution. A combination of widening earnings differentials, rising unemployment, and changes in social benefit policies and taxation have brought about increases in income inequality on a scale not hitherto experienced during this century.

Between 1886 (when records were first kept) and 1979, wages and salaries rose greatly, but the differential between higher and lower earnings did not change much, with the top decile of earnings normally between two-and-a-quarter and two-and-a-half times the bottom decile. Since 1979, at the top, there have been remuneration increases of many times the rate of inflation for top executives; at the bottom there has been erosion of the wages of the lowest paid following the abolition of wages councils; and in between a general widening of differentials reflecting increasing demand for scarce skills and diminishing trade union influence. The result has been that earnings of the top decile have been rising more than twice as fast as the bottom decile[94], and it can be calculated that, if this pattern were to continue, by 2010 the gap between the top decile of earnings and the bottom decile would be nearly double what it was in 1979, and far greater than at any time in the previous hundred years.

There has been no comparable widening in earnings distribution in other European countries. The shift in Britain brings it broadly into line with the high dispersion in earnings in France, but takes Britain to a much more widely dispersed pattern than in most other EU countries [95].

It used to be provided that pensions and other security benefits were indexed to go up automatically each year in line with prices or average earnings, whichever was the greater. Since, 1982 however, they have been linked only to the prices index, so that in real terms their value is frozen while other incomes go on rising. Consequently, their value in relation to other incomes has been falling; the value of the basic retirement pension, for example, has since 1983 fallen by about one-fifth relative to average incomes and is currently worth only about 15 per cent of gross average earnings. It can be calculated that, if real average incomes increase by an average of 2 per cent a year, by the year 2030 the national insurance basic retirement pension will be worth only about 7.5 per cent of average earnings[78].

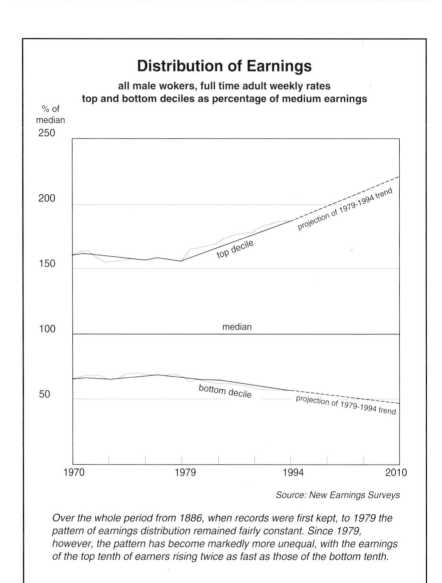

**Distribution of Earnings**
all male wokers, full time adult weekly rates
top and bottom deciles as percentage of medium earnings

% of median

*Source: New Earnings Surveys*

*Over the whole period from 1886, when records were first kept, to 1979 the pattern of earnings distribution remained fairly constant. Since 1979, however, the pattern has become markedly more unequal, with the earnings of the top tenth of earners rising twice as fast as those of the bottom tenth.*

In addition, some universal benefits, such as maternity grant and death grant, have been abolished; some benefits, such as unemployment and sickness benefit, have had earnings-related supplements removed; most benefits have had their conditions of eligibility tightened, with some whole categories of claimant, such as young people for unemployment benefit, removed altogether; some benefits, such as child benefit, have not always been increased even to take account of inflation; some benefits, such as homes for old people, have been made subject to means test; and some needs formerly met by cash grants are now covered only by loans, which are subject to cash-limited budgets.

At the same time, more people are in need of social benefits because of the rise in unemployment and the rise in broken marriages and lone-parent families. Thus the gap between earners (with rising incomes) and those dependent on social security benefits (fixed in real terms or falling) has been widening over a period when the numbers dependent on social security benefits has been increasing.

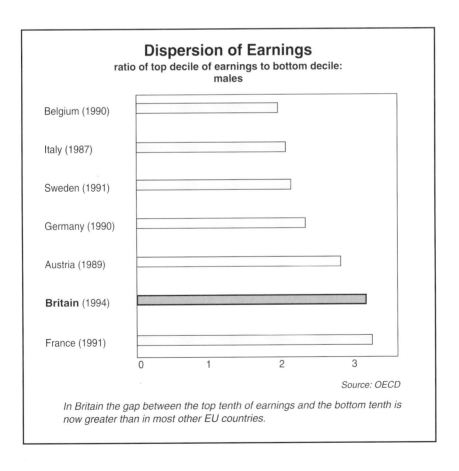

## Dispersion of Earnings
ratio of top decile of earnings to bottom decile: males

*Source: OECD*

*In Britain the gap between the top tenth of earnings and the bottom tenth is now greater than in most other EU countries.*

A third set of changes has been in taxation, where a succession of new taxes and changes in rates, bands and conditions have tended to favour those with higher incomes at the expense of those with lower incomes. The better-off have been the main beneficiaries of the Business Expansion Scheme and Personal Equity Plans, of reduced rates of Inheritance Tax and Capital Gains Tax, of the abolition of higher rate Income Tax and the Investment Income Surcharge, and of the separate taxation of husbands and wives. And the less well-off have been the main losers from the shift from Rates to the flat-rate Poll Tax, and subsequently to the Council Tax (which, unlike Rates, only partly reflects differences in property values), from the imposition of VAT on domestic fuel (which accounts for a larger part of spending by those with small incomes than by those with large ones), and from the general shift from direct taxes on income (which tend to be progressive) to indirect taxes on spending (which tend to be regressive.)

Since 1979, the result of these changes has been `a major redistribution from those on low incomes to the better-off'[96]. The Institute for Fiscal Studies has calculated that the tax changes between 1985 and 1995 have had the effect of reducing the incomes of people in the four lowest income deciles, increasing the incomes of people in the next five deciles, and increasing much more markedly the incomes of people in the richest decile[97].

The combined effect of changes in earnings differentials, in taxes, in benefit payments, and in the numbers dependent on benefits has been to bring about the sharpest widening in income inequalities this century. Over the period 1961-1979 real incomes went up roughly in line with the average for all income groups except the bottom decile, whose incomes went up about half as much again as the others[98]. Over the whole period 1979-1992, in contrast, the higher the income group the greater the increase, with the top decile (richest tenth) getting an increase of 61 per cent in real incomes, and the bottom decile (poorest tenth) experiencing an actual *fall* in real incomes of 18 per cent[98].

It is probable that some very small incomes are under-reported in surveys, thus exaggerating the difference between the top and the bottom; and it is also the case that people with the highest incomes are

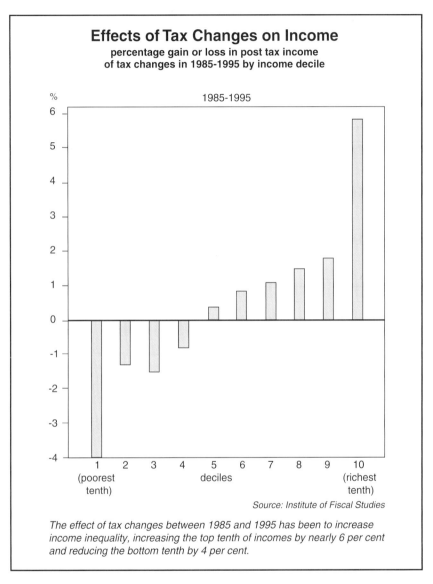

**Effects of Tax Changes on Income**
percentage gain or loss in post tax income
of tax changes in 1985-1995 by income decile

%                    1985-1995

Source: Institute of Fiscal Studies

*The effect of tax changes between 1985 and 1995 has been to increase income inequality, increasing the top tenth of incomes by nearly 6 per cent and reducing the bottom tenth by 4 per cent.*

better able and more inclined to save a part of them, while people with the lowest incomes have more need to dis-save or borrow, in so far as they are able to, in order to keep up their living standards - particularly if their incomes have recently fallen sharply (for example as a result of redundancy) or if they hope they will rise again shortly (for example as

# Changes in Income
### percentage changes in real net income, excluding housing costs, by decile

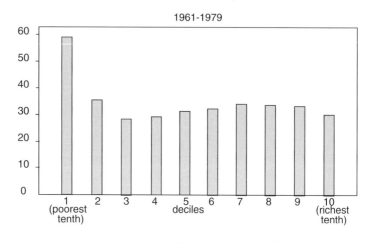

1961-1979

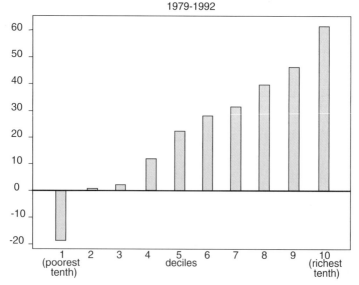

1979-1992

*Source: IFS, DSS*

*Between 1961 and 1979 incomes at all levels rose at a similar rate, except for the bottom tenth which rose faster than the others. Between 1979 and 1992 higher incomes rose much faster than lower ones, with the richest tenth's rising by 61 per cent and the poorest tenth's falling by 18 per cent.*

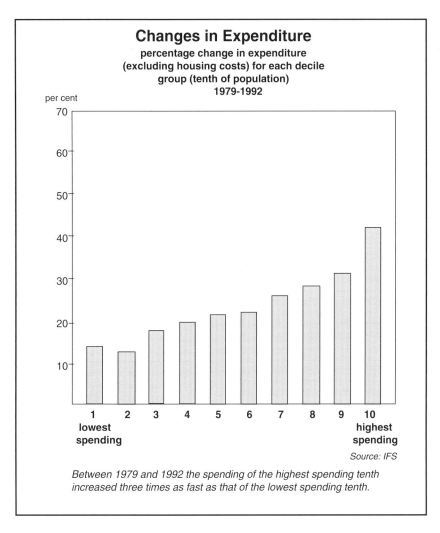

## Changes in Expenditure
percentage change in expenditure
(excluding housing costs) for each decile
group (tenth of population)
1979-1992

per cent

*Source: IFS*

*Between 1979 and 1992 the spending of the highest spending tenth
increased three times as fast as that of the lowest spending tenth.*

a result of getting a new job). Recent research suggests that people with
the lowest incomes have quite high ownership rates of consumer
durables[99] and often spend above their incomes[100]. Also there is
substantial movement between income groups from one year to the
next[101]. Accordingly differences in *living standards*, as measured by actual
expenditure, tend to be smaller than differences in *incomes*. But while
there is much argument over whether income, as indicator of
*opportunity*, or expenditure, as indicator of *current living standards*, is the

better measure of welfare, it is striking that even on the expenditure measure there has been a considerable widening of inequality, with the expenditure of the highest decile going up three times as fast as the lowest over the period 1979 to 1992[100].

The standard way of expressing degrees of inequality in a single figure is the Gini coefficient, which varies over a range where 0 is complete equality and 1 is complete inequality. Over the period 1961 to 1979 the Gini coefficient varied over a range of .245 to .276. After 1979 it went far outside this range to reach a new high point of .365 in 1991[98].

International comparisons of inequality are difficult because of differences in measures, but one of the few on a comparable basis (102) shows Britain in 1986 as having a Gini coefficient slightly lower than France and Italy, but higher than the Netherlands, West Germany, Sweden and Finland. Since 1986 inequality has continued to increase sharply in Britain, while in other European countries it has increased more slowly, or decreased, suggesting that by now inequality is probably greater than in France and Italy as well as the other countries[103].

One consequence of the widening of the gap between high- and low-incomes has been that, over the same period, the numbers in poverty *rose* from 9.3 per cent of the population to 24.3 per cent[98]. (This is on the basis used by the European Commission where poverty is defined as having incomes below half the average, implying social exclusion from the way of life of the rest of the community. However, the increase is similarly sharp if the alternative definitions of 40 per cent below or 60 per cent below are used.)

It may be supposed that if there is a continuation of this widening of inequality, with an absolute fall in the lowest incomes and further increases in the numbers in poverty, social tensions will be likely to increase and ultimately pose a threat to the cohesion and stability which are usually thought of as characteristic of British society. And if accompanied by continuing high unemployment and increasing

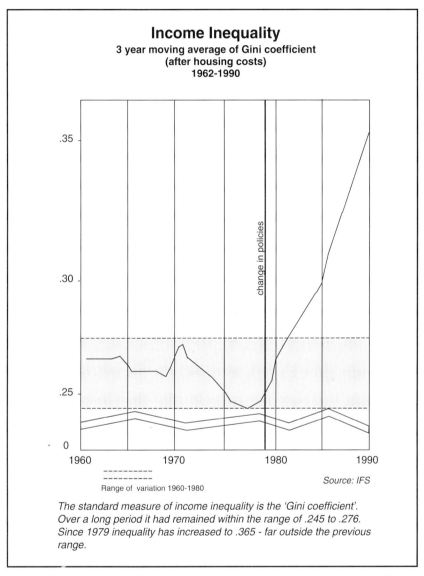

**Income Inequality**
3 year moving average of Gini coefficient
(after housing costs)
1962-1990

change in policies

.35

.30

.25

0

1960      1970      1980      1990

Range of variation 1960-1980

*Source: IFS*

*The standard measure of income inequality is the 'Gini coefficient'.
Over a long period it had remained within the range of .245 to .276.
Since 1979 inequality has increased to .365 - far outside the previous
range.*

numbers of people dependent on social benefits and services, it may be
expected to place increasing strains on the welfare state - particularly if
superimposed on the expected demographic and social changes. Thus,
unless the trends are reversed, there is a risk of increasing social division
and economic difficulty.

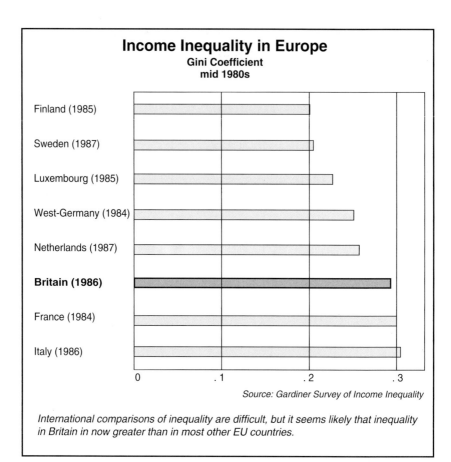

**Income Inequality in Europe**
Gini Coefficient
mid 1980s

Finland (1985)

Sweden (1987)

Luxembourg (1985)

West-Germany (1984)

Netherlands (1987)

**Britain (1986)**

France (1984)

Italy (1986)

0          .1          .2          .3

*Source: Gardiner Survey of Income Inequality*

*International comparisons of inequality are difficult, but it seems likely that inequality in Britain in now greater than in most other EU countries.*

The increase in inequality in Britain has been associated with the free market/deregulation economic and social policies which have been followed. In most other EU countries, where more corporatist policies have been maintained, there has not so far been an increase in inequality comparable to that in Britain. However, concern has been expressed in a number of countries that recent or intended changes in economic policy to increase competitiveness may be leading to similar social consequences[3,4,5,9].

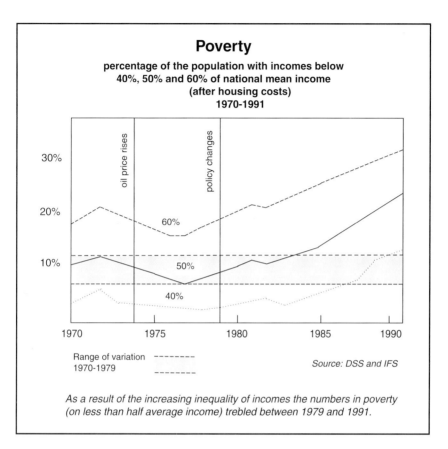

# Poverty

**percentage of the population with incomes below
40%, 50% and 60% of national mean income
(after housing costs)
1970-1991**

oil price rises

policy changes

30%

20%

60%

10%

50%

40%

1970           1975           1980           1985           1990

Range of variation ---------
1970-1979   ---------

*Source: DSS and IFS*

*As a result of the increasing inequality of incomes the numbers in poverty
(on less than half average income) trebled between 1979 and 1991.*

## Social policies

Faced with demographic and social changes, a need for maintaining
competitiveness in an increasingly global economy, and electorates
wanting both lower taxes *and* better social protection, the governments
of most of the countries in the European Union have been reviewing the
future of provisions for health, social security and welfare services. A
particularly worrying problem which many of them have not yet solved
is how to reconcile commitments to high levels of pensions with the
greatly increased number of people of pensionable age expected in the
future.

Different countries have modified their policies in different ways. In
Britain the government has sought to increase efficiency in provision of

services by introducing market competition and splitting the purchase of services from their provision. In the Netherlands there have been proposals to improve efficiency, reform the national insurance system, freeze pensions and cut other benefits[104]. In Germany the rapid rise in health spending has been checked and there are plans to limit some kinds of social benefits[105,106]. In France the period of contributions needed to qualify for a state pension has been extended, the social security tax has been increased, and there are plans to limit the rise in health spending[107]. In Italy the retirement age has been raised, the minimum contribution period for pensions has been increased, new private-funded pension schemes are being introduced, and steps are being taken to cut down on fraud in excessive payments of disability pensions[108,109]. In Portugal and Greece the pension retirement age has been raised[110]. And in Sweden unemployment, sickness and parental leave benefits have been cut[111].

The common assumption underlying most of the government responses is that, if costs are going up, the need is to cut the cost of provisions so as to prevent the need for higher taxes or social security contributions. This may be at variance with popular preferences. In Britain, for example, the British Social Attitudes Survey[112] found in 1983 that for every 9 people favouring a policy of reducing taxes and spending less on health, education and social benefits, there were 54 preferring to keep taxes and spending at existing levels, and 32 in favour of *increasing* taxes in order to spend *more* on health education and social benefits.

In subsequent surveys the proportions changed until, in the latest one in 1993, 63 per cent expressed themselves as in favour of tax increases to allow more social spending, and only 4 per cent in favour of tax reductions to allow less. When asked which areas spending should be on, 87 per cent wanted higher spending on health, 79 per cent on education and 78 per cent on pensions, compared with only 1 per cent wanting less on each of them. Now it may be that, in reality, many people want both lower taxes *and* better social services; and that, when asked to choose, tend to express a preference for better services in opinion polls, while behaving otherwise in the polling booths. Even so, the extent of expressed enthusiasm for the welfare state is impressive.

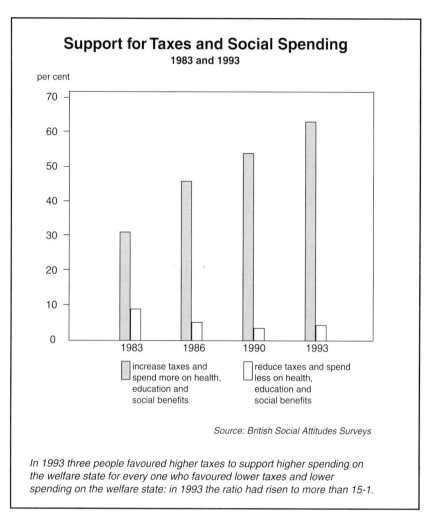

## Support for Taxes and Social Spending
### 1983 and 1993

per cent

*Source: British Social Attitudes Surveys*

*In 1993 three people favoured higher taxes to support higher spending on the welfare state for every one who favoured lower taxes and lower spending on the welfare state: in 1993 the ratio had risen to more than 15-1.*

And similarly in other countries, a Eurobarometer survey[113] found a majority in each of the member countries of the European Union in favour of the proposition that `the government must continue to provide everyone with a broad range of social security benefits, even if it means increasing taxes and contributions', and opposed to the proposition that `the government should provide everyone with only a limited number of essential benefits and encourage people to provide for themselves in other respects'.

## Support in Europe for Wide Range of Benefits
*the Government must continue to provide everyone with a broad range of social*
*security benefits, even if it means raising taxes and contributions:*
**percentage agreeing with statement, including don't knows**
**1993**

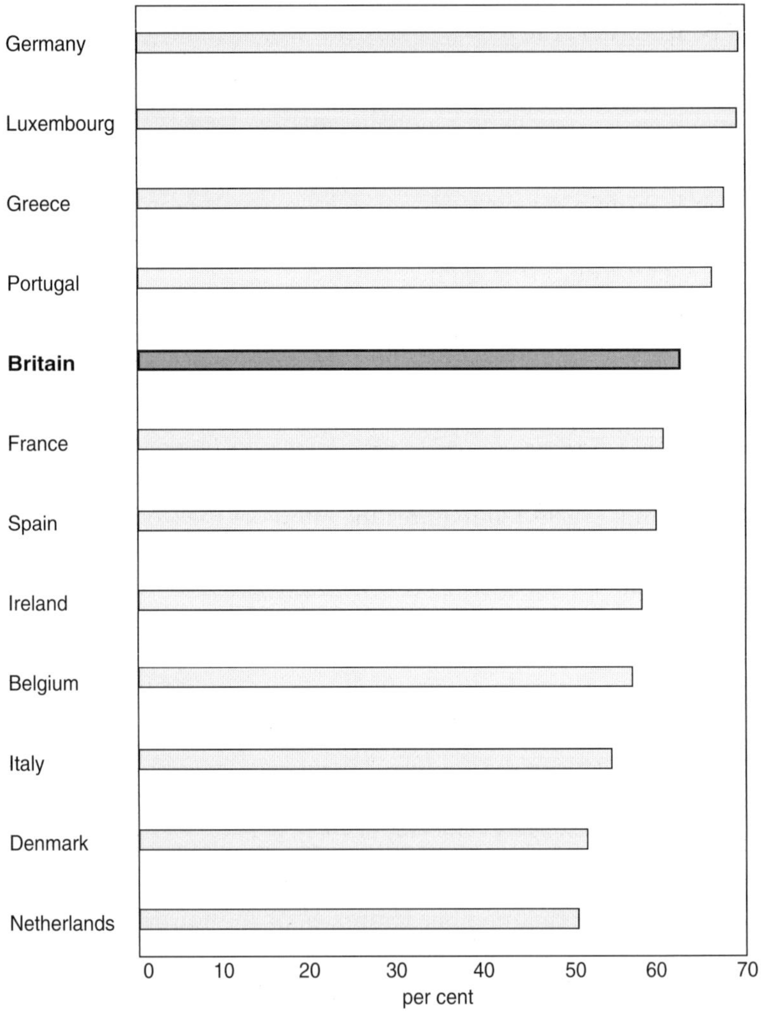

Germany

Luxembourg

Greece

Portugal

**Britain**

France

Spain

Ireland

Belgium

Italy

Denmark

Netherlands

0   10   20   30   40   50   60   70
per cent

*Source: Eurobarometer*

*In all EU countries there appears to be a majority in favour of maintaining the
welfare state, even if it means putting up taxes.*

The *desire* to maintain benefit levels is one thing; the *feasibility* of doing so may be another. In Britain it has been calculated that to keep social benefit levels going up in line with general living standards, despite the expected adverse demographic changes, would cost an additional 5 per cent of GDP[78]. This would be a very large increase; but it would be spread over several decades and would be no greater than the increase in public spending incurred *already* over only three years, 1989-90 to 1992-93, as a result of the recession[114]. Moreover, Britain would be better placed for this than most other EU countries because the demographic changes in prospect are less serious and government social spending in Britain accounts for a smaller proportion of GDP than in most other EU countries - a 5 per cent increase would bring it roughly into line with the European average.

Although most EU countries are facing broadly similar problems, the response to them has so far been predominantly at the national level - despite the passage in 1986 of the Single European Act which makes social policy a *European* issue. Article 118 calls on the European Commission to promote co-operation between the member states in the social field, and Article 130 requires the efforts of the Community to be designed to reduce the economic and social disparities between the regions and the backwardness of the least favoured regions[115]). The operation of the Single European Market can be interpreted as requiring harmonisation of social policies in order to ensure a level playing field for competition and to assist the free movement of labour between member countries. In 1990 the European Council stressed its commitment to give equal weight to the social and economic aspects of the Community, and the President of the Commission has declared that 'The social dimension permeates all our discussions and everything we do'.

So far the Commission has undertaken relatively minor anti-poverty initiatives, and taken more substantial action through the regional and structural funds, but it has not yet embarked on moves directly aimed towards the harmonisation of social policy - with the important exception of social policy in the employment field, which is considered in chapter 6.

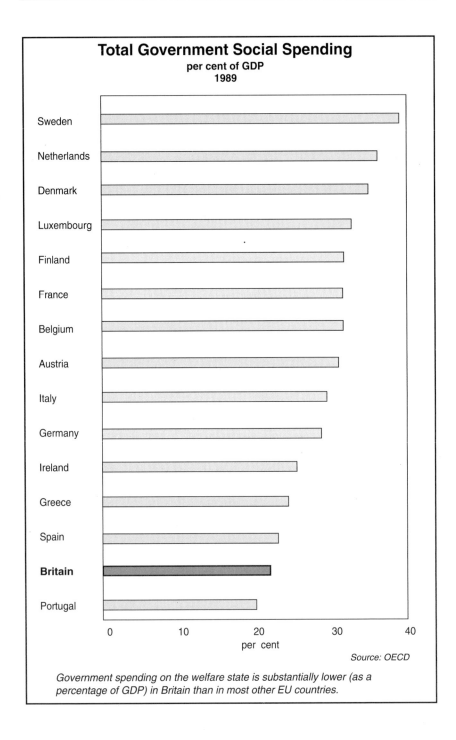

## Total Government Social Spending
### per cent of GDP
### 1989

Sweden
Netherlands
Denmark
Luxembourg
Finland
France
Belgium
Austria
Italy
Germany
Ireland
Greece
Spain
**Britain**
Portugal

0          10          20          30          40

per cent

*Source: OECD*

*Government spending on the welfare state is substantially lower (as a percentage of GDP) in Britain than in most other EU countries.*

This is partly because social policy is a sensitive area where, in many countries, there are likely to be strong feelings in favour of keeping national or local control and preserving distinctive national or local features. The same survey which showed widespread support for the welfare state also showed strong preferences in the majority of countries for policies to be decided by national governments rather than jointly by the European Union.

And it is partly because, if a decision were taken to try to harmonise the policies, there would be serious practical problems due to the differences between the countries: in the kinds of benefits provided; in the levels at which, and the terms on which, they are provided; and in the ways in which they are financed. For example, the proportion funded by contributions from employers and employees ranges from 44 per cent in France, through 17 per cent in Britain, to only 3 per cent in Denmark. The differences between arrangements in the various member countries are so great that it would be extremely difficult to make them broadly comparable in value, let alone uniform in operation.

Thus while full eligibility for locally available benefits would make easier the mobility of labour envisaged in the Single Market - and in the longer term it is hard to see how goals of greater cohesion and equality can be achieved without social policies playing some part in it - it none the less seems that national sensitivities and technical difficulties will preclude any attempt at wide-scale social harmonisation for the foreseeable future, except in the employment field. Accordingly, this is an area where the principle of subsidiarity - allowing decisions to be taken at the lowest feasible level - is likely to be applied with general agreement.

## Key Points for Europe    Population and Social Change

Falling fertility rates in all the countries of the European Union are bringing a levelling off in total population growth and an older age structure.

Between 1990 and 2020 it is expected that:
-   the proportion of people under 15 will fall by a quarter;
-   the proportion over 65 will rise by a third, and the proportion over 80 by a half; and
-   there will be a drop from 4 to 3 in the number of people in the active age groups available to support each older person.

These changes will make it easier to improve education standards, but bring problems in pensions, welfare services and health care - where people over 85 cost 15 times as much per head as people aged 5-64.

In varying degrees all EU countries are also experiencing social changes, with rising rates of divorce, cohabitation, children born outside marriage and one-parent families. These changes, together with high unemployment, are putting further strains on social services.

In Britain the projected demographic changes are less than in most other EU countries; but the social changes experienced so far have been greater.

In most countries governments are reviewing policies, wondering how far it will be possible to maintain the welfare state in a world of rising demands on social protection services, declining willingness to pay high taxes and contributions, and increasing need to improve international competitiveness.

Although the Single European Act brings social policy within its remit, the European Commission has not so far attempted to harmonise social policy, except in the field of employment.

Public opinion appears willing to pay more, if necessary, to maintain the welfare state, but social protection is seen as primarily a matter for national governments, not for Europe-wide decisions.

# 5. The Environment

Some areas of environmental policy, such as town and country planning, are essentially a matter for local decision; but other European countries with similar problems have dealt with them in different ways, and there is much to be learnt from their experience. Some environmental issues, such as air and water pollution and long-distance transport networks, extend across national frontiers, and some degree of joint EU action will be needed for dealing with them effectively. And other environmental problems, such as ozone depletion and climate change, are essentially global in their causes and effects; a united European approach can be a major force in helping to achieve the necessary international co-operation.

Environmental concerns have been assuming increasing prominence in recent years, and their interdependence has brought a growing inclination to take a holistic approach and seek a general pattern of development that is sustainable in the longer term. Environmental protection is an area in which there is much support for action at European rather than national level, and where the global consensus achieved at the Rio summit has given a powerful stimulus to environmental action in both industrial and developing countries.

## Countryside

The United Kingdom is one of the more densely populated countries in Europe and England is the most crowded of all, with the great majority of the population living in large towns and conurbations. It is therefore not surprising that the distinctive qualities of the countryside are deeply cherished and there is much controversy surrounding the major changes which have been happening in recent decades and the further ones which are in prospect.

### Population
Since the Second World War there have been substantial movements of population from Scotland, Wales and the North of England to Southern England; and also from the inner areas of the larger towns to the more

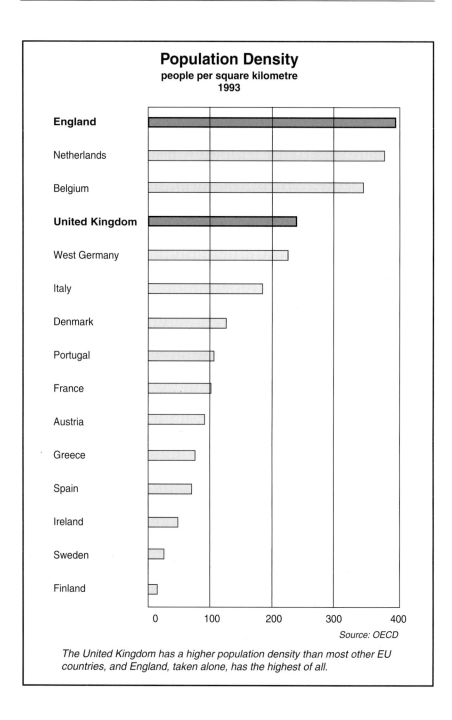

**Population Density**
people per square kilometre
1993

| | |
|---|---|
| **England** | |
| Netherlands | |
| Belgium | |
| **United Kingdom** | |
| West Germany | |
| Italy | |
| Denmark | |
| Portugal | |
| France | |
| Austria | |
| Greece | |
| Spain | |
| Ireland | |
| Sweden | |
| Finland | |

0   100   200   300   400

*Source: OECD*

*The United Kingdom has a higher population density than most other EU countries, and England, taken alone, has the highest of all.*

spacious suburbs, and beyond them to small country towns and villages as people have sought increasing prosperity in the form of living in more agreeable places. It is estimated that over the three decades 1971-2001 there will have been substantial population rises in a crescent from Cornwall to Lincolnshire, with increases of more than fifty per cent in Cambridgeshire and Buckinghamshire and of more than thirty per cent in Hereford and Worcestershire, Wiltshire, Suffolk, Lincolnshire, Hampshire, Norfolk and Oxfordshire, but *decreases* in Durham, Humberside, Cleveland and all of the metropolitan counties[116].

These changes from North to South and from town to country have been driven by changes in employment, by acceptance of long-distance commuting to town jobs from homes in the country, and by retirement moves from town to country and coastal areas - in six counties more than a quarter of the total population increase is attributed to retirement moves.

These moves are bringing important changes to country areas. The newcomers are from an urban background and tend to bring different life-styles and attitudes which can cause friction with traditional-minded existing communities. They also bring more wealth - it is, on the whole, the more affluent people in the cities who can afford to move. And this too can bring tensions, for the effect can be to drive up local prices, particularly for housing, beyond the levels which local people on low incomes, particularly young people, can afford.

One of the characteristics of the lifestyles of the newcomers is that this lifestyle is heavily dependent on the use of the motor car, both for social and shopping trips to nearby towns, and for longer journeys to commute to jobs. It will therefore be vulnerable in the future to the steep rise in motoring costs and other policies to discourage car use, as well as to rising property prices.

*Agriculture*
The second great change has been in agriculture, with more intensive methods and concentration of output in larger units - fifty-six per cent of output from the eleven per cent of largest farms - the bringing into use of large areas of marginal land, new methods of intensive animal rearing, an eight-fold increase in use of agricultural chemicals, and

improved varieties of crops and livestock. The result, compared with pre-war, has been some large increases in output - for example, a doubling of output of milk, a five-fold increase in wheat and a six-fold increase in barley. At the same time labour productivity has been greatly increased - the higher output has been achieved with a work force only one quarter of the 1945 level.

These changes have brought higher incomes to farmers, and also public disquiet over some of the consequences: large-scale loss of hedgerows and ancient woodlands, the effects of pesticides on food safety and fertilisers on water quality, and the treatment of battery hens and other farm animals with new intensive-rearing techniques.

Further changes in new directions are currently under way as a result of the reform of the European Union's Common Agricultural Policy (CAP). With a view to reducing the output surpluses which have been generated in the past, lower support prices have been introduced and arrangements made to pay farmers for a proportion of their land 'set aside' from agricultural production. The result is expected to be that output, incomes and employment will be lower than they would have been otherwise; and that there will be some stimulus to less intensive kinds of farming and to replanting of deciduous woodland, and incentives to embark on non-agricultural activities, such as rural handicrafts and tourism; and there will be a fall in the area of land under crops - it has been falling since 1987, and in one year, 1993, it fell by 4,600 km$^2$ (9.3 per cent), with most of the land reverting to rough grazing or falling into disuse[117].

*Recreation and tourism*
This release of cropland for alternative uses is giving a boost to the third main change in the countryside - the increasing use of country and coastal areas for tourism and recreation. In addition to more walking, riding, cycling, fishing and shooting, there have been great increases in a wide range of activities such as motor-biking, mountain-biking, hang-gliding, model aircraft flying, sailing, power-boating, water-skiing, archery, pigeon-shooting, war-gaming and golfing. To meet these demands, about a quarter of all farms now run some form of tourist activity, and there are also larger scale commercial developments such

as racetracks, marinas, theme parks, leisure complexes and golf courses. It is estimated that golf courses alone already cover about 1/2 of 1 per cent of the total land area of England; new ones are being built at an average rate of one-and-a-half a week[118], and planning permission has already been given for more than 600 additional ones.

These recreational activities are bringing changes to the distinctive sounds, smells and visual appearance of the countryside. Also, they are mostly dependent on the motor car for access, and are increasingly bringing traffic jams to rural areas, particularly along the coasts, in the national parks and in places of natural beauty. The Lake District, for example, often becomes such a traffic jam that it is effectively closed to further visitors.

*Policy controversies*
The three changes - in population, agriculture and recreation - have given rise to multi-dimensional conflicts: between newcomers and original populations; between city attitudes and rural ones; between residents and visitors; between agriculture and recreation; between employment and conservation; between recreation of humans and habitats of wildlife; between development of new facilities and preservation of 'natural' conditions; between greater access to peaceful and beautiful places and the erosion of their peace and beauty through excess of visitors.

In most of the other EU countries there have been similar developments, with people moving out of the towns, greater use of the countryside for recreation and tourism and falling employment in agriculture - although in all the other countries agriculture still accounts for a much greater share of total employment than in Britain, and has considerable political influence.

The conflicts arising from these changes seem bound to continue, and to be resolved in different ways in different places. The issues are, for the most part, essentially local, and give rise to strong feelings at times when national governments try to intervene, and even more outrage when there is intrusion from Brussels. Since most of these issues have no direct impact on people in other countries, and since there is great diversity in acceptable solutions in different places, it may be supposed that this is an area where subsidiarity will hold sway, with decisions being taken as often as possible at local level.

There is, however, one area in which the issues have a strong European dimension - agriculture. The Common Agricultural Policy has been much criticised by consumers, for bringing high prices, and by taxpayers, as a costly, cumbersome and inefficient mechanism which soaks up half of the Union's budget. It has also been criticised by producers in other countries as an unfair form of competition which generates surpluses which destabilise international markets.

However, the support system is strongly defended in countries in which the agricultural community is much larger than in Britain, as a means of ensuring self-sufficiency in food and of making possible the continuance of a distinctive way of life in rural areas. All changes in the CAP are hotly, even violently, opposed by farmers in the countries which benefit most from it.

The CAP was a major area of contention in the protracted Uruguay Round of GATT negotiations in which the European Union eventually had to agree to cuts in farm support and export subsidies as a condition for getting agreement on liberalisation of trade in manufacturing and services. It seems that in the future there will have to be further major changes, in order to release its half of the Union budget for other uses and to accommodate the large agricultural sectors of the countries of Central and Eastern Europe when they join the Union. (See Chapter 10.) The changes may involve reducing support prices to near international market levels, reducing the level of external protection, and phasing out the milk and sugar quotas - and hence in reducing farm incomes significantly. The savings might be used to promote new and environmentally-friendly kinds of rural development, particularly in low-income regions of the Union. But whatever form the changes take, and whatever kind of compensation is offered, the reform of the CAP will be sure to generate intense controversy.

## Towns

If more people are moving to country areas, fewer people are staying in the towns, particularly in the inner areas of the big conurbations. This is partly because people are seeking better living conditions in less congested areas. It is also because of changes in location of industry, offices, shops and recreation facilities.

For several decades industry has been moving out of the older inner city sites to get away from old buildings on cramped sites with poor access, high rates and high labour costs to go to new buildings on well-serviced modern industrial estates. More recently offices also have been moving out to get the benefit of newer buildings, lower rents and easier access by staff who also live in outlying areas.

There have also been major developments in retailing in the form of large supermarkets and of retail warehouses for bulky goods, such as furniture and electrical appliances, at the edges of towns and in out-of-town shopping centres, some of them offering a range of leisure and recreational facilities to provide 'a good day out for the whole family' for a catchment area population of half a million or more. Some of these out-of-town centres are very large: one near Sheffield has 110,000 m$^2$ of floorspace and parking for 12,000 cars[119]; one near Birmingham, if expansion plans go through, will have 215,000 m$^2$ of floorspace, the largest in Europe[120]; and a development in Avon has a floorspace greater than the centres of Bristol, Bath and all the other towns in the county combined[121].

Similar developments in the United States have led to the decline of retailing in existing city centres, followed by the departure to the suburbs of offices and recreational facilities, the depression of inner-city property values, the undermining of public transport system viability and the erosion of the municipal tax base. It has brought decay to central areas and traffic jams to suburban areas.

In most continental European countries, in contrast, it was felt that, with more constricted cities and better public transport systems, the dispersed car-based pattern of development followed in America would not be practical. Instead, a policy has been followed of improving existing city centres and access to them by public transport. This was followed almost everywhere, except in France and Germany, both of which allowed a number of major out-of-town developments in the

1960s, but which later brought in legislation to restrict them, in 1973 in France, and in 1968, 1977 and 1986 in Germany[122].

In many major cities in continental Europe, instead of developing new out-of-town complexes, the emphasis has been on strengthening existing city centres by:

- building new shopping and leisure complexes on city centre sites;

- upgrading existing shopping streets by covering them over to make weather-proof arcades;

- creating large traffic-free pedestrian precincts;

- improving access, with better public transport into and within shopping areas, and better facilities for pedestrians and cyclists; and

- restricting access by and parking of private cars.

Restrictions on car access are often opposed by retailers out of fear that business will suffer. Continental experience has been the reverse. When streets have been pedestrianised it has made them more attractive to shoppers and led to *increases* in turnover; for example, in Munich, which has a largely pedestrianised city centre, exceptionally *low* parking provision and a particularly *good* public transport system, business turnover levels have been exceptionally *high*[122].

In Britain in the 1980s a *laisser-faire* approach to development was leading towards an American pattern of development, but recently there has been a shift in government policy to a more continental European approach with the announcement of planning policy guidelines to discourage out-of-town development in favour of town-centre revitalisation[123]; and a report by the House of Commons's Environment Committee has called for the guidance to be strengthened to include `a presumption that superstores are best located in or on the edge of town centres unless there are strong indications to the contrary'[124].

However, the change may have come too late. Between 1976 and 1990 a total of 17 million m$^2$ of new shopping centre floorspace was built; in the recession since then, another 2.1 million m$^2$; and a further 2.4 million m$^2$ is in the pipeline[125]. Altogether, between 1973 and 1993, the number of `superstores' increased from 43 to 776[124], and the share of retail trade taken by out-of-town shopping centres has risen from 8 per cent of the total in 1983 to 27 per cent of the total in 1994[125] - with a corresponding reduction in the share of city-centre and neighbourhood shopping centres, and the collapse of a number of retail chains based on them. Moreover, people who have got used to the convenience of shopping once a week by car are not likely to be keen to revert to taking their groceries home by public transport, even if the standard of services is greatly improved.

And while policy for retail development has changed, and it is now the aim to regenerate existing city centres, funds have not yet been provided for major investment in the centres themselves, or for the improvement of public transport facilities, or the promotion of `park-and-ride' schemes to draw people living in the suburbs into shops in the town centre.

It seems likely that, in the course of the coming decades, urban development policies in Britain will become more like those in other countries of the European Union because their experience will seem more relevant to our circumstances than that of North America - and also more widely observed, as increasing numbers of people visit European cities and see for themselves how things are done in other countries.

However, it is most unlikely that there will be a European dimension in the sense that an attempt will be made to harmonise the policies of the different countries. Urban development policies affect mainly the inhabitants of the cities concerned and have little direct impact on people in other countries. This is therefore an area where the principle of subsidiarity is likely to remain unchallenged.

## Transport

The car is one of the most popular products ever invented, offering the attraction of quick, safe, comfortable, door-to-door transport for people and their possessions. As people's incomes improve, one of their first priorities is usually to get a car - and then a larger, faster or newer one, or a second one. As a result, whereas in 1951 six households in seven in Britain had no car, now only one household in three has no car, and one household in five has two or more cars[126]. Car traffic doubled between 1960 and 1970 and doubled again between 1970 and 1990[126]; and the Department of Transport forecasts that it will rise further by 33-53 per cent between 1990 and 2010, and by 60-93 per cent between 1990 and 2025[126]. This forecast is compatible with past trends. The lower figures require only a moderate rate of economic growth (which seems likely); and the higher figures imply a rise in traffic much faster than the rate of economic growth (which is what has happened in the past). Even so, there are a number of reasons why this particular forecast seems unlikely to prove correct.

### Traffic problems

Continuing increases in car ownership look like being self-defeating because of the steady worsening of traffic congestion. Despite a great variety of measures taken to mitigate it, peak-hour congestion in Britain's towns gets worse, and spreads over longer periods and wider areas, and congestion is also growing in smaller towns and in country and seaside areas at weekends and holiday periods.

In London it has become particularly bad. Between 1981 and 1991, the population of Greater London fell slightly from 6.6 million to 6.3 million but car ownership rose by 20 per cent and the number of cars trying to get in and out of London each day rose by 25 per cent[127]. In *Central* London there was no increase in car numbers because saturation had already been reached, but average speeds fell to only ten miles per hour[127] - only one mile per hour faster than in 1912 and two miles per hour faster than was achieved with horses and carriages in 1890[128]. Not only private cars are having to move more slowly, but fire engines and ambulances also are taking far longer to reach the scene of accidents [129].

At present only about one commuter in seven comes into Central London by car[126], and to try to enable the other six to do so would require the demolition of a large part of the inner area to provide seven times the road capacity and flattening the whole of the centre to provide

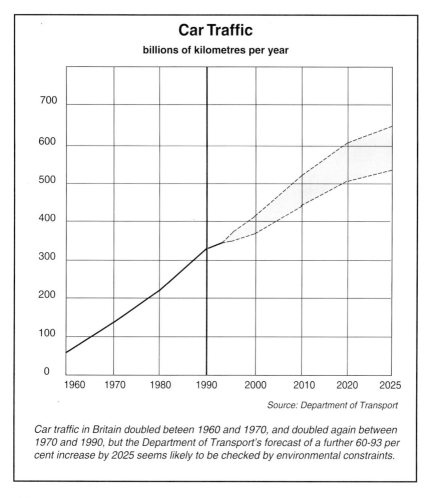

**Car Traffic**

billions of kilometres per year

Source: Department of Transport

*Car traffic in Britain doubled beteen 1960 and 1970, and doubled again between 1970 and 1990, but the Department of Transport's forecast of a further 60-93 per cent increase by 2025 seems likely to be checked by environmental constraints.*

additional parking space. The Los Angeles 'solution', which is not currently proving very satisfactory even in Los Angeles, would be physically impossible in the more cramped conditions of London and most other cities in Europe.

And building more new roads in other areas is becoming a less attractive proposition because of the high costs and the increasingly determined objections to the majority of new schemes - it is reported, for example, that a study by the Department of the Environment of 243 road schemes in the current programme found 103 likely to engender 'high controversy', and 118 likely to have a particularly damaging effect on the environment due to their effect on conservation areas, sites of special interest or other valuable land[130].

There is also the problem that experience has shown that the construction of new roads tends to generate extra traffic to fill them [131], and a report by a government advisory committee has stressed that this can be `a matter of profound importance' in invalidating the cost/benefit justifications for new road projects[132]. This was demonstrated with the M25 London orbital motorway, most sections of which, within three years of its opening in 1986, were already having jams as a result of carrying more traffic than the upper limit forecast for 2001[133].

Finally, there is the problem of accidents[134]. Although the figures have been coming down, there are still more than 3,500 deaths a year on the roads - equivalent to a jumbo jet crashing every month with the loss of all on board.

In other European countries also there has been a great increase in car ownership, and in the richer countries ownership levels are higher than in Britain[135]. But, while in most of them the percentage increase in ownership between 1971 and 1992 was greater than in Britain, in the richer countries the percentage increase was mostly less than in the poorer ones, and the increase was particularly small in two of the richest - Denmark and Sweden[135]

Other EU countries have also experienced great increases in car traffic, in congestion, and in road accidents - *all* the others have road death rates even higher than Britain's[135].

*Traffic policies*
In short, both policy-makers and consumers are beginning to weaken in their enthusiasm for the car. There is still great reluctance to face up to the constraints that traffic problems are highlighting, but local, national and EU policies are increasingly coming to recognise the limitations of increasing car use and increasing road construction to accommodate it. Accordingly, attention is being focused on the cities which have had some success by putting the emphasis on:

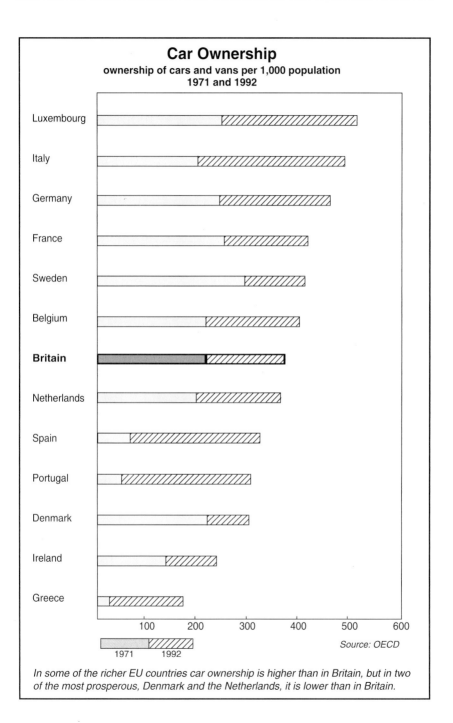

# Car Ownership
**ownership of cars and vans per 1,000 population**
**1971 and 1992**

Luxembourg

Italy

Germany

France

Sweden

Belgium

**Britain**

Netherlands

Spain

Portugal

Denmark

Ireland

Greece

100    200    300    400    500    600

1971    1992

*Source: OECD*

*In some of the richer EU countries car ownership is higher than in Britain, but in two of the most prosperous, Denmark and the Netherlands, it is lower than in Britain.*

107

**Road Deaths**
number killed per year per 100,000 population
1993

|  | |
|---|---|
| Britain | |
| Sweden | |
| Netherlands | |
| Finland | |
| Denmark | |
| Ireland | |
| Germany | |
| Italy | |
| Austria | |
| Belgium | |
| Spain | |
| France | |
| Greece | |
| Portugal | |

*Source: OECD*

In Britain there are fewer deaths on the road per 100,000 population than in any other EU country. Even so, the toll of more than 3,500 a year is equivalent to the loss of a jumbo jet every month.

- improved metro, light-rail and commuter train systems;

- faster and more frequent bus services, with priority lanes;

- better provision for cyclists and pedestrians;

- tougher enforcement of traffic regulations, particularly bus lanes and parking restrictions;

- charges for use of new motorways;

- discouragement of cars through restrictions on access and parking; and

- high petrol prices and other motoring costs and subsidies for public transport.

In Copenhagen, where plans for urban motorways were dropped and priority bus-and-cycle lanes were introduced instead, between 1970-90 car use *declined* by 10 per cent, between 1980-90 use of bicycles *increased* by 80 per cent, and now about one third of commuters use bicycles, compared with about 4 per cent in London[136]. Thanks to better provision for cyclists in the Netherlands, 27 per cent of commuter journeys are made by bicycle[137]. And in a number of cities in Italy, Switzerland, Germany and France car traffic in central areas has been successfully reduced.

In Britain policy has been influenced by a reluctance to offend motorists, by a reluctance to undertake heavy investment to improve public transport services, and by a reluctance to subsidise public transport fares. In consequence, fares in London are the highest of any city in the European Union and encourage people to use their cars for inner-city journeys.

A study by David Pearce[138], Professor of Environmental Economics at University College London, and former adviser to the Department of the Environment, estimates that the full social and environmental costs arising from private road users in Britain amount to between £22.9bn

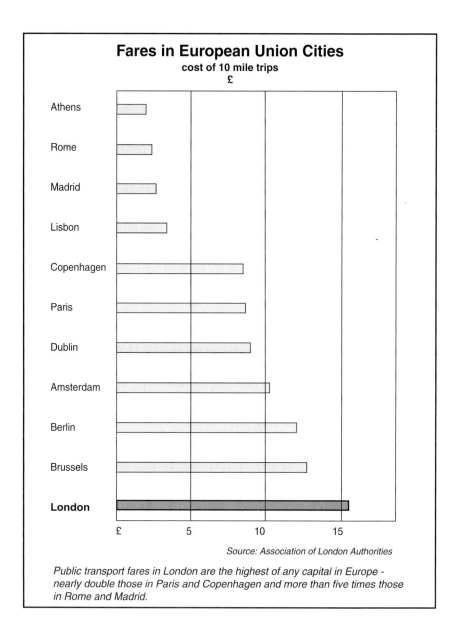

**Fares in European Union Cities**
cost of 10 mile trips
£

*Source: Association of London Authorities*

*Public transport fares in London are the highest of any capital in Europe - nearly double those in Paris and Copenhagen and more than five times those in Rome and Madrid.*

and £25.7bn a year - in, for example, physical wear on roads, traffic congestion, air pollution, noise pollution and accident costs. This compares with a total of about £14.7bn a year they pay in taxes. They would therefore need to pay at least a further £11bn a year - an extra

£500 a car - to cover their full social and environmental costs. Another study[139] estimates the gap between costs and tax receipts at twice as much, equivalent to a subsidy of about £1,000 a year per car.

As considerations such as these become more widely understood and accepted, it seems likely that motoring costs will be significantly increased, and the projected increase in traffic slowed down, as policies in Britain are reconsidered[140] and move nearer to those in continental countries. There are already some early indications of this with: the announcement in the 1993 Budget of an annual escalation of 5 per cent in real terms of road-fuel duties; plans to introduce charges for use of motorways[141] and inner-city roads[142]; cuts in the motorway building programme[143]; signs of a more sympathetic approach to the bicycle[144]; and the broadly sympathetic reception given to the report of the Royal Commission on Environmental Pollution, Transport and the Environment[145], which has called for a programme to cut down the forecast increase in traffic with a programme including:

- an increase in the proposed annual increase in the price of petrol from 5 per cent to 9 per cent;

- the end of tax concessions for company cars;

- legislation for tighter emission standards and a 40 per cent improvement in fuel efficiency by 2005;

- a halving of investment in motorways and trunk roads; and

- use of the saving to increase investment in public transport so as to raise the miles travelled on public transport from 12 per cent of the total in 1993 to 30 per cent by 2020.

*Public attitudes*
Part of the explanation of past public policies in Britain probably lies in the belief that public opinion is strongly in favour of unfettered use of the private motor car. This is not borne out by the findings of the 1994/95 British Social Attitudes Survey[146]. It found there were large majorities in favour of: doing more to improve public transport, even if

## Attitudes to Transport Policy in Britain
### 1994

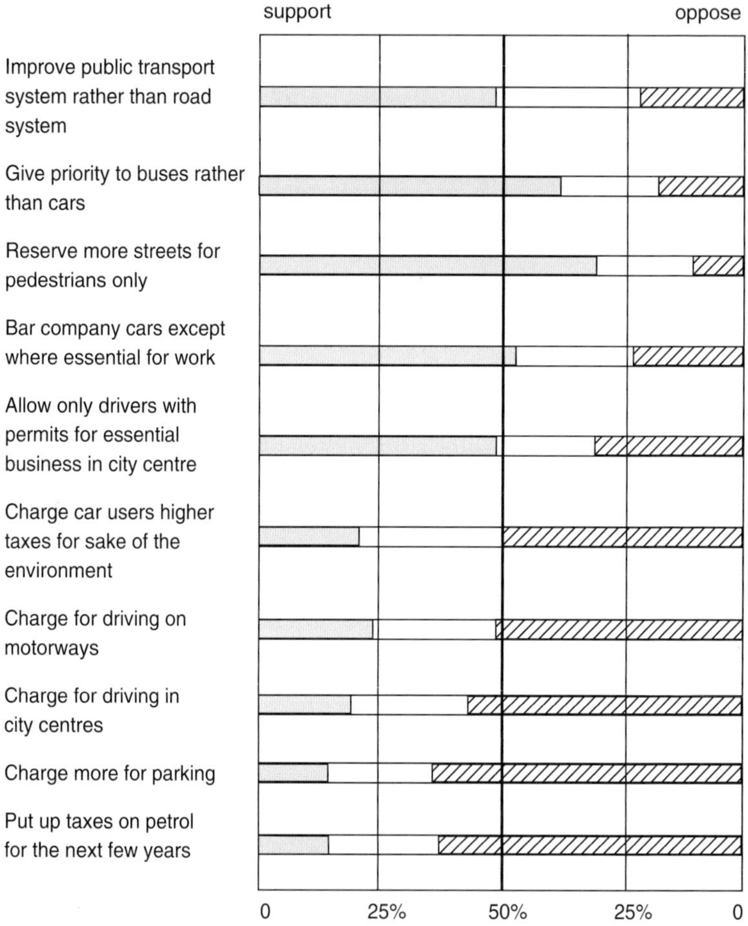

| | support | | | | oppose |
|---|---|---|---|---|---|

Improve public transport system rather than road system

Give priority to buses rather than cars

Reserve more streets for pedestrians only

Bar company cars except where essential for work

Allow only drivers with permits for essential business in city centre

Charge car users higher taxes for sake of the environment

Charge for driving on motorways

Charge for driving in city centres

Charge more for parking

Put up taxes on petrol for the next few years

0    25%    50%    25%    0

*Source: British Social Attitudes Survey 1994/95*

*Public opinion in Britain appears to favour giving more priority to public transport and pedestrians and measures to discourage the use of private cars - but only provided they do not put up the cost of motoring.*

the road system suffers; giving buses priority over private cars; reserving more streets for pedestrians; banning company cars except where essential for the work; and allowing only drivers with permits for essential business into city centres in working hours. On the other hand, it also found large majorities *against* dearer petrol, higher parking charges, or tolls for use of motorways or city-centre roads.

In short, the attitude now seems to be: `Yes, we need better public transport and more restraint on the use of *other* people's cars, but I can't do without *mine*' - still only half-way there, but an advance on the position a few years ago.

A survey of all the European Union countries[147] produced broadly similar findings, with large majorities in all countries in favour of giving public transport, cyclists and pedestrians priority over private cars in traffic-planning decisions; and in favour of solving traffic-congestion problems by developing public transport, creating more pedestrian areas, and limiting car traffic in town centres; but majorities in all countries *against* higher petrol prices and tolls on entering city centres; and a wide spread of national attitudes on tighter parking restrictions and construction of new urban highways. There was also a majority in every country that felt that political decision-makers had a false perception of public attitudes: in reality, people are more opposed to policies favouring unrestrained use of the car than is supposed. It may be that the way people respond to opinion poll questions differs from the way they vote in elections, and evidently people are not keen on actually *paying* more for their motoring. Nevertheless it appears that there is more support for less car-dominated policies than is often supposed.

### Long-distance links

Another area in which British practice has differed from continental is in the carriage of freight. Between 1961-93 the percentage of freight carried by road rose from 51 per cent of the total to 64 per cent, and the percentage carried by rail dropped from 28 per cent to 7 per cent[126] - with consequential increases in numbers of heavy goods vehicles, road wear, pollution and traffic congestion. In most continental European countries investment in railways has been much greater and policies

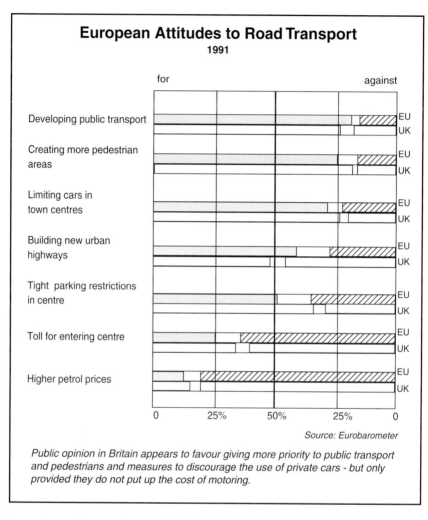

**European Attitudes to Road Transport**
1991

Public opinion in Britain appears to favour giving more priority to public transport and pedestrians and measures to discourage the use of private cars - but only provided they do not put up the cost of motoring.

have been directed towards keeping as much long-distance freight traffic off the roads as possible, with the result that in most of them a far higher proportion of freight travels by rail than in Britain[135].

Currently, policies in a number of European countries are being made more stringent with new levies on trucks using motorways in Germany, Belgium, Luxembourg, the Netherlands and Denmark[148], a proposal to force all foreign trucks crossing Switzerland to go by train from 2004[149] and similar proposals in Austria.

The opening of the Channel Tunnel provides new scope for fast through rail freight services to continental destinations, providing the speedier deliveries and longer hauls necessary for effective rail competition with road transport.

Probably no less important than the opening of the Channel Tunnel is the development of a pan-European network of high-speed rail links. These offer the prospect of bringing, not only Paris and Brussels, but

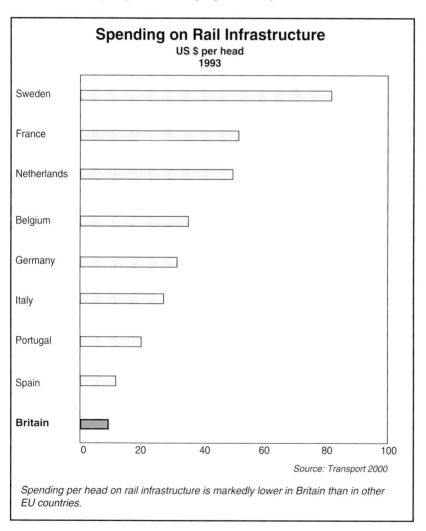

**Spending on Rail Infrastructure**
US $ per head
1993

*Source: Transport 2000*

*Spending per head on rail infrastructure is markedly lower in Britain than in other EU countries.*

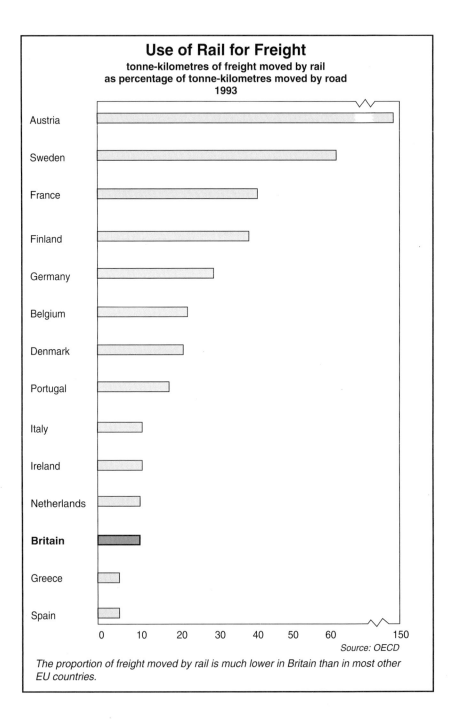

## Use of Rail for Freight
**tonne-kilometres of freight moved by rail
as percentage of tonne-kilometres moved by road
1993**

*Source: OECD*

*The proportion of freight moved by rail is much lower in Britain than in most other EU countries.*

also Amsterdam, Lyon and Bordeaux closer to London than Glasgow and Edinburgh are at present; and of bringing cities such as Berlin, Munich, Vienna, Milan, Barcelona and Madrid, and many holiday destinations also, within an overnight twelve-hour sleeper journey from London.

These developments offer the potential to 'de-peripheralise' Britain, bringing its exports and its businessmen much closer to the heart of Europe, and shrinking some of the psychological and material disadvantages previously experienced. It might have been expected that there would be a push to capitalise on the possibilities by pushing ahead with promoting through rail services to continental destinations and rapidly completing a connecting network of high-speed rail links within Britain. In the event, very little has so far been done to realise the scope for through rail services, the high-speed link between the Tunnel and London is unlikely to be ready until eight years after the opening of the Tunnel itself, and plans for other high-speed links to connect the Tunnel to the rest of Britain are still remote and uncertain[150].

The main explanation is that, whereas the French government has been ready to invest considerable public money in developing a major infrastructure network for the future, in Britain the scope for quick progress has been constrained by a reluctance to invest public money, an insistence on a high and early commercial rate of return for whatever is invested, and an insistence on the use of private-sector funding; while the scope for major future initiatives is likely to be constrained by the fragmentation of the network after privatisation. The outcome is likely to be the balancing of financial budgets in the short-term, but at the expense of the rapid creation of an asset of key importance in the longer term.

The construction of the Channel Tunnel has already required close Anglo-French co-operation; and the design and construction of a pan-European high-speed rail network which transcends national frontiers will require all the national rail undertakings to work closely together. The need for co-ordination of standards and policies for international road and sea and air freight will also oblige the member countries of the Union to work effectively together. Accordingly, the European Commission has prepared a policy statement seeking a sustainable

# Planned European High Speed Train Network 2010

New lines 250 km/h

Lines upgraded to 200 km/h

*Source: European Commission*

*Planned new high-speed rail links will bring European centres closer together and reduce the growth in air and road traffic. However, development of new rail links in Britain is less advanced and more uncertain than in other EU countries.*

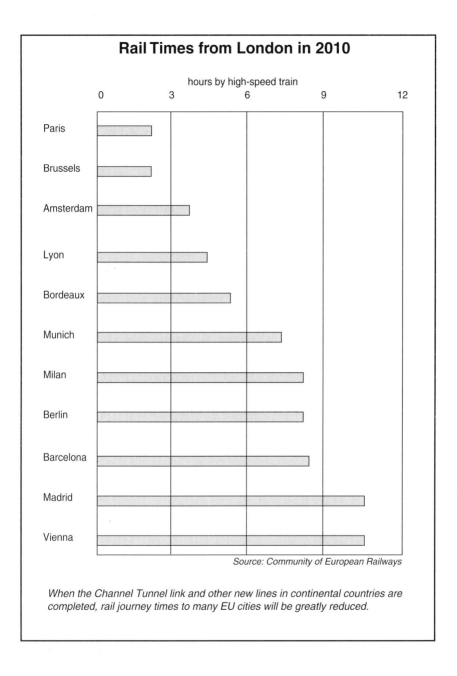

# Rail Times from London in 2010

hours by high-speed train

|  | |
|------|--|
| Paris | |
| Brussels | |
| Amsterdam | |
| Lyon | |
| Bordeaux | |
| Munich | |
| Milan | |
| Berlin | |
| Barcelona | |
| Madrid | |
| Vienna | |

*Source: Community of European Railways*

*When the Channel Tunnel link and other new lines in continental countries are completed, rail journey times to many EU cities will be greatly reduced.*

119

common approach for the development of rail networks on a European scale; but, more controversially, for pan-European motorway networks also [151].

On the other hand, policies for municipal and other internal transport are matters which countries are likely to be content to leave their partners to handle as they see fit - except where they have environmental effects which cross national borders.

## Water and waste

There are four main causes of contamination of drinking water in Britain:

- nitrates from excessive use of fertilisers, which leach through the soil to the water table below, over long periods of time, so that in some areas nitrates released now will still be causing trouble in fifty years' time;

- toxic chemicals, such as pesticides and herbicides, which can also leach into the water table and present risks;

- hydrocarbons shed from coal-tar linings in water mains which are thought to contain carcinogens, a risk which can only be removed by replacement of the linings, which would be very expensive - an estimated £1bn for the Thames Water area alone; and

- lead in domestic water pipes, mostly in older houses, which it is estimated would cost £8.5bn to replace in Britain and even more in France and Italy [152].

In 1980 the European Commission set standards for drinking water purity and since then considerable progress has been made in improving water quality. Even so, in Britain, as in several other countries in the European Union, there are still areas in which quality standards are not fully met [117].

With liquid waste, the main area of international contention in the past has been the practice in Britain, alone of North Sea countries, of discharging untreated sewage from many coastal towns directly into the sea, leading to contamination of bathing beaches in Britain and, it has been claimed, potentially in other countries also. Also about one-third of treated sewage sludge was dumped in the North Sea. In response to protests from other countries, agreement was reached on a programme of new treatment plant, incineration facilities and landfills to make it possible to end the dumping of sludge by 1998, and on an end to the discharge of untreated sewage by 2000[153]. However there have been delays in some of the projects[154]. In 1993 the amount of dumped sewage sludge had not yet fallen[117], and in 1994 18 per cent of Britain's beaches were still failing to meet the standards set by the European Commission for bathing water cleanliness[117].

Agreement was also reached to reduce the quantities of a number of toxic pollutants going into the North Sea to half the 1985 levels by 1995. Between 1985-93 there were big reductions in discharges from Britain of cadmium, mercury, copper and lead, but not of zinc or nitrates[117], and it now seems likely that Britain, together with some of the other North Sea countries, will fail to meet all the 1995 targets[155].

The quality of water in rivers in Britain has been improving, but the National Rivers Authority has urged the need for a £900m programme to secure further improvements[156]. In continental European countries river pollution is also a problem, which becomes an international one when major rivers flow across national boundaries. For example, Netherlands, which gets about 40 per cent of its drinking water from the Rhine and the Meuse, has suffered from heavy pollution of the water by chemical plants in other countries upstream[11]. However, negotiations have resulted in plans for major improvements.

The arrangements in Britain for disposal of toxic and hazardous solid waste have long been a matter of concern, leading to a highly critical report by the parliamentary Environment Select Committee[157] and the assertion by its chairman that Britain has come perilously close to suffering a disaster from its `appalling' waste disposal system[158]. However, controls have since been strengthened; and it is hoped that the introduction of a landfill tax in 1996 will reduce the proportion of general waste that is dumped rather than disposed of in more environmentally satisfactory ways.

Concern in continental Europe has been focused more on general household waste, particularly packaging waste, of which there is an estimated 50 million tonnes a year in the European Union as a whole [159]. In the European Union as a whole an average of 18 per cent of it is recycled, but the recovery rate varies greatly between different countries. European Union agreement has been reached on a 1998 target of recovery of a minimum of 50 per cent of packaging waste, with 25 per cent of it recycled[160]. This target, subject to a 'substantial increase' for 2003, is much less ambitious than the targets previously envisaged of 90 per cent recovered and 60 per cent recycled[160]. It is also less than the target of 50 per cent recycled by 2000 set for Britain[161], and far less than the targets already set by a number of other countries, such as Germany which has a recycling target of 60 per cent for 1995[160].

There have been complaints from other countries that in Germany the setting of targets were over-ambitious in relation to domestic recycling capacity and that this led to the accumulation of 'waste mountains' which other countries then had to take away; and arguments about what proportion of waste is worth recycling; the high cost of plastics recycling; the feasibility of schemes for recycling cars and domestic appliances; and the relative merits of glass-bottle recycling versus re-use, and of paper recycling versus incineration for heat and energy production[159,162,163]. This is an area in which agreement on concerted European action may make possible more progress than would be achieved with each country working alone.

## Air pollution

Air pollution has become a matter of growing concern in most of the countries of Western Europe over the past two decades and, more recently, in Eastern Europe also where past policy errors have resulted in particularly heavy pollution. The main pollutants are sulphur dioxide, mainly from power stations and industrial plants, which falls as acid rain causing damage to trees, crops, buildings and people; and nitrogen oxides, mainly from vehicle exhausts, power stations and industry, which damage air quality and injure health. There are also problems with other pollutants, such as lead, particulates and carbon monoxide, all from vehicles, and all posing a threat to health.

The cost of the damage done by air pollution is hard to measure but clearly considerable. In Britain, for example, estimates of the cost of the damage done by acid rain vary from £1.3bn to £3.3bn a year[138].

A characteristic of air pollution is that much of the pollution generated in one country blows across national borders to drift down as acid rain in neighbouring countries. It is estimated, for example, that more than half the sulphur dioxide emitted in Britain and Germany lands as acid rain in other countries[164]. The problem is particularly acute in smaller countries; for example, it is estimated that more than three-quarters of the acid rain falling in the Netherlands and in the Scandinavian countries is of external origin, while more than half of their own emissions are exported to other countries[11,164]. Hence the Dutch argue that, if they want to improve air quality in the Netherlands, they need to invest not so much to reduce their own emissions, which are among the lowest per head in Europe, as to reduce them in countries, such as Poland, where emissions per head are five times as high and total emissions are thirteen times as high[165].

East Germany has abundant supplies of brown coal and suffers from the legacy of irresponsible past policies, under which coal was subsidised and made available at about a quarter of its real cost[6], resulting in the generation of air pollution on a massive scale, with sulphur dioxide emissions per head four times as high as in the United States[165]. Similar policies in Poland have led to emissions per head as high as in the United States, despite the much lower level of industrial development. However, in Britain also, emissions are higher than in most other counties in Western Europe - for example about four times as high per head as in West Germany and the Netherlands, and six times as high as in Switzerland[165].

With nitrogen oxides the countries of Eastern Europe, with their low vehicle populations, do not compare so badly, but here too Britain is one of the countries with relatively high emissions per head. There are therefore likely to be continuing pressures from other countries for Britain to become a 'good neighbour' and reduce the emissions which blow across to damage neighbouring countries.

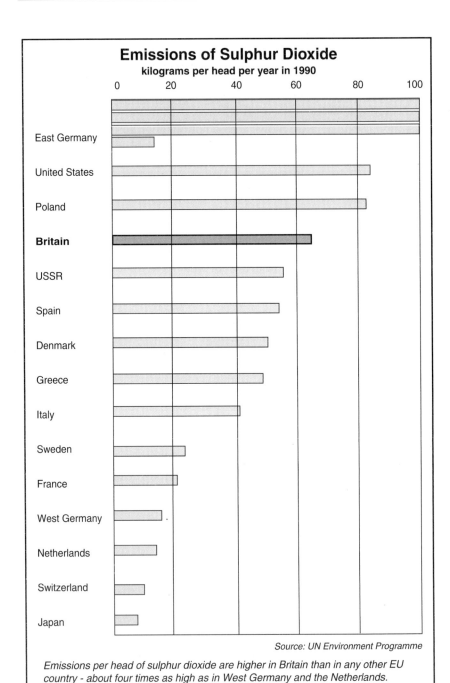

**Emissions of Sulphur Dioxide**
kilograms per head per year in 1990

*Source: UN Environment Programme*

*Emissions per head of sulphur dioxide are higher in Britain than in any other EU country - about four times as high as in West Germany and the Netherlands.*

# Emissions of Nitrogen Oxides
**kilograms per head per year in 1990**

| | |
|---|---|
| United States | |
| Greece | |
| Denmark | |
| **Britain** | |
| West Germany | |
| East Germany | |
| Netherlands | |
| Poland | |
| Italy | |
| France | |
| Switzerland | |
| Spain | |
| USSR | |
| Sweden | |
| Japan | |

*Source: UN Environment Programme*

*Emissions per head of nitrogen oxides are higher in Britain than in most other EU countries, and there has been little progress in meeting targets for reductions - lower power station emissions have been offset by increased road traffic.*

125

In response to the mutual interest in achieving a general reduction in emissions, the European Environment Council reached agreement for phased reductions of sulphur dioxide emissions to 60 per cent below the 1980 level by 2003, and reductions in nitrogen oxide emissions to 30 per cent below by 1993. It had been envisaged that the targets for Britain would be met largely by fitting expensive desulphurisation plant to the largest power stations and low-$NO_x$ burners to all twelve of the major coal-fired power stations at a total cost of about £2bn. However, a cheaper way of reducing emissions has instead been adopted, in the form of increased use of low-sulphur coal imports and greater reliance on gas-fired generating plant.

A further major step has been taken by the European Commission, following the lead given by the United States, in setting emission standards for new cars which, for the larger ones at least, can only be met by the fitting of catalytic converters to their exhausts.

In the event, by 1993 emissions of sulphur dioxide in Britain had been reduced to 35 per cent below the 1980 level; but emissions of nitrogen oxides by only 2 per cent - lower emissions from power stations having been offset by higher emissions from road traffic; while emissions of carbon monoxide actually *increased* by 15 per cent[117].

The introduction of a small tax differential was largely responsible for sales of lead-free petrol rising to 58 per cent of the total in 1994, when lead emissions from motor vehicles in Britain dropped to 82 per cent below the 1980 level, but there is still concern about high emissions of benzene and other dangerous volatile organic compounds from road vehicles[117].

Overall, the World Bank estimates[166] that air-pollution levels are very high and still rising in cities in low-income countries; less high and falling in cities in middle-income countries; and much lower and falling to within acceptable limits in cities in high-income countries. In the industrialised countries, emissions of sulphur dioxide have fallen to about half the levels of the early 1970s, due to tougher emissions regulations, but also due to changes in energy prices after the oil shocks in the early 1970s, the use of more efficient technologies, and slower rates of economic growth[165]. However, not only in Britain, but in most of the other industrialised countries also (except Japan) emissions of nitrogen oxides have *not* been falling, indeed have been tending to go on rising, largely because of the continuing increase in vehicle traffic [165].

It is the major contribution which road traffic makes to air pollution in cities that led the Royal Commission on Environmental Pollution to recommend a package of measures to encourage a shift from private cars to public transport[145], and which is likely to result in increasingly stringent vehicle emissions standards on a Europe-wide basis.

## Biodiversity

An environmental area of concern which applies to all scales of development, from the local to the global, is biodiversity. At present knowledge is very incomplete about the exact number of species currently in existence, about the proportion of them threatened with extinction, and about the consequences if they do indeed become extinct. It is clear, however, that many natural habitats have been destroyed in Europe as a result of agricultural activities and the expansion of towns and roads and, more importantly, in the tropical developing countries by the destruction of forests which are particularly rich in the variety of wildlife they support. Studies undertaken for the World Bank estimate that in Sub-Saharan Africa and in South and South-East Asia more than half the forest, savannah and mangrove habitats had already been destroyed by 1986[166], and the world's remaining tropical forests are estimated to be disappearing at the rate of 0.9 per cent a year[166]. Other studies[167] estimate that in Brazil alone an area of forest three times the size of Wales is being cleared each year.

It is estimated that the number of extinctions of mammal species this century has been about double that of the last century and about five times that of the century before[168]; the current rate of loss is estimated to be more than 100,000 times the 'natural rate'[169] and, if it continues, a quarter or more of the species of organisms on the earth could be eliminated within fifty years[170].

Already about a quarter of all medicines are based on plants and microorganisms, with a total value of $40bn a year[169]; and these are the fruits of investigation of perhaps as little as one in a hundred of the earth's plant species. Hence it is impossible to calculate the scale or form of the future loss if a sizeable fraction of all species become extinct.

Probably more important, but less well understood and even harder to measure in economic terms, is the role played by particular species in complex ecosystems. There is the risk that further mass extinctions will upset natural balances and bring gravely damaging biological, physical or climate changes. It will therefore be prudent to document more fully the range of existing species and their rates of extinction, and to make more strenuous efforts to preserve the natural habitats of endangered species, particularly the eighteen 'hot spots', comprising a mere 0.5 per cent of the earth's surface, which have been identified as the homes of a full 20 per cent of all the earth's plant species[169]. The eventual gain may be hard to quantify but, as Sir Crispin Tickell has said[171]:

We have to value the things that count rather than the things that can be counted.

With a view to mobilising a global response to these challenges, the UN Rio Earth Summit adopted the Biodiversity Convention and established the Global Environmental Facility, with a budget of $150bn over three years, nearly half of it aimed at conserving biodiversity. In Europe the Commission has promulgated the Habitats Directive, to seek to preserve what remains of biodiversity within Europe; but the main European contribution to the global effort is likely to be not so much within Europe itself as through provision of funding and scientific expertise to help preserve biodiversity in some of the species-rich developing countries.

## Ozone depletion

The use of chlorofluorocarbons (CFCs) in aerosols, foams, solvents and refrigerants leads to a depletion of the earth's protective ozone layer in the upper atmosphere, bringing increased risk of skin cancers to humans and possible risks also to animals and plants. Although the . phenomenon had only recently been identified, the international response was relatively quick, with an international conference in Montreal in 1987 getting agreement on a 50 per cent world reduction in

CFCs by the year 2000. When it was subsequently established that this would not be sufficient, further meetings agreed successively on a complete phasing out by 2000, and later still on a complete phasing out by 1997. In the European Union an even more stringent phase-out has been agreed, with all production of CFCs stopped by the end of 1994.

World output of CFCs in 1993 was already 60 per cent below the 1988 peak[172], and the 1997 world target is expected to be met; and the European Union target of a phase-out by the end of 1994 has been met already. In the achievement of this outcome the European Union has played a leading part, both in pressing for concerted international action and in setting for itself a timetable faster than was acceptable to other countries.

It is important and encouraging for the future that, in the face of a severe global threat, needing a global response to deal with it, the international community was able to react with a globally-accepted and effective response. Even so, the outcome is less than perfect. First, because of time-lags in the process, means that the ozone hole will continue to grow, as a result of past emissions, for many years after production of CFCs has ceased, and it will be several decades before ozone levels return even to 1988 levels. Second, some of the substitutes that have been developed, it transpires, are themselves major contributors to the 'greenhouse effect', and so will need to be phased out in their turn[173]. And third, there is doubt whether a full solution has in fact been found. It appears that the ozone reduction in the northern hemisphere has been between two to four times as great as can be explained by CFCs alone, and there are reasons for believing that much of the balance may have been caused by nitrous oxide emissions from jet aircraft - which are still growing with the increase in air traffic[174].

Also it has to be remembered that speedy global agreement was only possible because reasonably satisfactory substitutes were available (which could profitably be produced by the companies which previously made CFCs), and CFCs are not a major element in the economy of any country - it was therefore not very difficult for the industrialised countries to make the necessary changes, or to provide sufficient economic and technical help to enable the developing

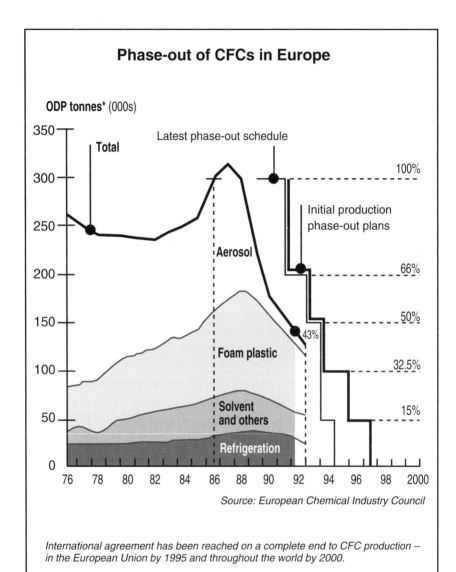

## Phase-out of CFCs in Europe

ODP tonnes* (000s)

Total

Latest phase-out schedule

Initial production phase-out plans

Aerosol

Foam plastic

Solvent and others

Refrigeration

100%

66%

50%

43%

32.5%

15%

*Source: European Chemical Industry Council*

*International agreement has been reached on a complete end to CFC production – in the European Union by 1995 and throughout the world by 2000.*

countries to co-operate also. However, if it is confirmed that international air traffic is a major cause of ozone depletion, it will be a great deal more difficult to find agreement on an effective solution to the problem.

## Global climate change

In recent years many scientists have been concerned that the burning of increasing quantities of fossil fuels in the course of economic growth was giving rise to increasing emissions of carbon dioxide, and also of other gases such as methane, CFCs and nitrous oxides; and that these were accumulating in the upper atmosphere, allowing short-wave solar radiation to reach the earth, but preventing longer-wave infra-red heat from escaping into space - thus bringing about a `greenhouse effect' and giving rise to a long-term rise in world temperatures.

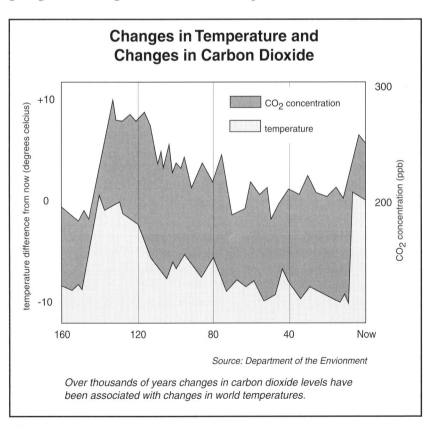

**Changes in Temperature and Changes in Carbon Dioxide**

*Source: Department of the Envionment*

*Over thousands of years changes in carbon dioxide levels have been associated with changes in world temperatures.*

This theory was hotly disputed, not least by governments who were uneasy about the implications for future energy consumption. Accordingly, they resolved to establish the facts beyond all reasonable doubt by setting up the Intergovernmental Panel on Climate Change (IPCC) to investigate the matter. The project was staffed by more than 200 scientists from all the world's leading institutions in this field, and was sponsored jointly by the United Nations Environment Programme and the World Meteorological Organisation. When the report[175] was published in 1990 its findings were unanimous and unequivocal:

> We are certain that emissions resulting from human activities are substantially increasing the atmospheric concentrations of the greenhouse gases: carbon dioxide, methane, CFCs and nitrous oxide. These increases will enhance the greenhouse effect, resulting on avenge in an additional warming of the world's surface.

> Based on current model results, we predict, under the IPCC 'business-as-usual' emissions of greenhouse gases, a rate of increase of global mean temperature during the next century of about .3°C per decade (with an uncertainty range of 0.2°C to 0.5°C per decade), greater than that seen over the past 10,000 years.

Many of the large and complex processes involved are still not fully understood and the report points out that much uncertainty remains about the size, timing and distribution of the temperature changes in prospect, and still more about their consequences. There is the possibility of negative feedbacks, dampening the effects of the increased greenhouse gas emissions[176]; but also the possibility of *positive* feedbacks[177,178,179,180] which could lead to *faster* rises in temperature, and conceivably to other more suddenly catastrophic effects.

If greenhouse gas emissions continue to rise on a 'business-as-usual' basis, the IPCC report predicts that by the end of the next century the earth will have become hotter than at any time in the past two-million years, with more violent storms, floods and droughts, and with most serious consequences for many kinds of plant and animal life, for food output[181] and for human welfare generally. Accordingly, the IPCC report urgently recommends a cut of 60 per cent in the level of greenhouse gas emissions.

In the years since the original report there has been an accumulation of further evidence - including recently the dramatic detachment from the Antarctic Peninsula of an iceberg the size of Oxfordshire[182] - and John Gummer, the UK Environment Secretary, has expressed the view that the evidence for global warming is now `pretty conclusive'[183]. While there is much that is still not fully understood, forecasts for particular areas are still not possible, and some of the general forecasts (for example of a rise in sea levels) have been modified, the IPCC has seen no reason to depart from its central finding - of an inexorably continuing rise in global temperatures as a result of rising greenhouse gas emissions - or its central recommendation - that a 60 per cent cut in emissions is needed.

In response to this threat, the 152 countries signed the UN Convention on Climate Change at Rio in 1992. They were only able to agree, however, on an emissions target much more modest than that proposed by the IPCC - they agreed that the industrial countries should bring their emissions of carbon dioxide back to 1990 levels by the end of the century. This target is likely to be reached without much difficulty due to the combined effects of economic recession, a switch from coal to natural gas (which is `cleaner' in the sense of emitting less carbon dioxide than coal of equivalent thermal value), and some very limited measures for greater economy in the use of energy. But it will not be enough.

A follow-up international conference was held in Berlin in April 1995. It failed to reach agreement on any further commitments, but it did agree to prepare emissions targets for further years, such as 2005, 2010 and 2020 for consideration at a conference to be held in Japan in 1997.

An earlier international conference in Toronto in 1988 set a somewhat more ambitious target - to bring emissions down to 20 per cent below the 1988 level by the year 2005. And several of the countries in Europe have been setting the pace in pressing for joint international action to reduce emissions, and in setting for themselves targets more ambitious than for most other countries. For example, Germany has set itself the target of cutting its emissions to 25 per cent below the 1998 level by 2005, and Denmark plans to cut emissions to 20 per cent below 1987 by the year 2000.

They would like the European Union, as an entity, to take a prominent part, since Europe as a whole may be expected to carry more weight in the world than some of the individual countries acting alone. However, the countries looking for a strong EU line are mostly the richer, more environmentally-conscious ones of the North; other, less prosperous, countries in the South are more reluctant to put at risk their plans for rapid economic growth by accepting constraints on their future emissions. Thus it seems likely that the target for the Union as a whole will end up being less ambitious than some in the North would have hoped; and that it will be achieved by allowing some increases for the poorer countries in the South, which will need to be offset by the richer countries in the North making additional cuts to compensate.

In this Europe is a microcosm of the wider world, where the richer countries in the North, with high current emission levels, will in due course need to accept disproportionately large reductions in order to reach whatever overall level of reduction is required, and need also to provide economic and technical help to some of the developing countries, in order to persuade and enable them to make an appropriate contribution to the common objective. It is clear that the more closely Europe is united, and able to speak with a single voice, the more strongly placed it will be in the long and difficult negotiations which undoubtedly lie ahead.

The uncomfortable underlying fact is that at some stage there will be a need for cuts on a much more severe scale than at present contemplated. And whatever the target set, there will surely be dispute as to how it should be shared between different countries. The industrialised countries, with heavy existing energy consumption, may argue that any cuts should be in terms of a standard percentage reduction from a base of current or recent carbon dioxide emission levels. However, developing countries will see this as unfair and unacceptable. They regard the high emission levels of the richer

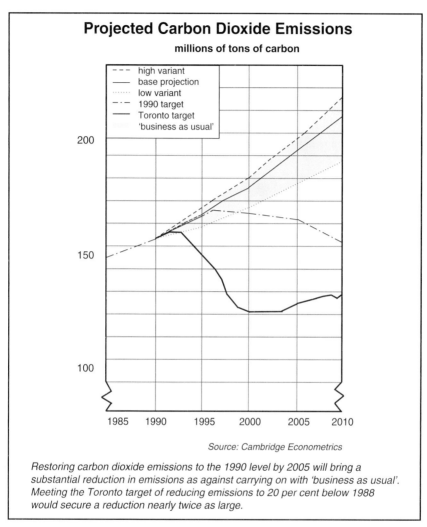

## Projected Carbon Dioxide Emissions
**millions of tons of carbon**

- - - high variant
—— base projection
.......... low variant
— ·— 1990 target
—— Toronto target
'business as usual'

Source: Cambridge Econometrics

*Restoring carbon dioxide emissions to the 1990 level by 2005 will bring a substantial reduction in emissions as against carrying on with 'business as usual'. Meeting the Toronto target of reducing emissions to 20 per cent below 1988 would secure a reduction nearly twice as large.*

countries as the main cause of the problem. They therefore insist that the industrial countries should make proportionately greater cuts to leave room for the developing countries to have some increase in their emissions as their economies grow towards the levels of the richer countries.

In this connection it is relevant to note that Britain is the seventh largest generator of carbon dioxide emissions in the world; and in terms of emissions per head of carbon dioxide, Britain's level is about half that of the United States, broadly similar to other countries in Western Europe (except for those which rely mainly on hydro or nuclear power), and rather more than double the average for the world as a whole[165]. Thus if an overall reduction of 60 per cent took the form of reducing the emissions per head of every country to 40 per cent of the present world average, this would imply a reduction in Britain of 80-85 per cent, and in the United States reductions of more than 90 per cent.

Because fossil fuels are the main source of energy in most countries, and because energy is a key element in the economies of all countries, it is clear that very large reductions in greenhouse gas emissions will not be easy to achieve, and there will be major conflicts of interest between different countries and between different interests within them. Hence, if the need for very large reductions is confirmed, and the need for universal agreement remains, it may be expected that international negotiations on how to achieve the reductions will be very long and difficult - indeed will probably be the main area of international dispute in the early decades of the next century. It is therefore fortunate that the problem is a long-term one which can be tackled in stages, over decades, rather than promptly over a few years.

## Energy

The need to reduce greenhouse gas emissions will cause attention to be focused increasingly on energy - on generating it in ways which release less carbon dioxide, or none at all, and in using it more efficiently.

### Fossil and nuclear energy

In Britain there is already a shift from coal and petroleum in thermal power stations to natural gas, which releases less carbon dioxide per unit of power generated, but which also depletes a resource which has world reserves which are only one-tenth as plentiful as coal. There is also likely to be increasing interest in combined heat-and-power units which make use of heat which in conventional power stations is wasted, thereby raising overall thermal efficiency from about 35 per cent in a coal-fired power station and about 45 per cent in a gas-fired one to as much as 80 per cent for a combined-use unit[166].

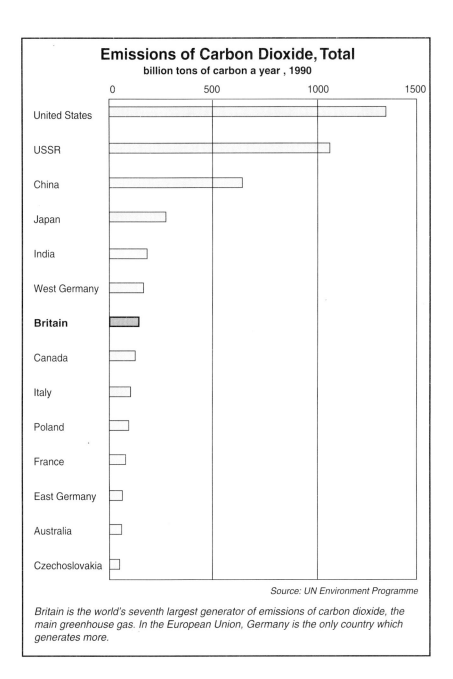

## Emissions of Carbon Dioxide, Total
### billion tons of carbon a year , 1990

*Source: UN Environment Programme*

*Britain is the world's seventh largest generator of emissions of carbon dioxide, the main greenhouse gas. In the European Union, Germany is the only country which generates more.*

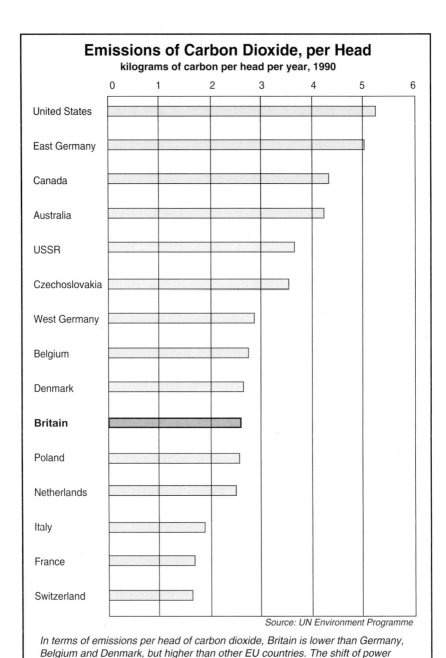

**Emissions of Carbon Dioxide, per Head**

kilograms of carbon per head per year, 1990

*Source: UN Environment Programme*

*In terms of emissions per head of carbon dioxide, Britain is lower than Germany, Belgium and Denmark, but higher than other EU countries. The shift of power stations from coal to natural gas will help Britain meet current modest international targets.*

And there is likely to be pressure to improve efficiency in power generation. The World Bank estimates that improving efficiency alone could cut emissions of pollutants by more than a fifth[107], the most important measure needed being the ending of the high subsidies on energy in many countries. The Bank estimates that electricity tariffs in developing countries average only about half those in the OECD countries, and energy prices used to be heavily subsidised in the Soviet bloc countries also; the removal of energy subsidies is estimated by 1995 to have already had the effect of reducing by 4 per cent the developing countries' share of global carbon dioxide emissions, and by 7 per cent the Soviet bloc's share[166].

There is also likely to be renewed interest in nuclear power, which produces no greenhouse gases or air pollution at all. However, public concern about the possibility of nuclear accidents (particularly in ageing plants in the former Soviet bloc countries), long-term problems of high-level waste disposal and decommissioning, and concerns about the security implications of generating weapons-grade plutonium, have caused most western countries to pause before embarking on the construction of additional capacity, and some of them to contemplate phasing out their existing capacity. In Britain the decisive factor has been costs - in practice nuclear power has turned out to be far more expensive than power from other sources, and would become even more so if used for more than base load, or if the full costs of decommissioning and waste disposal were included. Hence, barring a break-through in nuclear fusion, it seems unlikely that nuclear-power capacity will be expanded beyond its present share of primary energy - 10 per cent in Britain and 8 per cent worldwide[184,185].

### Renewable energy

There is likely in the coming decades to be a considerable expansion in the use of alternative, renewable energy sources. At present they account for only about 0.5 per cent of primary energy consumption in Britain and for about 3.7 per cent in the European Union as a whole. However, the European Commission has embarked on a renewable energy development programme which aims to double the share by 2005[186].

*Biomass and waste*
Energy from municipal, household and industrial waste, sewage sludge and landfill sites is at present the biggest source of renewable energy, accounting for 60 per cent of the total in Britain and 64 per cent in the European Union as a whole. In relatively low-use countries, such as Britain, there is evident scope for increasing production. In France and Spain energy from this source accounts for more than 4 per cent of total consumption, in Germany and Italy for more than 6 per cent, and in Portugal for more than 12 per cent[186].

*Hydro*
Hydroelectricity accounts, at present, for the bulk of the remainder of renewable energy - 38 per cent of primary energy in Britain and 31 per cent in the European Union as a whole. Most of the best hydroelectric sites in Europe are already exploited, and there are often environmental problems in the development of new ones. Even so the Commission aims to increase hydroelectric power by 40 per cent by 2005[186].

*Geothermal*
Prospects in Britain appear limited, but in Italy geothermal energy accounts for 24 per cent of renewable energy and 1.3 per cent of total energy consumption.

*Wind*
In Denmark, Germany and the Netherlands the use of windpower has been increasing rapidly. In Britain windpower is, so far, on a much smaller scale, but the number of windfarms is expected to double by 2000[187].

*Solar*
The economics of solar power are not yet favourable in Northern Europe, but use is increasing in the sunnier countries of the South.

*Tide*
There is, at present, only one tidal-power installation in operation in Europe (in France), but there are sites in Britain which are suitable for major (but expensive to develop) tidal-power schemes.

*Wave*

There are no commercial wave-power installations yet in operation in Europe. However, Britain had a world lead in this technology until the research programme was stopped, and conditions around Britain are particularly favourable for this to become a major source of power in the future.

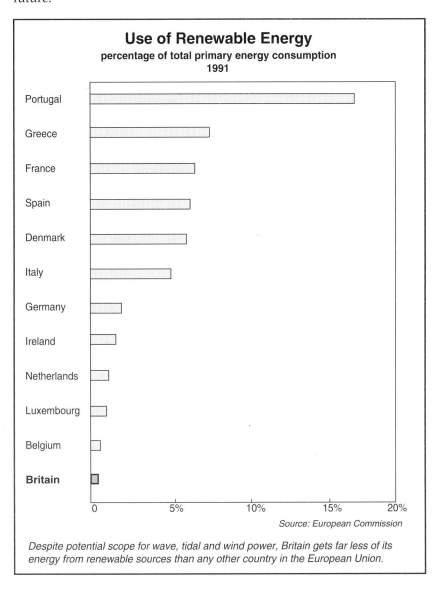

**Use of Renewable Energy**
**percentage of total primary energy consumption**
**1991**

*Source: European Commission*

*Despite potential scope for wave, tidal and wind power, Britain gets far less of its energy from renewable sources than any other country in the European Union.*

## Costs

In the past the main objection to most of the alternative sources of energy was that they were too expensive. However, costs have been coming down: wave power is already estimated to be less expensive than nuclear power[188]; costs at a demonstration biomass plant have been shown to be comparable to those at a conventional coal-fired power station, and capable of being made much lower[189]; US wind-energy costs have been reduced by two-thirds between 1981-85 and 1992-95, and are expected to be brought down by a further third by the turn of the century[190]; and the costs of photovoltaic systems is expected to halve between 1990 and 2000[191].

It is important to remember that most of the renewables are new technologies seeking to compete with nuclear-power technology which has been in use for fifty years and with thermal power which has been in use for more than a century. Although between them they have had the benefit of R&D expenditure, only about one-tenth of that invested in nuclear power[166], already costs have been falling sharply. With most of them it is reasonable to expect costs to fall substantially further as a result of a more strongly directed R&D effort in the future.

In Britain the Department of Energy has estimated that by 2025 renewables could be supplying up to 20 per cent of Britain's energy. For the European Union the Commission has set a target of 7.8 per cent of energy from renewables by 2005[186]. And the World Bank postulates that by 2050 renewables could be providing more than 60 per cent of total world energy demand - with the result that global annual carbon dioxide emissions would rise by about 25 per cent, compared with an increase of about 250 per cent with continued reliance on fossil fuels on a 'business-as-usual' basis[166].

### Energy conservation

However, it will take time to develop cleaner energy sources, and meanwhile there is much scope for economising in energy use - often in ways which have no serious disadvantages and which give rise to lower costs. Energy saving - through reductions in use and greater efficiency in use - is effectively a vast, if as yet inadequately tapped, source of power. There is still much scope for greater energy economy in

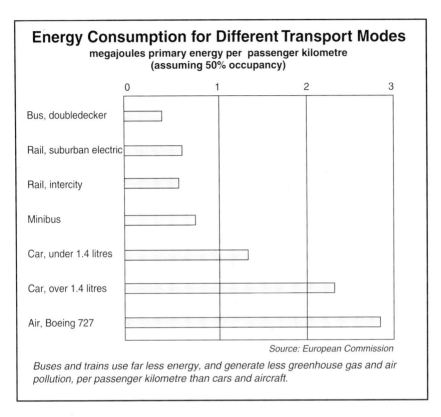

**Energy Consumption for Different Transport Modes**
megajoules primary energy per passenger kilometre
(assuming 50% occupancy)

*Source: European Commission*

*Buses and trains use far less energy, and generate less greenhouse gas and air pollution, per passenger kilometre than cars and aircraft.*

industrial machinery and heat-using processes; in the regulation and control of space heating; in the use of less energy-intensive materials and processes; in the use of more economical vehicle engines; in the use of bicycles, buses and trains instead of cars, and of telecommunications links in place of the physical transport of documents and people.

Insulation of buildings offers particular scope. Buildings account for nearly half of the total energy demand in Britain[192]. Yet many homes still do not have adequate insulation, or even draught-proofing, and many are totally reliant on electricity for heating. If the UK-building stock was uprated to the proposed new UK-building regulations' insulation standard, it would cut total UK-carbon dioxide emissions by 5 per cent; and if raised to the standards of the Danish-building regulations, it would cut them by 7 per cent[193].

Lighting also offers scope for easy savings. The new compact domestic fluorescent bulbs are more than four times as efficient as traditional bulbs, and cost less to run; and a new sulphur streetlamp bulb under development is expected to be twelve times as efficient as mercury lamps[194].

Domestic appliances are another area with great scope for energy economy. A study for the Department of Energy[195] found that in Britain the best larder refrigerator was nearly twice as energy-efficient as the average of the total stock, while the best fridge/freezer and the best chest-freezer were both more than twice as efficient. And recent tests by the Consumers' Association of washing-machines, tumble-driers, dish-washers and fridge/freezers found that a consumer buying the most energy-efficient model of each, instead of the least energy-efficient model, would use less than half the energy and save more than £100 a year[196].

A major international study has concluded that, if all the various energy- conservation possibilities were adopted, it would be feasible for the industrialised countries to maintain their present living standards in the year 2020 with total energy consumption of only half the present level; while the developing countries could enjoy Western European living standards with a total energy consumption only 10 per cent higher than it was in 1987[197].

Thus both through changes in the sources of energy and in the ways it is used, there is scope for making a major impact on the global-warming problem - much of it by doing things which involve little cost and are worth doing anyway on their own account.

The European Commission has sought to require member countries to adopt a common line in international negotiations and has sought to introduce measures specifically designed to reduce emissions of greenhouse gases. The most ambitious of these was a proposal for an annually- escalating tax, half carbon tax and half a general energy tax. Since a carbon tax is widely regarded as the most efficient tax instrument for reducing emissions, the Commission was criticised by environmentalists for diluting it with a general energy tax and, even more, for mitigation which was proposed to allow for heavy energy-using sectors - thereby seriously weakening its likely impact. The proposal drew strong opposition from some member governments, particularly Britain's (1984), and in the absence of unanimity it was impossible for the measure to be adopted. As a result, each country has been left to adopt its own measures. However, the Commission has worked out a framework for those countries which *do* wish to adopt a carbon tax, and will review the situation in 1998 with the aim of getting agreement on a harmonised target tax rate equivalent to $10 a barrel of oil by 2000[199].

One of the considerations which has made some countries reluctant to introduce a carbon tax or other measures to shift energy demand and cut energy consumption is apprehension that this would impede economic growth or impair competitive advantage. However, an exercise carried out by Cambridge Econometrics for PSI's *Britain in 2010* project[1] showed that if an escalating carbon tax was introduced at a level high enough to meet the Toronto target (getting emissions down to 20 per cent below the 1988 level by 2005), but if the tax was offset by equivalent reductions in VAT, the effect would be to bring a shift from coal to natural gas, to put up the cost of energy, and to bring a shift from more energy-intensive activities to less energy-intensive activities. This would *not* however reduce the rate of growth of GDP, or reduce the level of employment, or impair international competitiveness.

A more recent study by Cambridge Econometrics (in this case offsetting an escalating petrol tax or carbon tax with reductions in national insurance contributions) comes to broadly similar conclusions - but with the bonus of an increase of about 500,000 in employment[200].

Moreover, even if the unilateral imposition of a carbon tax *did* have the effect of impairing a country's competitive advantage, the fact that the bulk of the trade of EU countries is with one another means that if they all imposed the tax *at the same rate and at the same time* any impact on their trade would be small. Thus the introduction of a Europe-wide initiative offers the possibility for countries to do *together* things which each might find difficult to do *on its own*.

## Policies for sustainability

The various environmental issues are interdependent and come together in the need to evolve a pattern of development that is sustainable in the longer term. The prospects of this being achieved will be strongly affected by changes that are taking place in perceptions of environmental issues, in the policy instruments for dealing with them, in the performance of businesses and governments, in the common purpose of the international community, and in the underlying attitudes of public opinion.

### Perceptions

In recent years there has been a significant evolution both in the importance which is accorded to environmental issues and in the ways in which they are perceived.

*Before* attention was focused on monitoring and cleaning up specific environmental problem areas, such as domestic coal fires, discharges of effluent, disposal of nuclear waste.

*Now* the emphasis is more on *prevention* of pollution and waste, using better design, cleaner processes and environmentally-conscious management to economise on use of energy and materials, and minimise generation of waste and harmful substances.

*Before* the emphasis was predominantly on improving the production *processes* to make them less environmentally damaging.

*Now* there is interest in the environmental impact of the whole *product life-cycle*, including the production of the materials and energy used, the use of the product during its lifetime, the durability, reparability and length of life, and the scope for salvage and recycling at the end of its life.

*Before* the main attention was given to *key points* posing obvious threats, such as factory chimneys, river effluent outlets and nuclear power stations.

*Now* interest extends also to the cumulative effects of more dispersed kinds of problem such as car exhausts, non-biodegradable packaging and agricultural chemicals.

*Before*, when information was incomplete, there was usually a willingness to defer a response until there was *conclusive evidence* of the need for urgent action.

*Now*, when there is uncertainty, there is greater willingness to act on the *precautionary principle*, taking at least preliminary steps to be on the safe side lest the worst case turns out to be real.

*Before* most environmental problems were seen as *discrete*, limited and capable of being dealt with piecemeal.

*Now* they are increasingly seen as *interdependent* and capable of being adequately addressed only in a holistic way, concerned with the longer-term sustainability of the system as a whole.

*Before* environmental issues were widely regarded as little more than peripheral *nuisances* of relatively minor importance.

*Now* they are seen as a serious, conceivably even terminal, *threat* to our whole way of life.

*Performance*
These changes in perception are gradual and evolutionary rather than sudden and revolutionary, but they are none the less already having an effect on the ways businesses and other organisations see their objectives and carry out their operations.

At present there is no uniformity of business practice, but rather a wide-ranging continuum. At the top are firms which have integrated the environmental dimension into their whole way of thinking and operating, habitually, enterprisingly and profitably following the best available practice. Next are firms which in general seek to follow good environmental practice, provided it is not too costly and does not involve too much disturbance of their customary ways of operating.

Next are firms which are more sceptical, or in difficulty, which are prepared only to do the minimum to keep within the regulations. And finally there are some which are willing to cut corners and break the rules if it saves money and there does not seem much risk of getting caught.

The important point is that there is evidence[201] that firms are steadily moving up the hierarchy, consciously adopting more environment-friendly ways of operating. This is partly a matter of social responsibility, as directors become more aware of and concerned about environmental issues. It is partly because being seen to be environmentally responsible is increasingly regarded as good for the corporate image. And it is partly because environmentally-sound practices can be directly profitable - sometimes the processes involved turn out to be cheaper, and sometimes sales can be expanded by appealing to the growing market of `green' consumers. And the provision of environmental equipment and services is itself a huge market, estimated to amount to about $210bn worldwide in 1992, and expected to grow to more than twice that size by 2010[202].

### Policy instruments

A further factor has been the increasingly concerned attitudes of governments leading to stronger environment policies, which in the future will be put into effect by a widening range of policy instruments. In the past the main instrument of environmental regulation has been direct statutory controls - for example, banning outright the use of specified toxic substances, limiting permissible discharges from effluent pipes and chimneys, or requiring the installation of catalytic converters on cars. This type of control is effective and will continue to be used, but it has disadvantages: it tends to be crude and rigid, setting only basic *minimum* standards, with no incentive to improve on them, and no mechanism for ensuring that the improvement is achieved with greatest efficiency and minimum cost. Also it requires expensive machinery for inspection and enforcement.

In the future it seems likely that more important roles will be found for a number of other policy instruments which should be more flexible and, in combination, more effective.

*Taxes*

It is likely that taxes will be increasingly used to discourage environmentally-damaging activities, such as generating pollution or greenhouse gas emissions, or to encourage more economic use of energy and materials. These can `make the polluter pay', instead of `externalising' environmental costs by passing them on to the community, but leave firms to make their own decisions, so that the biggest adjustments will be made by those best placed to make them.

*Tradeable permits*

The sale of permits to pollute provides a mechanism for limiting (and over a period reducing) the total amount of a particular kind of pollution, while leaving the market to decide which firms should make the biggest adjustments.

*Product standards*

The setting of standards for the product, as opposed to the process, for example in terms of energy efficiency or material content, can stimulate design changes, particularly when more stringent future standards are announced years in advance.

*Life-cycle responsibility*

Producers may be required to accept some responsibility for their products over their whole life-cycle - for example for the salvage of old cars, to encourage design for longer life and easier recycling.

*Information*

Measures to improve general environmental awareness, combined with published company environmental audits and eco-labelling of products, can result in `green' consumers encouraging good environmental practice through the pressures of the market.

*Voluntary arrangements*

Increasing use is being made of voluntary arrangements of various kinds, such as the adoption of non-mandatory standards, the setting of voluntary targets, the initiation of collaborative research projects, and the work of business environment associations.

### United Nations Conference on Environment and Development

Since sustainability is essentially a global issue, a key factor is the role of world organisations such as the United Nations. Here the United Nations Conference on Environment and Development (UNCED) at Rio in 1992 was a crucial turning point in three ways. First, in anticipation of it, national governments were galvanised into thinking more specifically about environmental issues in order to prepare their positions for the conference.

Second the conference itself achieved world agreement on a Declaration on Environment and Development, the Agenda 21 action programme to give effect to them, and world conventions on climate change and biological diversity. While some of the agreements are in broad terms, and anyway subject to local interpretation, they are likely to have the effect of giving a boost to developments in areas such as: energy saving; pollution prevention and waste minimisation; priority for public transport, walking and cycling over private cars; greater exposure of business to environmental performance monitoring; inclusion of environmental indicators in national accounts; and growth of a major new service sector concerned with environmental management, information, training, repair and recycling.

Third, the conference provided for the momentum to be maintained in future years by setting up the Commission on Sustainable Development, establishing the International Environmental Information System, giving a bigger role to the UN Environment Programme, and restructuring the Global Environment Facility to provide better funding for environmental projects in developing countries. The machinery has been put in place to bring continuing pressure on governments to improve environmental performance, and to provide funding to help the developing countries play a full role.

### Public attitudes

Ultimately what businesses, governments, and international organisations do to safeguard and improve the environment will depend to an important extent on underlying public attitudes. There have been many surveys showing a high degree of public concern in Britain about most of the main environmental issues, but a recent one [203] has sought to put people's expressed concern in the context of their apparent willingness to act in support of it. According to this survey there is a high proportion of people who see things such as river pollution, air pollution, the greenhouse effect and nuclear power stations as `extremely' or `very' dangerous to the environment.

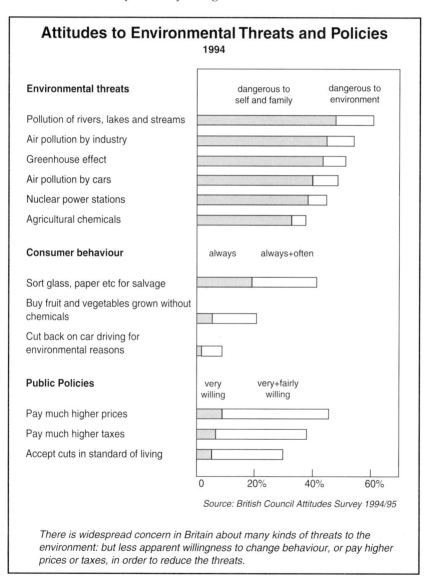

**Attitudes to Environmental Threats and Policies**
1994

Source: British Council Attitudes Survey 1994/95

*There is widespread concern in Britain about many kinds of threats to the environment: but less apparent willingness to change behaviour, or pay higher prices or taxes, in order to reduce the threats.*

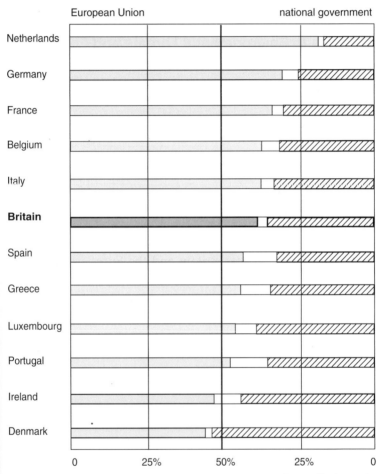

# Attitudes to Decision taking on Environmental Protection
**where decisions best taken**
**1994**

European Union                        national government

Netherlands

Germany

France

Belgium

Italy

**Britain**

Spain

Greece

Luxembourg

Portugal

Ireland

Denmark

0         25%         50%         25%         0

*Source: Eurobarometer*

*In Britain, and in the European Union as a whole, there is roughly a two to one majority in favour of decisions on environmental protection being taken at EU rather than national level. Only in Denmark (where national standards are particularly high) is there a majority in favour of decision taking at national level.*

However, the extent of concern does not seem to be correlated with the extent of scientific knowledge of the issues; the perception of danger to self and family is less than that of danger to the environment more generally; the proportion of people who are `very willing' to accept much higher prices or taxes or a lower standard of living are very small, and even the proportion `fairly willing' is less than the proportion expressing concern; the proportion always or often buying chemicals-free fruit and fresh vegetables is barely half the proportion seeing agricultural chemicals as dangerous; and the proportion always or often willing to cut back on their driving is less than a fifth of the proportion seeing air pollution from cars as dangerous. So it would seem that there is still an important gap between the extent of awareness of environmental dangers and the extent of willingness to make sacrifices to avert them.

On the question of the most appropriate level for policy decisions, environmental protection is an area where there is particularly strong public support for decision-taking by the European Union rather than national governments. A Eurobarometer poll[204] has found that there is a majority of two-to-one, in both Britain and the European Union as a whole, in favour of decision-taking at European level.

## Key Points for Europe        Environment

Most town and country planning issues have been, and are likely to continue to be, settled locally. The big exception is the EU's CAP, set up before Britain joined - but this is likely to be radically changed.

In many EU countries - especially Britain - transport policies tend to favour the private car over public transport. However in all EU countries public opinion appears to favour less car-dominated policies.

The Channel Tunnel and the high-speed rail and motorway links beyond will effectively bring Britain closer to continental Europe countries.

The European Commission has set standards for water quality, sewage disposal and waste management; but Britain is failing to reach some of the targets.

The European Union took a leading role in getting world action to stop the production of CFCs; but the ozone layer may face a new threat from the emissions of jet aircraft, and this could be more difficult to deal with.

Air pollution blows across national frontiers, and the European Union has agreed on joint action to reduce emissions from power stations and vehicles.

Global warming poses a threat to the whole world and the European Union has been trying to set an example in its response. Britain's government recognises that the evidence for global warming is `pretty conclusive'; but has blocked European Commission proposals for Europe-wide energy taxes to reduce greenhouse gas emissions.

The conversion of some of Britain's power stations from coal to natural gas will help reduce greenhouse gas emissions; but Britain's use of alternative renewable energy sources is much the lowest in the European Union.

Some countries worry that taking measures to protect the environment will impair their competitiveness; however, the trade of EU countries is now mostly with one another, so if they act *together* they can safely take measures which might seem risky if undertaken alone.

Environmental protection is an area in which there is a two-to-one majority in public opinion in Britain, and in the EU as a whole, in favour of decision-taking at EU rather than national level.

# 6 Employment

In the course of the past two decades there have been two recessions, the introduction of new technology, rising international competition, and pressures for reductions in operating costs, and these have led to drastic falls in employment in manufacturing. Recently there has been labour-shedding also in many large service organisations in both the private and the public sectors. There is a growing sense of insecurity, even among formerly `secure' professionals and managers, and concern for the future stability of a society with continuing high levels of unemployment and job insecurity.

Employment patterns will continue to change in the coming decades, with increasing proportions of people in services, in high-skill and professional jobs, in part-time jobs and self-employment, and with more flexible hours - both in Britain and in the other countries of the European Union. There will be greater use of new technologies and a need for further improvements in education and training to provide the higher skills levels required. Unemployment will continue to be a serious problem and policies to reduce it will be of central importance. Several of the measures in the package of policies envisaged will require a joint European approach.

## Changes in employment

Between 1971-93 total employment in Britain changed little, but there were important changes in the type of employment. Employment in agriculture continued its long-term decline and employment in manufacturing fell by more than a third between 1979-92; but there were increases in employment in services, particularly in professional, financial and business services. Employment of males has been falling a little; but employment of females has been rising. Full-time employment has been falling a little; but part-time employment has been rising, particularly for females. Salaried employment has been falling a little; but self-employment has been rising, and also casual employment and employment in second jobs. Average hours worked fell in the 1960s and 1970s, but have risen a little subsequently.

In other European Union countries there have been changes in type of employment broadly similar to those experienced in Britain, but not to the same degree. The drop in employment in agriculture has been greater than in Britain; but the decline in employment in manufacturing less steep[205]. Employment in financial and business services has risen in all European Union countries but (apart from Luxembourg) less strongly than in Britain; on the other hand most of the others have had a greater increase in employment in community, social and personal services than Britain[205]. Other European countries have experienced an increase in part-time employment; but the increase in self-employment has been much less marked in Britain than in all of them except Portugal[205]. The number of hours worked per week has been falling in all the other countries, and in Britain both men and women now work more hours per week on average than in any other country in the European Union[206].

Between 1990 and 2010 Cambridge Econometrics projections[1] envisage an increase in total employment in Britain of three-to-four million jobs, with a continuing decline in employment in agriculture and manufacturing (although with increasing output in both because of rising productivity), and a further increase in professional, financial and business services.   Similar sectoral changes are likely also in other European countries.

In the coming decades the Single European Market will make possible increasing mobility of labour within Europe, although the scale on which people in fact move from one country to another in pursuit of better work opportunities is likely to be constrained by linguistic and cultural differences and the reluctance of many people to contemplate moving to another country[207]. This is particularly likely as long as there is still substantial unemployment in prospective receiving countries; for everywhere unemployment tends to be much higher among new immigrants than among those already well established in a country.

## Labour standards

In most countries of the European Union the `social partners' (employers and trade unions) have machinery within firms and nationally for dialogue on matters affecting employment, and there are nationally-set labour standards on, for example, minimum wages, maximum hours,

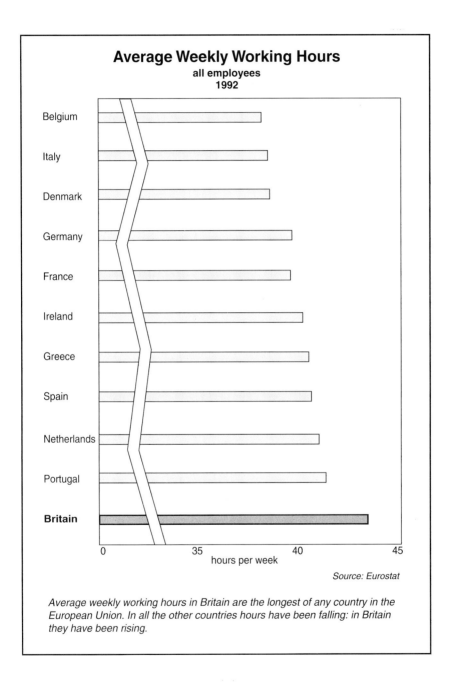

**Average Weekly Working Hours**
all employees
1992

Source: Eurostat

*Average weekly working hours in Britain are the longest of any country in the European Union. In all the other countries hours have been falling: in Britain they have been rising.*

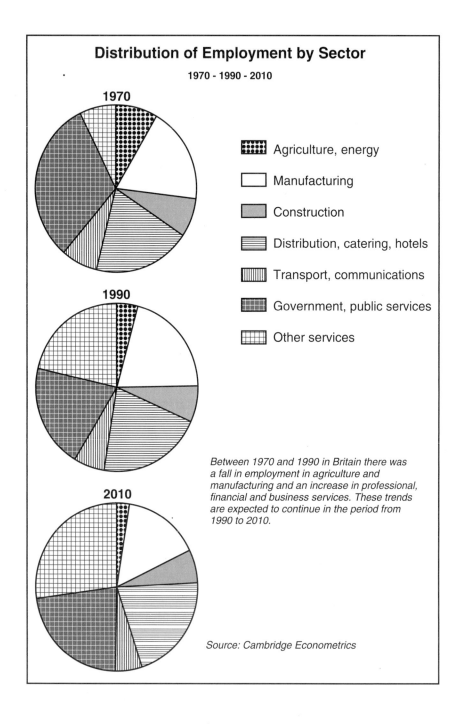

## Distribution of Employment by Sector

### 1970 - 1990 - 2010

**1970**

**Agriculture, energy**

**Manufacturing**

**Construction**

**Distribution, catering, hotels**

**Transport, communications**

**1990**

**Government, public services**

**Other services**

*Between 1970 and 1990 in Britain there was a fall in employment in agriculture and manufacturing and an increase in professional, financial and business services. These trends are expected to continue in the period from 1990 to 2010.*

**2010**

*Source: Cambridge Econometrics*

employment protection and employee representation in management. This is an area in which the position in Britain is quite different from the other countries. A study by the OECD[208] found that Britain has the least provision for national labour standards of any country in the European Union. It is the only one with no minimum wage or employment protection and one of the few without employee representation rights, regulation of fixed-term contracts or limits to working hours. In Britain 28 per cent of males work 48 hours or more a week, the proposed EU maximum. This is far more than in any other country in the European Union, and accounts for nearly half the EU total[209].

The aims of the European Union on labour standards are set out in the White Paper on social policy[210]:

> The key objectives have been both to ensure that the creation of the single market did not result in a downward pressure on labour standards or create a distortion of competition, and to ensure that the working people also shared in the new prosperity . . . The establishment of a framework of basic minimum standards . . . provides a bulwark against using low social standards as an instrument of unfair economic competition and protection against reducing social standards to gain competitiveness.

Under the policy common standards have been proposed in areas such as health and safety at work, maximum hours of work, rights of women, young people and part-time workers, rights to paternity leave, dismissal procedures and representation on works councils.

The objectives were incorporated in the Maastricht Treaty as the Social Chapter and accepted by all the member countries except Britain, which negotiated a derogation excluding it from this part of the treaty.

The practical effect of the derogation is probably less important than the friction generated by it might suggest. Many of the measures envisaged under the Social Chapter can instead be brought in under the provisions of the Single European Act - from which Britain has no derogation - and despite the opposition to many of the social measures proposed, Britain has in fact a 100 per cent record, the best in the Union, of actually putting EU social legislation into domestic law[211]. And some measures will be brought in by companies anyway, irrespective of the derogation. With the law requiring the larger multinationals to set up works councils, for example, it is estimated that, of the 300 British multinationals that would have been affected, about 100 will have to comply anyway because of their operations in other EU countries[212]; as will also continental European multinationals operating in Britain; and also foreign multinationals operating in other EU countries as well as Britain.

Even so, the British derogation has attracted much resentment in other EU countries. It is seen as being at variance with the general principle of the Union that all member countries accept the same commitments, and contrary to the specific requirement of the Single European Market for a 'level playing field'. The refusal by Britain to accept common minimum standards is seen as unfair competition which has the effect of 'exporting unemployment'. Accordingly, there are likely to be pressures for the Britain's derogation to be stopped at the end of the four-year period it runs for.

## Use of new technologies

The Single European Market (and beyond it an increasingly open global market) is likely to bring intense competition, with opportunities for the stronger companies to expand their sales in other countries, but also risks for the weaker companies of losing sales in their home markets to imports from outside. There will therefore be increased pressure on companies to strengthen their competitiveness by improving quality and design, which in turn will involve making full use of new technologies. (See Chapter 7.)

There has been concern at the possible implications of this for employment. In the early days of the 'microchip revolution' it used to be supposed that it would lead to widespread de-skilling and loss of jobs on a massive scale. In the event, actual job losses have turned out to be much smaller. Four major PSI surveys covering the whole of manufacturing industry[213,214,215,216] showed that the total direct loss of jobs due to the use of microelectronics in manufacturing processes and products was about 15-20,000 a year between 1981-83 and about 40-50,000 a year between 1983-87 (the latter equivalent to only about two jobs per factory per year); and parallel surveys showed a similar position in West Germany and France[217]. Further analysis of the UK data showed that the loss of jobs from all causes was actually *less* in the plants using microelectronics than in the ones which were not, and *less* in the plants using the most advanced applications than in those with relatively simple ones[218].

The reason for these employment effects was that new technology was being used not so much to cut jobs or costs as to raise *quality* and *output*, both in industry[216,219] and in offices[220]. In consequence the number of unskilled manual and clerical jobs in industry has been reduced as a result of the use of new technology, but the number of skilled manual and white-collar jobs has been *increased*[216], so that many firms now have a `leaner' labour force with a higher average skill level.

The largest survey ever undertaken in Britain on the effects of new technology on the workplace[221] has shown emphatically that the overall effect has been to require more skills rather than less, in both manual occupations and office ones; and likewise the introduction of new materials has also been found to result in new special skills needs[222]. And the need for *more* people with special skills has been found to be the prime requirement for making full use of new technology in similar surveys undertaken in Germany[223], France[224], Sweden[225], Denmark[226] and New Zealand[227].

Thus the threat from new technologies is *not*, as was once supposed, that it would remove the need for skills; but rather that, for its effective use, it *requires* a range of special skills. And while, like other changes which increase productivity, it destroys some jobs, but potentially generates new ones, the opportunities offered by the new jobs will only be realised if people are able to acquire the new skills needed for them.

## Education and training

It is thus clear that success in competition in the Single European Market, and in particular effective use of new technologies, will require more people with more skills at all levels: more highly-qualified managers; microelectronics engineers, materials scientists, microbiologists and other specialists with high-level skills; and, probably most important of all, a high general level of skills, including new technology skills and combinations of skills, right across the work force.

In this area Britain appears to be seriously behind its main European competitors. British managers tend to be less qualified than those in competitor countries and, probably even more important, a succession of international comparative studies have found the *general* level of education and skills qualifications to be lower in Britain than in competitor countries[228,229]. For example, only 18 per cent of Britain's work force is educated to craft level, compared with 33 per cent in France, 38 per cent in the Netherlands and 56 per cent in Germany[230]. In 1993, 27 per cent of the working age population in Britain had no qualification at all[231].

These low figures are the outcome of poor general education standards in earlier periods. Fortunately, in recent years there have been substantial improvements. For example, between 1980-81 and 1992-93 the number of students enroling in higher education more than doubled [231]. The percentage of young people going on from school to university is still relatively low, but this is partly offset by the relatively high proportion completing their courses and the relatively high proportion taking courses in science and technology[232]. Also in Britain, in addition to the 27 per cent going straight to full-time university courses, the equivalent of a further 12 per cent enrol on full-time courses later as mature students, and a further 17 per cent as part-time students, for example at the Open University. Hence it is calculated that altogether about 57 per cent of people will get a chance to start a university education at some stage[233].

There have also been important improvements in secondary education. Between 1982-83 and 1992-93 the proportion of 16-year-olds who stay on in full-time education rose from 52 per cent to 71 per cent[231]. Between 1980-81 and 1992-93 the proportion of 16-18-year-olds in full-time education rose from 29 per cent to 53 per cent[231]. And between 1984-93 the proportion of people leaving the education system with no qualification at all fell from 27 percent to 18 per cent[231].

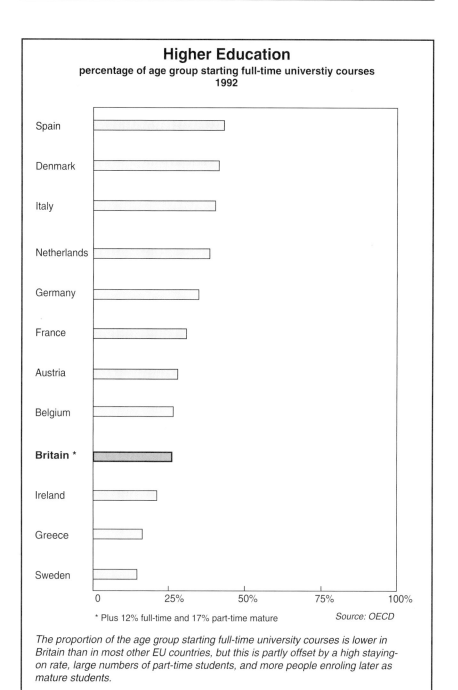

# Higher Education
**percentage of age group starting full-time universtiy courses
1992**

Spain

Denmark

Italy

Netherlands

Germany

France

Austria

Belgium

**Britain \***

Ireland

Greece

Sweden

0    25%    50%    75%    100%

\* Plus 12% full-time and 17% part-time mature          *Source: OECD*

*The proportion of the age group starting full-time university courses is lower in
Britain than in most other EU countries, but this is partly offset by a high staying-
on rate, large numbers of part-time students, and more people enroling later as
mature students.*

However, even the improved figures appear still to be behind those of comparable countries in Europe. In 1992, the latest year for which comparative OECD figures are available: the proportion of 16-18-year-olds in full-time education in Britain was the lowest in the European Union; the number of pupils per teacher was one of the highest; and the proportion of students in vocational training was relatively low[232].

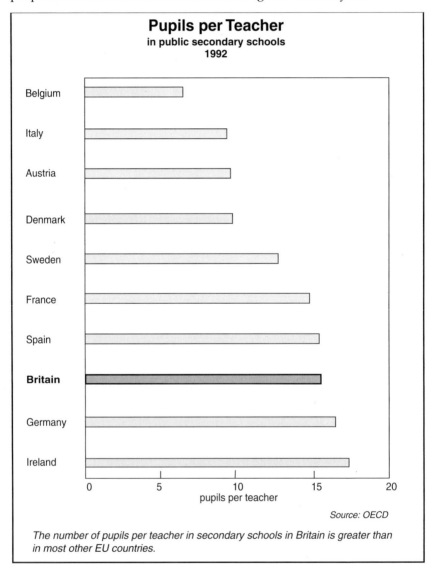

**Pupils per Teacher**
in public secondary schools
1992

*Source: OECD*

*The number of pupils per teacher in secondary schools in Britain is greater than in most other EU countries.*

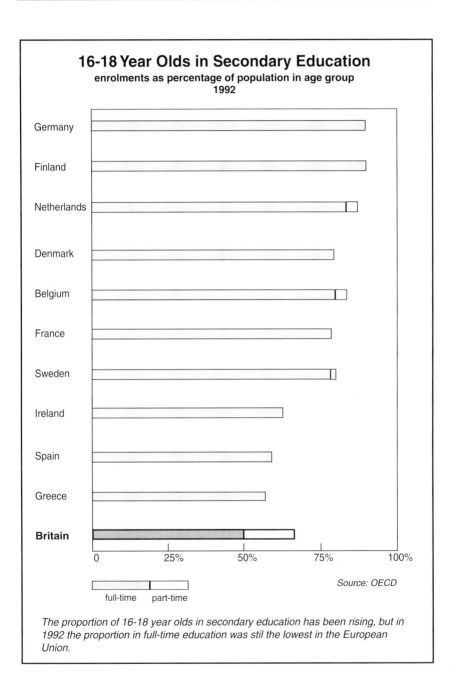

# 16-18 Year Olds in Secondary Education
### enrolments as percentage of population in age group
### 1992

Germany

Finland

Netherlands

Denmark

Belgium

France

Sweden

Ireland

Spain

Greece

**Britain**

0    25%    50%    75%    100%

full-time    part-time

*Source: OECD*

*The proportion of 16-18 year olds in secondary education has been rising, but in 1992 the proportion in full-time education was stil the lowest in the European Union.*

165

Other European countries have plans to raise their standards further in order to equip their people for the more demanding needs of the future. Britain will need to invest more than the others in order to close the present gap, to reach the higher standards planned in elsewhere in the future, and to compensate for the fact that the proportion of people aged 0-19 in the population, at present about the European average, is

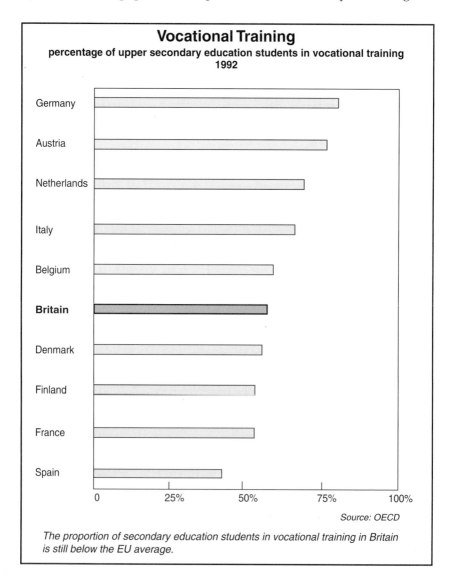

**Vocational Training**

**percentage of upper secondary education students in vocational training 1992**

*Source: OECD*

*The proportion of secondary education students in vocational training in Britain is still below the EU average.*

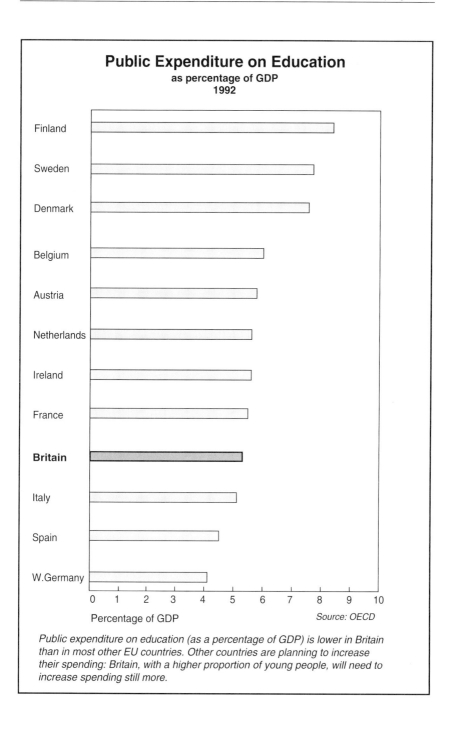

# Public Expenditure on Education
## as percentage of GDP
### 1992

| | |
|---|---|
| Finland | |
| Sweden | |
| Denmark | |
| Belgium | |
| Austria | |
| Netherlands | |
| Ireland | |
| France | |
| **Britain** | |
| Italy | |
| Spain | |
| W.Germany | |

Percentage of GDP

*Source: OECD*

*Public expenditure on education (as a percentage of GDP) is lower in Britain than in most other EU countries. Other countries are planning to increase their spending: Britain, with a higher proportion of young people, will need to increase spending still more.*

167

expected by 2020 to be about 4 percentage points above it. Spending on education in Britain is at present fairly low relative to other European countries[232], and is likely to have to be increased more than in the other countries in the future.

## Labour force

At present the proportion of the population in the most economically-active age groups (20-64) is lower in Britain than in any other country in the European Union except Ireland. The proportion is expected to fall a little further in Britain, but also in most of the other countries, so that by 2020 Britain will then still have the lowest proportion of any country except Ireland. Long-term demographic changes, therefore, will tend to reduce unemployment pressures in Britain and in most of the other EU countries also.

Activity rates (the percentage of the population aged fifteen and over who are in work or seeking it) are slightly higher in Britain than in most other European countries for men, and for women they are much the highest of any country except Denmark - nearly twice as high as in Greece, Spain, Belgium, Italy, Luxembourg and Ireland[234].

Over the coming decades it is expected that in Britain overall activity rates will fall slightly for men, and rise a little further for women, resulting in a very small reduction in the two combined (1). However, there could be a rather more substantial fall if the numbers of young people in education is greatly increased; or an increase if women's enthusiasm for careers increases, or if childcare arrangements are improved, or if the average age at which people become eligible for pensions becomes higher.

The combined effect of changes in demography and in activity rates is expected to result in a potential labour force in Britain in 2010 about two-to-three million higher - that is, an increase of possibly one million or so less than the increase expected in employment, implying the likelihood of some consequential reduction in unemployment.

In most of the other countries in the European Union there is the likelihood of substantial further increases in female activity rates, which

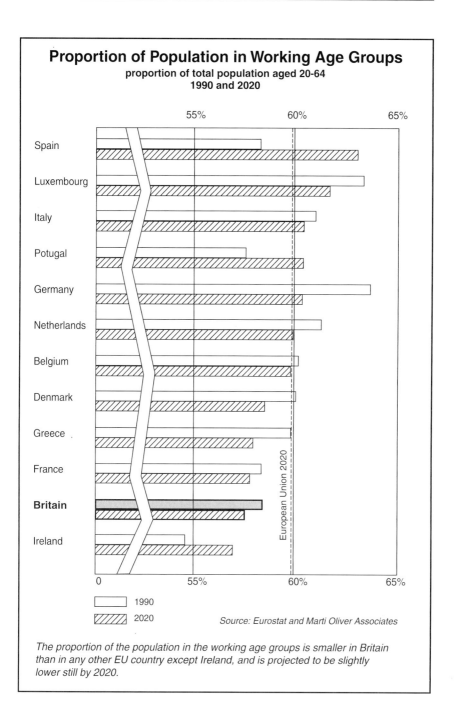

# Proportion of Population in Working Age Groups
## proportion of total population aged 20-64
### 1990 and 2020

*The proportion of the population in the working age groups is smaller in Britain than in any other EU country except Ireland, and is projected to be slightly lower still by 2020.*

Source: Eurostat and Marti Oliver Associates

169

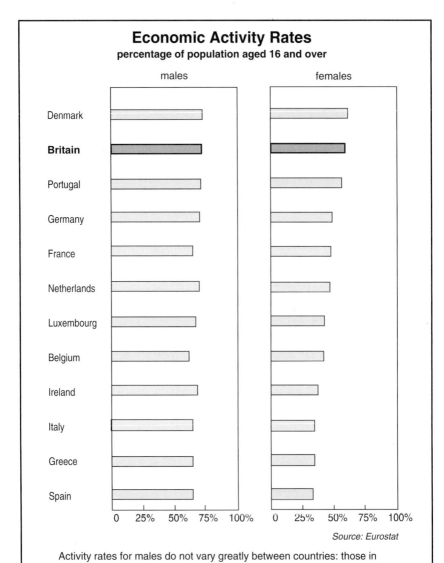

**Economic Activity Rates**

**percentage of population aged 16 and over**

Source: Eurostat

Activity rates for males do not vary greatly between countries: those in Britain are the second highest in the Union. Female activity rates vary far more widely: here too those in Britain are the second higest in the Union.

will tend to increase the labour force and add to unemployment problems; but also demographic changes which will tend to reduce them.

## Unemployment

Between the wars unemployment in Britain (and in many other industrial countries) rose to as high as 15 per cent, causing much economic waste and social hardship. In the 1950s and 1960s, unemployment in Britain was kept down to one-to-three per cent and the number out of work was often smaller than the number of unfilled job vacancies. Many, but not all, of the other industrial countries had a similar experience. It was widely believed that mass unemployment was a plague of the past and that, thanks to Keynesian macroeconomic policies, full employment could be maintained indefinitely.

However, after the oil-price shocks in the 1970s economic growth became slower in Britain and unemployment rose above 5 per cent; and after the adoption of new economic policies in 1979 unemployment rose to more than 11 per cent in some years. Thus in every year since 1981 there have been between 1.5 and 3 million people unemployed. In Britain the official unemployment figures are derived from claimant counts, which a report by the Royal Statistical Society says are unsatisfactory and should be replaced[235]. The basis of the figures has been changed about thirty times since 1979 and it can be argued that the true figure for total unemployment may have gone as high as four million[236,237] - even higher than the peak between the wars.

And in addition to those formally recorded as unemployed, there are others who have dropped out of the labour market altogether. The proportion of men, aged 16-64, who are not economically active has increased from 2.9 per cent in 1975 to 12.3 per cent in 1994, so that about 9 per cent of potentially active men have dropped out of the labour market, many of them as a result of inadequate employment opportunities[238,239].

On any reckoning the number of people unemployed has risen to many times the number of job vacancies, and is at a level where the costs are very great: economic costs in the form of lost output, lost tax and national insurance receipts, higher social security payments and de-skilled workers; and social costs in the form of poverty, insecurity, debt, stress, family tensions and break-up, and social isolation[240] and also, it is claimed, to mortgage repossessions and homelessness[241], worse health and earlier death[242,243] and increased rates of crime[244,245].

Other countries in the European Union have also experienced higher unemployment after 1973, and much higher unemployment in the 1980s and early 1990s, and also falling male activity rates as more men drop out of the labour market altogether. And, although in most of them the effects have been cushioned by unemployment benefits at higher rates, relative to previous earnings[205], the average level of unemployment in the European Union (about 11 per cent) has become a matter of considerable concern.

In Britain unemployment has been forecast to be still in excess of two million by the year 2005[246], and unemployment is expected to continue at high levels in most of the other countries of the European Union. Since unemployment is giving rise to increasing economic and social strains in all the countries, there is growing urgency in the search for policies to bring unemployment down to nearer the levels of the 1950s and 1960s.

## Employment policies

There has been much controversy over what are the main causes of recent high levels of unemployment, and many different policy approaches have been proposed for reducing unemployment in the future.

### Demand management
While all countries have had higher unemployment in the 1980s and 1990s than in the 1960s and 1970s, they have not all experienced this to the same degree. In the European Union as a whole unemployment has recently been at record levels of ten-to-eleven per cent, and in North America it has also been high, with cyclical fluctuations in the seven-to-ten per cent range. In striking contrast, however, in Japan unemployment has been kept down to around the three per cent level, and in the EFTA countries it has until very recently been kept to within the two-to-four per cent range.

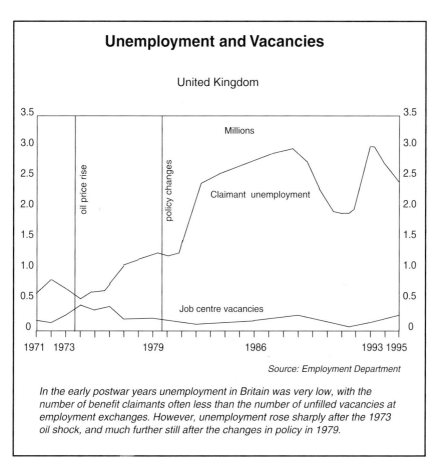

**Unemployment and Vacancies**

United Kingdom

Millions

oil price rise

policy changes

Claimant unemployment

Job centre vacancies

Source: Employment Department

*In the early postwar years unemployment in Britain was very low, with the number of benefit claimants often less than the number of unfilled vacancies at employment exchanges. However, unemployment rose sharply after the 1973 oil shock, and much further still after the changes in policy in 1979.*

One factor in this has been the shift in emphasis in policy objectives in Britain and other European countries from maintaining full employment and economic growth to containing inflation and public borrowing. Recently this has been reinforced by the aim of meeting the convergence criteria for European Monetary Union. In France, for example, the objective of maintaining the parity of the Franc relative to the Deutschmark, at a time when German interest rates were high as a result of reunification, brought a need for higher rates of interest in France and rates of unemployment even higher than they would have been otherwise. Accordingly, it is argued that reversion to a less deflationary stance in monetary and fiscal policy will help reduce unemployment.

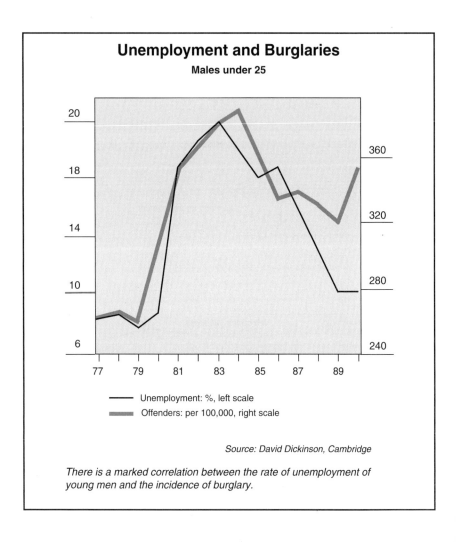

**Unemployment and Burglaries**
**Males under 25**

— Unemployment: %, left scale
▬ Offenders: per 100,000, right scale

*Source: David Dickinson, Cambridge*

*There is a marked correlation between the rate of unemployment of young men and the incidence of burglary.*

However, it appears that, following the oil shocks in the early 1970s, and the recession in the early; 1980s, there has been a shift in the behaviour of European economies with the effect that an expansion of demand tends to bring overheating and inflation at much higher levels of unemployment than in the 1960s[247]. For example, it has been estimated that in the four largest economies of the European Union the rate of unemployment below which there are likely to be inflationary wage increases has risen from about 4 per cent in the 1973-79 period to

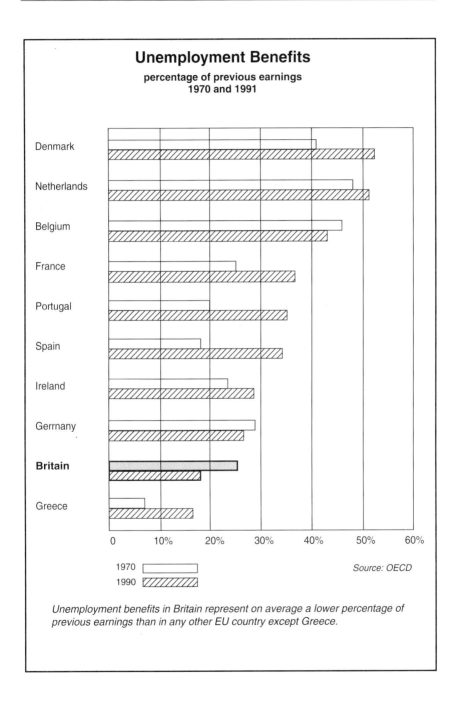

## Unemployment Benefits
**percentage of previous earnings
1970 and 1991**

Denmark

Netherlands

Belgium

France

Portugal

Spain

Ireland

Gerrnany

**Britain**

Greece

0    10%    20%    30%    40%    50%    60%

1970

1990

*Source: OECD*

*Unemployment benefits in Britain represent on average a lower percentage of previous earnings than in any other EU country except Greece.*

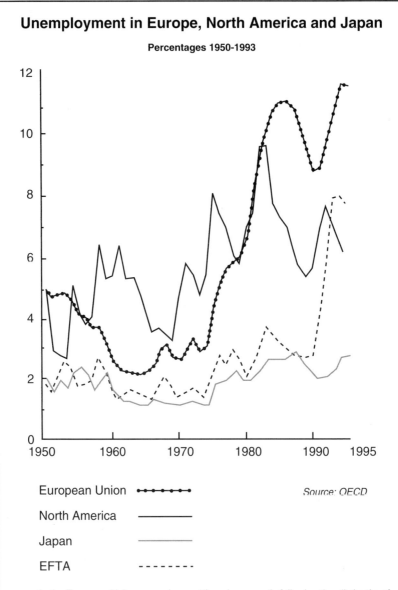

**Unemployment in Europe, North America and Japan**

Percentages 1950-1993

European Union •—•—•—•

North America ——————

Japan ——————

EFTA - - - - - - -

Source: OECD

*In the European Union unemployment has risen greatly following the oil shocks of the 1970s and the adoption of more deflationary economic policies subsequently. In North America, where unemployment used to be higher, it has risen less. In the EFTA countries, where it used to be lower, it has risen only more recently. And in Japan it has remained low.*

about 9 per cent in 1994[248]. Consequently, reliance on a policy of demand expansion alone would imply high rates of inflation.

Recent research[249] suggests that the rise in unemployment in Europe is associated primarily with a decline in the growth of the stock of productive capital, which between 1973-92 grew at only about half the rate that it did in the 1960-73 period. This means that, when demand is increased, capacity constraints are reached earlier than before, halting the growth in jobs while unemployment is still at a high level. It has been calculated that, if Western Europe's growth of investment had been just one per cent higher over the past twenty years, employment now would be about eight million jobs greater[249]. On this analysis, the key to higher future employment is to increase the level of productive investment.

*Labour market deregulation*
Between 1965 and 1995 economic growth rates in the North America and the European Union have been similar, but employment has grown five times as fast in North America. It is argued[205] that in Europe there have been relatively inflexible labour markets with high minimum labour costs because of minimum-wage legislation and, in some countries, high social contributions charged to labour. This has meant that the fall in demand for unskilled workers resulted in their being priced out of the market, with job shedding and higher unemployment. In the United States, in contrast, with a more flexible labour market, a similar fall in demand for unskilled workers brought a fall in their wages and the creation of new jobs instead of the higher unemployment experienced in Europe.

However, it appears that more than half of the increase in jobs in the united States can be explained as resulting from growth in population [249], many of the new jobs have been low-skill, low-pay, part-time ones, average wages have not risen and there has been a marked widening of income differentials. There has also been an increase in poverty, and over half the families in poverty are ones with at least one member *in* work, but with pay too low to keep above the poverty line[250].

In Britain also government policies have sought to achieve a more flexible labour market, with fewer national agreements and lower social contributions than in most other European countries. However, the new jobs created have been predominantly part-time, low-skill, low-pay ones, and unemployment has remained high. Many of these jobs have been taken by women wishing to work part-time, but relatively few by the low-skilled men who predominate among the long-term unemployed.

### Secondary labour markets

In some countries unemployment has been kept low partly through the expansion of sectors which do not have to face direct competition in international markets. In the EFTA countries the expansion of employment between 1974-92 was almost entirely in the public sector, where expansion of social services provided jobs for people who would otherwise have been unemployed[205,247]. And in Japan the increase in employment has been in the private sector, but predominantly in services which, compared with manufacturing, are `inefficient' and `over-manned'[205,247]. In both cases there have been advantages in the form of lower levels of unemployment, but at the cost of higher taxes in the EFTA countries and more expensive services in Japan.

It is suggested that in other countries too it may be possible to build up secondary markets to engage people who would otherwise be unemployed, for example in social projects, with lower skill demands and rates of pay, and subsidised or protected from the competitive market in one way or another. In the United States there have been experiments with `workfare' - requiring unemployed people to take part in work projects as a condition of receipt of welfare benefits. And in Britain there are experiments with `Workstart' under which there will be concessions in National Insurance contributions, speeding up of benefits payments and cash subsidies to employers for a limited period when they take on people who have been unemployed for a long time.

These and other schemes to supplement or bypass the `normal' labour market all involve difficulties, but may turn out to have a useful role to the extent that other measures do not fully succeed.

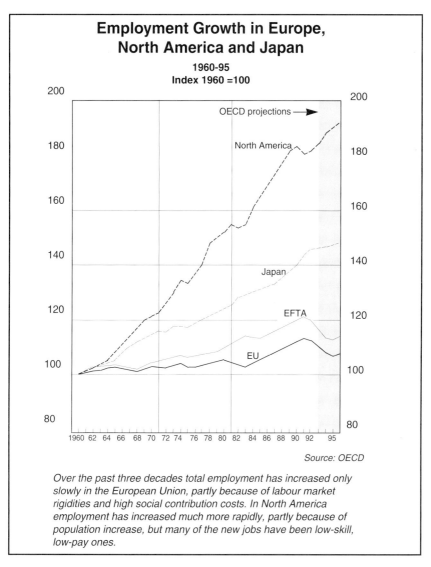

## Employment Growth in Europe, North America and Japan

**1960-95**
**Index 1960 =100**

OECD projections ⟶

North America

Japan

EFTA

EU

1960 62 64 66 68 70 72 74 76 78 80 82 84 86 88 90 92 95

*Source: OECD*

*Over the past three decades total employment has increased only slowly in the European Union, partly because of labour market rigidities and high social contribution costs. In North America employment has increased much more rapidly, partly because of population increase, but many of the new jobs have been low-skill, low-pay ones.*

### Shorter working hours

It is anomalous that most people have more work than they want, while a sizeable minority have no work at all. Between 1960-80 average working hours fell by 15-20 per cent in most European countries[251], but since then in some countries the trend towards shorter hours has slowed down. In Britain average working hours have actually *increased*

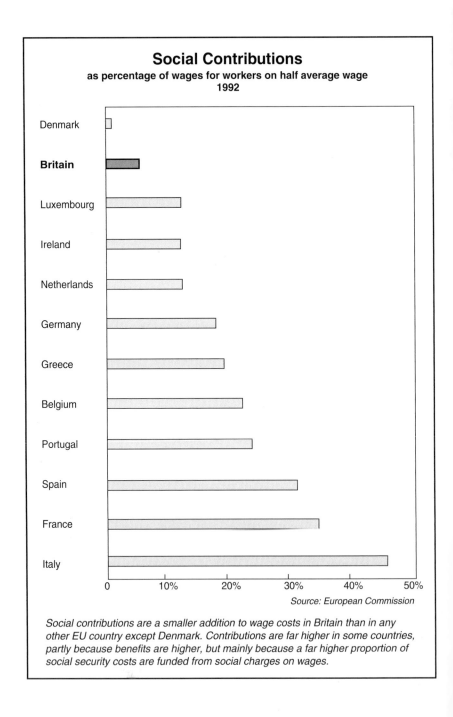

## Social Contributions

**as percentage of wages for workers on half average wage**
**1992**

*Source: European Commission*

*Social contributions are a smaller addition to wage costs in Britain than in any other EU country except Denmark. Contributions are far higher in some countries, partly because benefits are higher, but mainly because a far higher proportion of social security costs are funded from social charges on wages.*

over the past decade as people on low incomes have sought to supplement them with overtime earnings, while people with special skills in senior executive and professional jobs have been under competitive pressure to work longer hours.

In Britain opinion polls suggest that the majority of people in work would rather work for fewer hours than they actually do[270] and an EU survey has found that the same is true of other European countries[207]. However, when asked to choose between shorter hours and higher pay, in Britain and in all the other EU countries except Denmark and the Netherlands, a majority of people express a preference for more pay [207]. However, the majority in favour of more pay tends to be greater in the poorer countries, and it may be expected that as living standards rise the preference for more leisure will tend to increase.

There have been examples of workers accepting shorter hours and *lower* pay when the alternative has been substantial redundancies, but in general people who are already in a job have shown reluctance to work shorter hours if this means a proportionate drop in earnings. However, in the future it may be possible to get people to take a greater part of the fruits of rising productivity in the form of shorter hours, particularly if this can be linked with schemes for limited-period subsidies for employers who take on  people who were previously unemployed.

*Tax changes*
Another proposal is to change the tax system so as to alter the effective costs of different factors of production, shifting some of the burden away from labour (which we would like to use more of) and on to energy and natural resources (which we need to use less of). At present taxes on income from labour are one of the main sources of government revenue in Britain and all other EU countries, and social security contributions, which are a direct charge on labour, in many countries add significantly to labour costs. In Britain personal income tax and social security contributions account for nearly half of all central government revenue, and in the European Union as a whole they account for substantially more than half the total[252]. A shift in taxes away from them would have the effect of making labour cheaper and

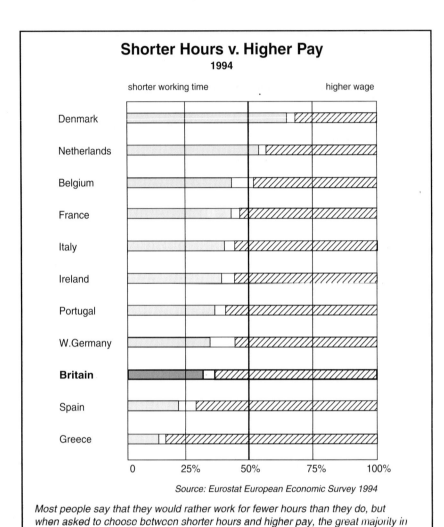

### Shorter Hours v. Higher Pay
#### 1994

shorter working time           higher wage

Denmark

Netherlands

Belgium

France

Italy

Ireland

Portugal

W.Germany

**Britain**

Spain

Greece

0      25%      50%      75%      100%

*Source: Eurostat European Economic Survey 1994*

*Most people say that they would rather work for fewer hours than they do, but when asked to choose between shorter hours and higher pay, the great majority in most EU countries, including Britain, opt for higher pay.*

encouraging greater use of it. And if instead higher taxes were levied on energy, pollution and environmentally-damaging activities, it would make these more expensive and help to protect the environment.

In Britain the Government has already introduced a 5 per cent additional tax on petrol which it is intended to escalate by a further 5 per cent a year in the future. It has been calculated that if this escalation is maintained at 5 per cent a year, and if the proceeds were used to reduce national insurance contributions, the effect would be to increase employment by nearly 200,000 by 2005; while an escalating road fuel tax of twice the size should increase employment by about 500,000; and a carbon tax of a size equivalent to the doubled escalating road fuel tax should also increase employment by about 500,000, while reducing carbon dioxide emissions by more than twice as much as the road fuel tax[253]. Calculations for the European Union as a whole suggest that if reductions equivalent to about one per cent of GDP were made in social security contributions on low incomes, and the lost revenue replaced by a carbon tax equivalent to about $10 a barrel, this could be expected to reduce the unemployment rate by about two percentage points[252].

There is thus the possibility of a single package of tax changes achieving both an increase in employment and an improvement in the environment. However it has been calculated that if such measures are introduced unilaterally in Britain only, they will not result in loss of economic growth or serious damage to international competitiveness [253]. Changes of this kind would be more effective if carried out on a Europe-wide basis, and the Commission put forward proposals for the introduction of a combined energy and carbon tax throughout the European Union. It was not adopted, however, partly because of the opposition of the government of Britain.

### European Commission White Paper

At the end of 1993 the European Commission produced its White Paper on *Growth, Competitiveness, Employment: the challenges and ways forward into the 21st century*[252], which began with the question: `Why this White paper?', and gave the answer: `The one and only reason is unemployment'. The White Paper puts forward a package of proposals designed to create at least fifteen million new jobs and halve the rate of unemployment across the Union by the year 2000. Among its proposals are:

- Completing the establishment of the Single European Market in order to provide favourable conditions for higher investment, improved competitiveness and faster economic growth;

- Helping small and medium enterprises (which provide 70 per cent of present employment in the Union and are considered to be the greatest potential new job creators) by alleviating the constraints which hamper them and improving the financial resources available to them;

- Stepping up co-operative research efforts in order to make the fullest use of new technologies;

- Improving education and training arrangements to give people the higher skills levels that will be needed in the future;

- Promoting sound financial policies to prevent inflation, ensure exchange rate stability and achieve lower interest rates; and suitable macroeconomic policies to even out cyclical fluctuations and encourage growth;

- Reforming social security systems to reduce the burden on labour costs and help unemployed people to get back into work;

- Encouraging shorter working hours;

- Adopting more active labour market policies and removing inflexibilities impeding employment growth; and

- Three major pan-European infrastructure projects in information technology, transport and energy, with a total cost by the year 2000 of over Ecus400bn, to provide immediate jobs in their construction and, by improving competitiveness, provide improved employment prospects in the longer term.

The White Paper represents a combined package in two senses. First, it sees the issues of employment, competitiveness and growth as interrelated and needing a package of policies to address all three in combination. And second, while some of the measures will require action mainly at national level, others can only be put into effect fully, or indeed at all, by joint action by the European Union as a whole. The three infrastructure projects, in particular, are not only conceived as joint European projects - they are also consciously designed to have the effect, when completed, of bringing the member countries physically closer together.

The White Paper highlights the potential within Europe for co-ordinated investment in skills and in employment-generating and wealth-generating sectors. For its success in bringing higher levels of employment it will depend on achieving a greater sense of solidarity between well-off regions and nations and poorer ones, and between those in jobs and those who are unemployed or in low-paid marginal activities; it will also depend on the extent to which it will be possible to establish a more successful economy - which is the subject of the next chapter.

**Key Points for Europe**                    **Employment**

The central issue will continue to be unemployment which is still unacceptably high in all the countries of the Union.

Demand-management should still have a role in raising employment levels - but only a limited one unless there are common European fiscal and financial policies.

A shift away from taxes on income and labour should help increase employment - but this will be easier to bring about if environmental taxes are introduced on a Europe-wide basis.

Future employment growth will be mainly at the upper end of the market and, to get the higher skills levels needed, education and training standards will have to be improved - in all European countries, but particularly in Britain where general education and training levels have lagged behind.

The Single European Market will bring keener competition, particularly in quality, which will increase the need to make full use of new technologies, and to build up the skills base to prevent this resulting in higher unemployment.

The Single Market requires competition to be on a `level playing field', and other EU countries interpret this as including common minimum labour standards. Britain's refusal to accept them is seen as `exporting unemployment' and will bring pressure to end Britain's derogation from the Social Chapter when it expires after four years.

The European Commission has proposed a package of policy measures for tackling unemployment and other economic problems, including investment in pan-European infrastructure networks in information technology, energy and transport. They are based on joint action by the countries of the Union.

# 7 The Economy

Over much of the postwar period the performance of the British economy has been weaker than that of most of the other countries in the European Union. However, other EU countries also face serious economic worries and there is a widespread perception that competitiveness needs to be improved. Key requirements will be raising skill levels, increasing investment and making the fullest use of new technologies. The Single European Market and the emerging global market system will offer new opportunities, but also present new problems which will have an important bearing on the way the European Union develops.

## Economic growth

Britain's economy has become `mature' in the sense that over a long period it has been growing less rapidly than other 'younger' industrial economies, and its share of total world output and trade has been falling. Britain was the first country to have an industrial revolution, and was for many years the world's leading industrial economy. For more than a hundred years, however, its position has been slipping as other countries have also industrialised, and currently it accounts for less than five per cent of total world output[254] and about five per cent of world trade[255].

The long-term decline has been relative, not absolute. In the 1960s and early 1970s up until the time of the oil-price shocks in 1973, the economy grew moderately, if somewhat unevenly, at an average of about 3.2 per cent a year. In the two years after the oil shock, Gross Domestic Product (GDP) actually *fell* for the first time since the war and, although it recovered in some of the subsequent years, average growth in the period 1973-79 was only about 1.5 per cent a year - less than half the previous rate. Since then growth has been high in some boom years, but negative in two periods of recession, with the result that over the whole period 1979-94 the increase in GDP has averaged only about 1.8 per cent a year, barely more than half as much as in the 1960s and early 1970s[256].

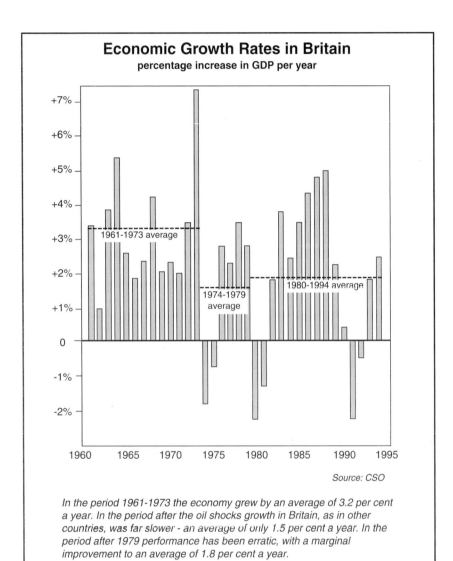

**Economic Growth Rates in Britain**
percentage increase in GDP per year

*Source: CSO*

*In the period 1961-1973 the economy grew by an average of 3.2 per cent a year. In the period after the oil shocks growth in Britain, as in other countries, was far slower - an average of only 1.5 per cent a year. In the period after 1979 performance has been erratic, with a marginal improvement to an average of 1.8 per cent a year.*

In the 1960s and early 1970s other EU countries had rates of economic growth on average half as fast again as Britain, and Japan had a growth rate three times as fast. In the 1974-79 period, after the oil shocks, economic growth in other EU countries fell to about half the previous level, but was still substantially faster than in Britain. In the period since 1979, however, the average growth rate of EU countries has fallen further and has in recent years been broadly similar to Britain's [257].

The cumulative effect of four decades of economic growth has been considerable. In Britain, for example, real GDP per head in 1992 was 129 per cent higher than in 1950[258]. However, economic growth was faster in *all* of the thirteen other EU countries for which comparable figures are available, with the result that, for example, Italy and Austria, which in 1950 had a GDP per head only about half of Britain's, by 1992 had one that was higher. The overall outcome of a less successful economic

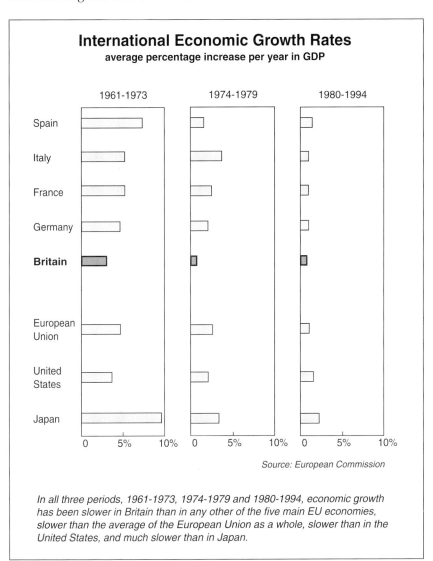

**International Economic Growth Rates**
average percentage increase per year in GDP

*Source: European Commission*

*In all three periods, 1961-1973, 1974-1979 and 1980-1994, economic growth has been slower in Britain than in any other of the five main EU economies, slower than the average of the European Union as a whole, slower than in the United States, and much slower than in Japan.*

performance was that Britain, which in 1950 was the richest of the fourteen countries, by 1973 had become only the sixth richest, and by 1992 had fallen into ninth place[258].

In a projection made for the *Britain in 2010* project, Cambridge Econometrics envisage an average future rate of growth in the British economy of about 2-2.5 per cent a year leading cumulatively to a total growth of about one half over the two decades 1990-2010. Imports are expected to grow nearly twice as fast, nearly doubling over the period; and exports will need to grow rather faster, to pay for the imports and remove the overseas payments deficit, more than doubling over the period [259].

Forecasts for other European Union countries on a similar basis are not available for so far ahead, but projections for 1992-98 envisage an average annual rate of growth of 2.2 per cent a year, and a slightly faster one of 2.5 per cent a year in the United States and Japan[260]. In the European Union as a whole it is expected that imports and exports will rise at about twice the rate of GDP[260].

In Britain between 1970-90 output in manufacturing rose more slowly than in other sectors, but between 1990 and 2010 it is expected to rise more quickly, accounting for an increasing share of the total. Within manufacturing, much the fastest rate of increase will be in electronics, which, by 2010, will be the largest industry in terms of net output. In other sectors the biggest decline, in terms of share of total net output, will be in government and public services and the biggest increases will be in communications, financial and other business services[259].

Similarly in the European Union as a whole the biggest increases are expected to be in electronics and in communications, financial and other business services[260].

## Overseas balance

Britain's relatively poor economic performance has been particularly evident in overseas trade. Over the period 1970-94 the volume of imports of manufactures rose twice as fast as the volume of exports, and the volume of imports of *finished* manufactures rose three times as fast[257].

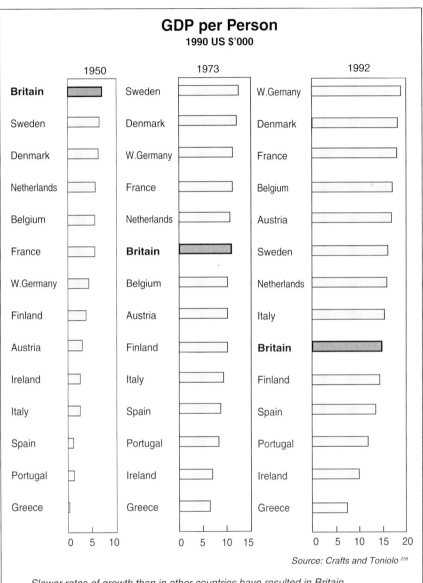

# GDP per Person
## 1990 US $'000

| 1950 | 1973 | 1992 |
|------|------|------|
| **Britain** | Sweden | W.Germany |
| Sweden | Denmark | Denmark |
| Denmark | W.Germany | France |
| Netherlands | France | Belgium |
| Belgium | Netherlands | Austria |
| France | **Britain** | Sweden |
| W.Germany | Belgium | Netherlands |
| Finland | Austria | Italy |
| Austria | Finland | **Britain** |
| Ireland | Italy | Finland |
| Italy | Spain | Spain |
| Spain | Portugal | Portugal |
| Portugal | Ireland | Ireland |
| Greece | Greece | Greece |

*Source: Crafts and Toniolo* [258]

*Slower rates of growth than in other countries have resulted in Britain experiencing a relative decline, from having the highest income per head of the present 15 EU countries in 1950, to the sixth highest in 1973, and only the ninth highest in 1992.*

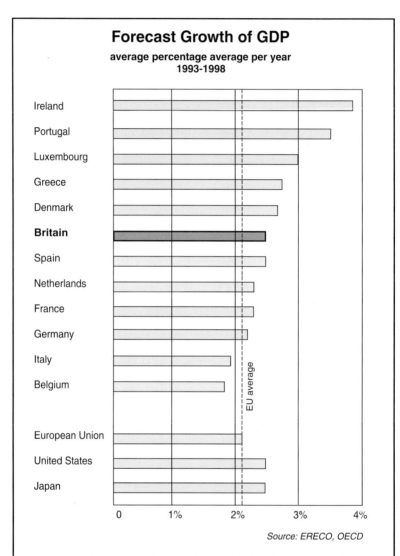

**Forecast Growth of GDP**

average percentage average per year
1993-1998

*Source: ERECO, OECD*

*Over the period 1993-1998 economic growth in the European Union is expected to be marginally less than in the United States and Japan, but growth in Britain marginally above the EU average.*

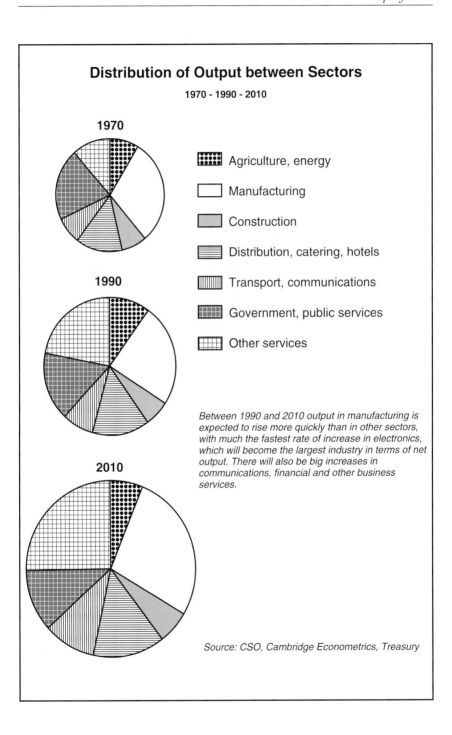

# Distribution of Output between Sectors
### 1970 - 1990 - 2010

**1970**

| | |
|---|---|
| ▓▓▓ | Agriculture, energy |
| ☐ | Manufacturing |
| ▨ | Construction |
| ☰ | Distribution, catering, hotels |
| ▥ | Transport, communications |
| ▦ | Government, public services |
| ▦ | Other services |

**1990**

*Between 1990 and 2010 output in manufacturing is expected to rise more quickly than in other sectors, with much the fastest rate of increase in electronics, which will become the largest industry in terms of net output. There will also be big increases in communications, financial and other business services.*

**2010**

*Source: CSO, Cambridge Econometrics, Treasury*

In most of the main manufacturing sectors during the 1970s and 1980s imports accounted for an increasing proportion of home-market consumption, and exports accounted for a diminishing proportion of manufacturers' sales[256]. Britain's share of total OECD-manufactured exports fell from 10.4 per cent in 1970 to 8.9 per cent in 1990[261].

The decline in manufacturing performance has been going on for a long time, from the early 1950s when the surplus of exports over imports was equivalent to about ten per cent of GDP, and paid for imports of food, energy and raw materials, until the early 1980s when the balance turned into a deficit[262]. For most of the 1950s, 1960s and early 1970s the diminishing surplus on manufactures was broadly offset by a diminishing deficit on food and raw materials as a result of falling world commodity prices[262].

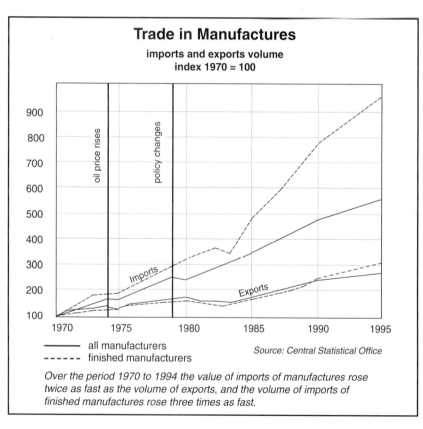

## Trade in Manufactures
### imports and exports volume
### index 1970 = 100

all manufacturers
- - - - - finished manufacturers

*Source: Central Statistical Office*

*Over the period 1970 to 1994 the value of imports of manufactures rose twice as fast as the volume of exports, and the volume of imports of finished manufactures rose three times as fast.*

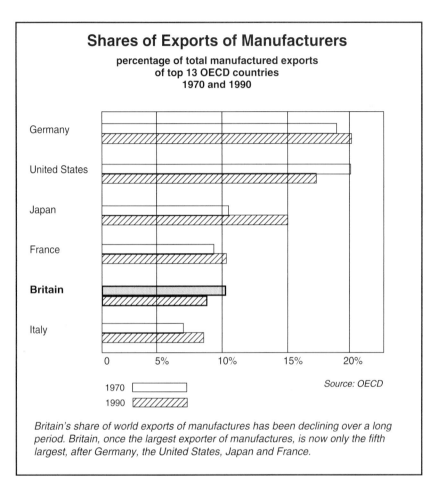

**Shares of Exports of Manufacturers**
percentage of total manufactured exports
of top 13 OECD countries
1970 and 1990

Germany

United States

Japan

France

**Britain**

Italy

0    5%    10%    15%    20%

1970

1990

*Source: OECD*

*Britain's share of world exports of manufactures has been declining over a long period. Britain, once the largest exporter of manufactures, is now only the fifth largest, after Germany, the United States, Japan and France.*

After 1973 the balance of payments on current account was thrown into deficit by the sudden increase in world oil prices; but in the early 1980s production of North Sea oil came on stream and benefited from the high prices, transforming an oil deficit of more than £4bn in 1976 into a surplus of more than £7bn in 1985[256]. After 1985, however, oil prices fell sharply back, and North Sea production declined a little, with the result that by the end of the 1980s the oil surplus had virtually disappeared[256].

During the early 1980s there was also an upsurge in net earnings from invisibles (mainly shipping, aircraft, tourism, business and financial services, dividends and interest and government overseas spending), but they declined again later in the decade, and in the early 1980s the surplus on invisibles was once again quite small compared with the deficit in manufactures[256].

What has happened, then, is that the poor international performance of Britain's manufacturing industry has in the course of four decades turned a large surplus in trade in manufactures into a large deficit; but this was offset for the first three decades by a diminishing deficit on primary products, and then in the early 1980s by large surpluses from oil and invisibles, providing a substantial surplus in the total balance of payments; but when both of these fell away later, there was nothing to offset the continuing decline in manufactures, with the result that the deficits in the total balance of payments reached unprecedented levels[256].

A major factor in the poor international performance of British manufacturing in recent years has been the high exchange rates which resulted from the early 1980s North Sea oil boom, and was maintained subsequently as a result of the policy of shadowing the Deutschmark and then joining the European Monetary Mechanism (ERM) at a high parity. This was highly damaging to manufacturing industry in Britain by making exports to other markets unduly expensive and imports to the home market attractively cheap, so that many enterprises which would have been competitive at a more realistic exchange rate were placed at a serious price disadvantage.

At the same time, in order to defend the over-valued currency, it was necessary to keep interest rates significantly higher than in other centres, particularly in Germany where interest rates were exceptionally high as a result of problems following reunification. This made it more difficult for industry to finance investment for modernisation in order to compete with industry in other countries with access to cheaper finance. In addition there was a recession, the longest and deepest in the postwar period. The combined effect of overvalued currency, high interest rates and general recession put a severe squeeze on manufacturing, with the result that manufacturing output fell after 1989 and took until the last quarter of 1994 to get back to the level it had reached five years before[263].

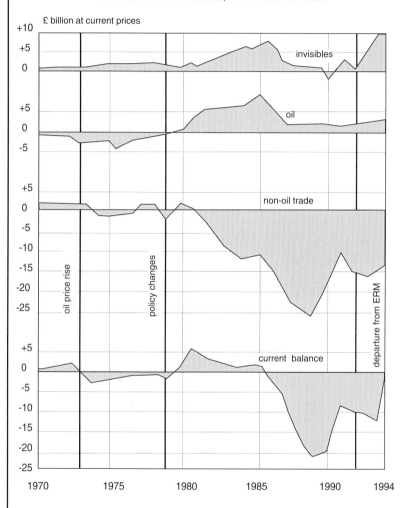

# Balance of Payments

**balance of payments on current account and
net balances on invisibles, oil and non-oil trade**

£ billion at current prices

invisibles

oil

non-oil trade

oil price rise

policy changes

departure from ERM

current balance

1970    1975    1980    1985    1990    1994

*Source: Department of Trade and Industry, Central Statistical Office*

*Poor performance in manufactures, together with falling earnings from oil and
invisibles, have brought record overseas payments deficits in the late 1980s
and early 1990s. However, since the enforced devaluation in 1992, the
balances on both manufactures and invisibles have improved.*

However, the enforced departure from the ERM in September 1992, and the subsequent depreciation of Sterling, greatly improved price competitiveness and, after a time lag, performance. Between 1993 and 1994 exports of goods increased twice as fast as imports, and the surplus on invisibles increased from £1.6bn to £10.4bn[263]. This turnaround shows the damage done by being tied into the ERM at too high a rate, and the advantage of being released from it subsequently; and the danger were Britain to join the proposed European Currency Union at too high a rate.

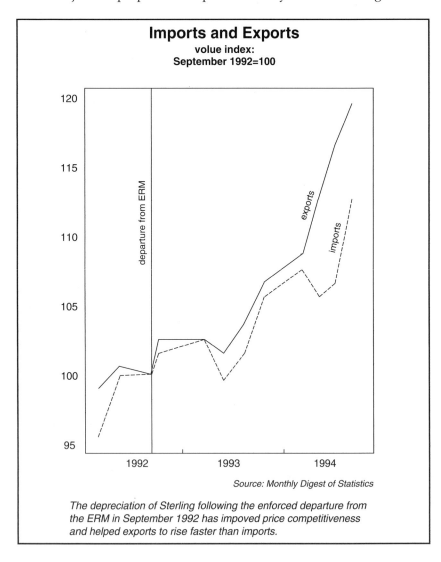

**Imports and Exports**
value index:
September 1992=100

*Source: Monthly Digest of Statistics*

*The depreciation of Sterling following the enforced departure from the ERM in September 1992 has impoved price competitiveness and helped exports to rise faster than imports.*

While in Britain attention has been focused primarily on the balance of overseas payments, particularly the size of recent deficits, there are too other aspects of the overseas position which are also of significance. One is the *direction* of trade.

Largely because of the customs union, and more recently the Single Market, there has been a major shift in the direction of Britain's overseas trade. Trade with the other eleven members of the European Union has increased from 22 per cent of the total in 1958 to 53 per cent in 1992, plus a further 10 per cent with other Western European countries, some of which joined the European Union in 1995 and others of which may join later[257].

There has been a similar shift in the trade of other countries in the Union, with the proportion of their total trade, that is with one another, increasing from 36 per cent in 1958 to 60 per cent in 1992, plus a further 11 per cent with other western European countries which were not members in 1992[257]. It seems likely that with the further development of the Single Market this trend will continue. And it may be expected to be further reinforced if there is a single currency, the introduction of which will mean that this trade will be converted from `international' to `internal'.

The second aspect of significance is the changing *composition* of international trade, with the growing importance of internationally traded services and other `invisible' items. Indeed, it is often argued that we are now in a 'post-industrial society', that manufacturing does not matter any more because we can pay our way in the world by selling services, such as banking, insurance and various business services to other countries.

It is true that for many years the total value of credits and debits of invisibles has been of the same order of magnitude as the value of exports and imports of physical goods. However, it is important to recognise that invisibles are not likely to offer the same scope as exports of manufactures for increased earnings to pay for higher levels of imports in the future.

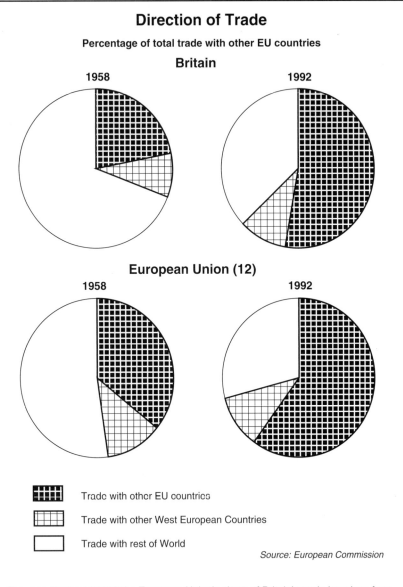

# Direction of Trade

**Percentage of total trade with other EU countries**

## Britain

1958       1992

## European Union (12)

1958       1992

Trade with other EU countries

Trade with other West European Countries

Trade with rest of World

*Source: European Commission*

*Between 1958 and 1992 the European Union's share of Britain's trade has risen from 22 per cent to 53 per cent of the total. In the European Union countries as a whole, the share of their trade that is with other EU countries has risen from 36 per cent of the total to 60 per cent.*

About two-thirds of invisible earnings are from private-sector interest, profits and dividends. Between 1983-93 earnings under this head increased by £31bn (74 per cent); but, unfortunately, over the same period, payments *out* increased by a similar amount; and in order to achieve the £31bn increase in earnings it was necessary to spend more than *twenty-eight times* this amount in new investments overseas [256].

The next most important categories of invisibles are tourism and financial and other services, which were adversely affected, just like trade in physical goods, by excessively high exchange rates. In 1983 tourism spending and receipts were roughly in balance; but by 1993 this had turned into a net deficit of £3bn [254].

Almost certainly, the best prospects for higher earnings on invisibles are in financial and other business services. Net earnings under this head doubled between 1983-93, and if they could be doubled again it would bring in an extra £18bn - enough to turn the balance of payments deficit into a comfortable surplus in every past year but two [256].

However, the scope for achieving such an increase may be limited by the fact that Britain has such a large part of the market already. Banking and insurance already account for 31 per cent of the total value added in services in Britain - more than twice the European Union average[264]; and London already accounts for 44 per cent of total equity market capitalisation in the European Union[265]. To double the stockmarket business would imply taking over *all* the business of Frankfurt, Paris, Milan and Madrid - not an easy task when these and a number of new centres are pressing hard to take business from London, and when the new European Monetary Institute, forerunner of the proposed European Central Bank, has gone to Frankfurt, not to London.

It can be calculated that earnings equivalent to a doubling of financial and other services would be gained from an increase of a mere 18 per cent in exports of manufactures[256]; and this looks like a much more feasible target to achieve. Accordingly, while increased earnings from invisibles will doubtless be sought as well, it seems likely that in the future more attention will be given to fostering the expansion of industry in order to increase the export earnings from manufactured goods - as has been the policy all along in most other European countries.

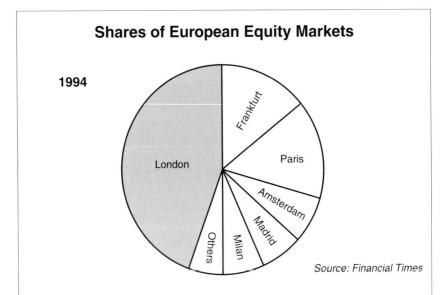

**Shares of European Equity Markets**

1994

Source: Financial Times

*London, along with New York and Tokyo, is one of the three great capital markets of the world. It accounts for 44 per cent of total European equity trading - three times as much as Frankfurt or Paris.*

In Britain imports increased from 21 per cent of GDP in 1970 to 33 per cent in 1990 and are forecast to increase further to 42 per cent in 2010, when they are expected to be equivalent of 68 per cent of consumers' expenditure (259). Similar increases in imports are likely also in other European countries; and the need to find ways of earning enough to pay for them is causing increasing attention to be focused on international competitiveness.

## International competitiveness

There will be no point in seeking to become more competitive by cutting wages - pay levels in many developing countries are only a tiny fraction of those in Europe, and it would be impossible to match them even if it were thought desirable to. The way to a more prosperous future will be by becoming more competitive in productivity and quality. This will need improvements in three areas.

First, it will be necessary to raise skill levels through changes in education and training. (See Chapter 6.)

Second, it will be necessary to increase productive investment, for this is a key factor in faster economic growth, greater productivity and higher employment[266]. Between 1960-73 and 1973-92 the rate of growth in the capital stock fell by about a half in most industrial countries, and in Britain by a third. In the 1973-92 period the rate of growth in capital stock in Britain was lower than in other European countries, barely a third of the rate in the United States and only a fifth of the rate in Japan[266]. Fixed investment per year in manufacturing in Britain in 1992-94 was *lower* than in 1961-73, more than two decades before [256].

Although the rate of investment in Britain has been lower than in other countries, one area in which Britain has been *more* successful is in attracting inward investment *from* other countries. Britain has received more inward investment from within the European Union than any of the others - about a fifth of the total; and far more from other parts of the world - no less than 45 per cent of the total, with more than twice as many new plants from the United States and Japan as any other country in Europe[267].

There are a number of different considerations which attract companies to Britain, but one of the more important ones is Britain's membership of the European Union, which means that the products of plants sited in Britain can have easy access to consumers in all the other countries of the Single Market. A further consideration is the language. English is becoming increasingly strongly established as the second language in Europe (as many people are able to use it as a second language for all the other languages combined), and this gives English-speaking exporters an important advantage[268].

There are many factors affecting rates of investment, but among the more important ones are stable economic conditions to give confidence in future markets for the output resulting from increased capacity, and low-interest rates to make projects viable at a lower rate of return. In recent years real interest rates in Britain and other EU countries have been higher than in earlier periods, causing companies to set high hurdles when appraising investment projects. A CBI survey has found that most companies expect payback in only two-to-three years or (a fifth of them) at a real rate of return of 20 per cent or more[269].

One of the *aims* (although not necessarily one of the *outcomes*) of the proposed European Monetary Union will be to establish stable economic conditions and make possible lower interest rates.

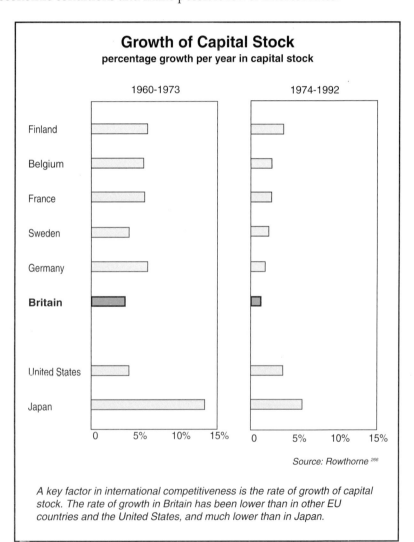

**Growth of Capital Stock**
percentage growth per year in capital stock

*Source: Rowthorne* [266]

*A key factor in international competitiveness is the rate of growth of capital stock. The rate of growth in Britain has been lower than in other EU countries and the United States, and much lower than in Japan.*

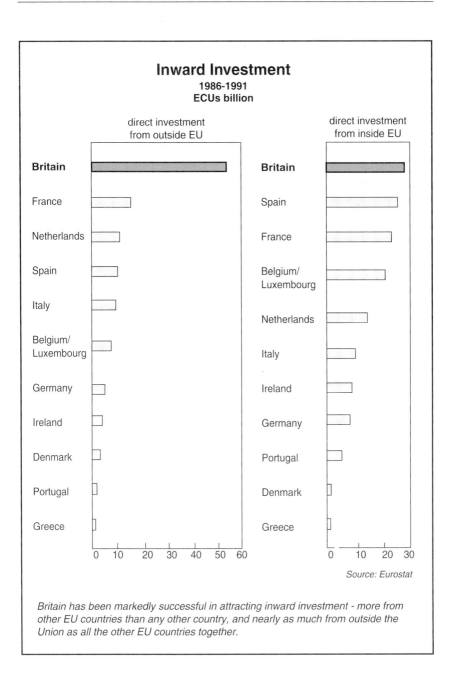

# Inward Investment
**1986-1991**
**ECUs billion**

direct investment
from outside EU

direct investment
from inside EU

| | |
|---|---|
| **Britain** | **Britain** |
| France | Spain |
| Netherlands | France |
| Spain | Belgium/ Luxembourg |
| Italy | Netherlands |
| Belgium/ Luxembourg | Italy |
| Germany | Ireland |
| Ireland | Germany |
| Denmark | Portugal |
| Portugal | Denmark |
| Greece | Greece |

0  10  20  30  40  50  60

0  10  20  30

*Source: Eurostat*

*Britain has been markedly successful in attracting inward investment - more from other EU countries than any other country, and nearly as much from outside the Union as all the other EU countries together.*

205

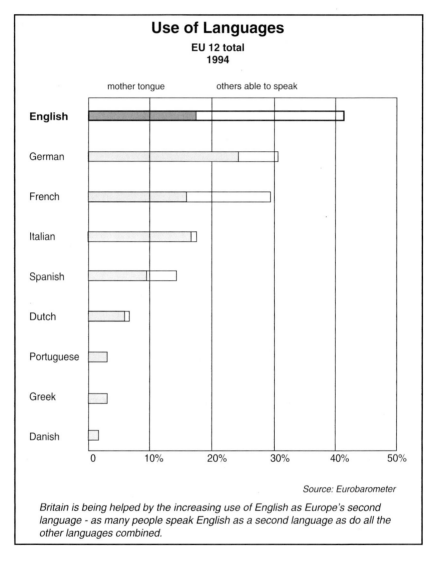

## Use of Languages
### EU 12 total
### 1994

mother tongue                others able to speak

*Source: Eurobarometer*

*Britain is being helped by the increasing use of English as Europe's second language - as many people speak English as a second language as do all the other languages combined.*

And the third requirement will be to make the fullest use of new technologies - which will need both higher skill levels and more investment. It will also need a high level of well directed Research and Development. In 1992 total business R&D spending was higher in Germany than in any other EU country; in France it was two-thirds as great as in Germany; in Britain half as great; and in other countries far less. However, even in Germany total business R&D spending was only half as great as in Japan and a third of that in the United States [270].

R&D spending by government can be important in supporting and complementing private R&D. In 1993 government R&D spending also was highest in Germany. In France it was almost as high, but a third of it was on defence work. In Britain it was lower, and nearly half of it was on defence work, with the result that the amount spent on *civilian* applications was not only much less than in Germany and France, but also much less than in Italy. Government spending on non-defence R&D in Germany was slightly more than in Japan, but only about 30 per cent of that in the United States [270].

European countries are at a competitive disadvantage in that the R&D effort in each of them is on a different scale from that in the United States and Japan. However, taken together, their *combined* business R&D is greater than that of Japan, and their combined non-defence government R&D is greater than that of Japan and the United States together; but this is a point of only hypothetical interest as long as Europe's R&D efforts are *not* in fact combined. Accordingly, the European Commission has been active in schemes to encourage major European companies to pool their R&D efforts in collaborative projects and in getting EU governments to co-ordinate their R&D policies. This has been done mainly through a series of four Framework programmes (and the separate Eureka project) which have resulted in many joint programmes and the setting up of joint centres for work in fields such as space, nuclear fusion and microbiology.

Expenditure on R&D by the European Commission is planned to increase by 72 per cent between 1992-97, but even in 1997 it will represent less than 5 per cent of the Commission's total budget and only about 4 per cent of the total R&D spending of member governments [271].

## Globalising forces

The recent increase in concern about competitiveness has been brought about partly by a perception that Europe is losing ground to Japan, the United States and the newly emerging dynamic economies in East Asia. For example, the European Union's share of world exports of

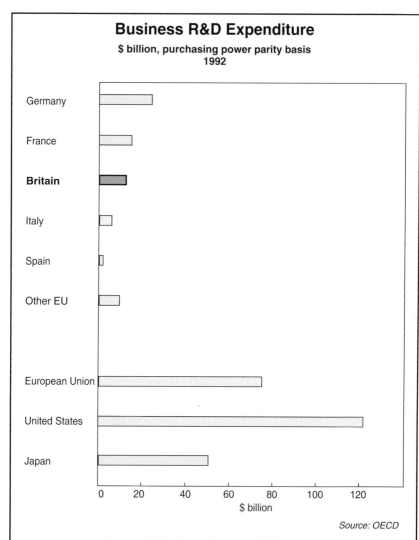

**Business R&D Expenditure**
$ billion, purchasing power parity basis
1992

*Source: OECD*

*Business expenditure on R&D in Britain is substantial: but in Germany it is twice as great, in Japan four times as great, and in the United States nine times as great. However, the combined expenditure of the European Union as a whole is two thirds of that of the United States and half as great again as that of Japan.*

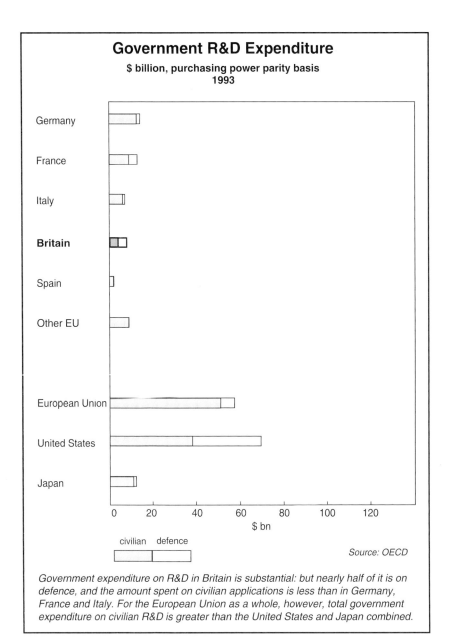

# Government R&D Expenditure
## $ billion, purchasing power parity basis
### 1993

Germany

France

Italy

**Britain**

Spain

Other EU

European Union

United States

Japan

0   20   40   60   80   100   120

$ bn

civilian   defence

*Source: OECD*

*Government expenditure on R&D in Britain is substantial: but nearly half of it is on defence, and the amount spent on civilian applications is less than in Germany, France and Italy. For the European Union as a whole, however, total government expenditure on civilian R&D is greater than the United States and Japan combined.*

209

manufactures fell from 29 per cent of the total in 1980 to 24 per cent in 1992[272]. It is also based on the perception that competitive pressures will get sharper in the future as a result of underlying longer-term changes in the world economy which are having the effect of making it operate increasingly as a single market system. Some of these changes have been happening already over several decades, and some are more recent; but all are likely to continue, and to have, in combination, increasingly important effects.

### Removal of trade barriers

Between 1947 and 1979, seven successive rounds of cuts under the auspices of the General Agreement on Tariffs and Trade (GATT) have led to a widespread dismantling of tariff barriers. The average tariff level on manufactures in the industrialised countries has come down from about 40 per cent in the late 1940s to about 5 per cent in 1993[273]. These GATT deals also secured agreement on codes for technical barriers, government procurement, dumping and subsidies, although these only went a limited way towards removing non-tariff barriers, and did not extend to the increasingly important international trade in services.

### Developments in transport

Over the past three decades there has been a revolution in transport technology which has improved reliability, reduced journey times and cut dramatically the cost of international movement of goods and people with:

- a ten-fold increase between 1960 and 1990 in typical oil-tanker sizes and the introduction of bulk carriers for grains, ores and heavy chemicals;

- containerisation, with giant ocean carriers, roll-on/roll-off vehicle ferries and special trains and lorries for shipment of manufactured goods;

- larger lorries, using modern motorways;

- the replacement of steam locomotives by diesel and electric ones running on modernised signalling systems; and

- the introduction of faster and larger jet aircraft.

*Developments in communications*

Telephone and computer links have become more convenient and reliable, and cheaper to use, as a result of improvements in instruments and switchgear and the use of fibre-optic cable networks, VHF and satellite links. New services such as telex, fax and mobile phones have been introduced and widely adopted. These improvements in communications have made it far more feasible than before to integrate international financial, production, sourcing and marketing operations, and to manage them efficiently from a distance.

*Changes in financial institutions*

Many countries have abolished foreign exchange controls and restrictions on movements of capital, providing the possibility of moving funds from one country to another to take advantage of widening market opportunities. At the same time improvements in communications technologies have made the transfer of funds easier, faster, securer and cheaper.

In most of the industrialised countries savings have become increasingly institutionalised in banks, insurance companies and pension funds, and these large organisations are much better equipped than most individual investors for making effective use of the new opportunities for placing and switching investments on an international scale. In some countries there has been considerable deregulation of the financial institutions and this has led to rationalisations, mergers and international link-ups, further increasing the proportion of business handled by large organisations and the volume of international transactions.

*Growth of multinationals*

The major multinational companies have been particularly well placed to make use of the removal of barriers to trade and financial movements and the improvements in transport and communications. Their international operations have expanded greatly and the United Nations has estimated that transnational corporations now account for a third of world production and that their sales have a value greater than the whole of world trade[274].

### Technology transfer

The effective use of new technologies in manufacturing production and design, and in the products themselves, has become a decisive factor in industrial success. With the accelerating pace of technological change, shortening product life-cycles, and increasing R&D costs, the rewards of being first with a winner have become very large while the penalties of falling behind have become disastrous. Accordingly, companies strong in technology have been keen to spread the cost of their R&D by getting it used more widely, while those in danger of falling behind have been keen get access to it from elsewhere - in both cases without much concern for national boundaries.

This has given an impetus to international technology transfer in many different forms: cross-border transfers between different companies within the same multinational group; licence arrangements; joint research and development projects; mergers and take-overs; and the more informal route of literature, international conferences and overseas education.

### Cultural convergence

There has been increasing global convergence of tastes and fashions due to the growing internationalisation of news and entertainment media, particularly the influence of television in increasing awareness of what people are doing, wearing, using, eating, drinking and listening to in other countries. There has also been more direct international experience, with growing numbers of people going to other countries for part of their higher education, for holidays, or for their companies.

The result of this increasing international awareness has been a tendency for more familiarity with, and acceptance of, foreign products and services; for the development of more similarity in consumer demands in different countries; and for scope for producers to achieve economies of scale by supplying a similar range of products or services to markets in a number of different countries.

### New transport links

The opening of the Channel Tunnel has provided an important material and psychological link between Britain and the rest of Europe, and a number of other bridges and tunnels are likely to  provide new links elsewhere, for example between Sweden and Denmark, Calabria and Sicily, Istanbul and Scutari and, possibly later, between Spain and Morocco, and between Ireland and Scotland.

At the same time the rapidly growing network of high-speed rail links will bring different parts of the European Union closer together, and similar links are likely to be important later in high-density routes in other parts of the world.

*Single European Market*
The passage of the Single European Act has created a single market in the European Union from the beginning of 1993, removing most of the remaining barriers to movement of goods, services and capital within the Union, and encouraging increased intra-EU trade. The Maastricht Treaty has taken economic integration a stage further by adopting a Social Chapter to harmonise labour markets and a timetable for eventual establishment of a common currency - although in both cases with reservations on behalf of Britain.

*Free trade areas*
Free trade areas have been, or are being, set up in many different parts of the world:

- EEA (European Economic Area): The countries of EFTA (the European Free Trade Association) formed closer links with the European Union in the form of the EEA which took effect from the beginning of 1994. Since then three of the member countries have joined the European Union, but the remaining members, Norway, Switzerland, Iceland and Liechtenstein, remain members of the EEA.

- NAFTA (North American Free Trade Association): in 1992 the leaders of the United States, Canada and Mexico signed an agreement to link the three countries in a free trade area which is expected to lead to substantial restructuring of industrial location and employment and a major increase in trade between them. It is hoped over time to widen it to include many other countries in Latin America, of which the first is likely to be Chile.

- MERCOSUR: Argentina, Brazil, Paraguay and Uruguay have established a free trade area which is to be transformed into a full customs union. It is estimated to have trebled trade between the four countries between 1990-94. Chile and Bolivia wish to join as free trade partners.

- Andean Pact: Bolivia, Colombia, Ecuador and Peru have set up a free trade area covering most of the rest of South America.

- ACS: the thirteen English-speaking Caribbean countries in CARICOM are joining with Cuba, the Dominican Republic, Haiti, Surinam, Colombia, Mexico, Venezuela and the counties of Central America to form a wider free trade area called the Association of Caribbean States.

- All Americas: it is hoped by 2006 to establish a free trade area covering thirty-four western hemisphere countries.

- SADC: the Southern African Development Community was formed by ten anti-apartheid Southern African states in 1992, and joined by post-apartheid South Africa in 1994. It aims to boost economic development by the creation of a common regional market, eliminating internal trade barriers within two years and establishing a common currency by the turn of the century.

- ASEAN: Indonesia, Malaysia, Singapore, the Philippines, Thailand and Brunei formed their association originally mainly for political reasons, but the emphasis has shifted more towards economic co-operation and the six countries are now working towards setting up a free trade area.

- APEC: Eighteen Pacific countries meeting in an Asia-Pacific Economic Co-operation conference in 1994 agreed to work towards the establishment by 2020 of a free trade area covering the whole of the Pacific region.

- CIS (Confederation of Independent States): the economy of the Soviet Union was highly centralised, but when it broke up the newly independent republics claimed economic sovereignty. Subsequently, however, most of them have seen advantage in re-establishing close economic links, including free trade, with Russia.

These and other prospective free trade areas may at some stage develop into protectionist economic blocs. Meanwhile, however, they increase trade within the areas covered and help prepare the conditions for a more global economic system.

### Former Soviet bloc

The fall of the Berlin Wall and collapse of Communism in Eastern Europe in 1989, and later the disintegration of the Soviet Union itself, have been followed by radical economic changes in Russia and in most of the countries of Eastern Europe. In the absence of suitable institutions, infrastructure, managers, entrepreneurs and financial backing, the attempted move to a market system has run into major difficulties almost everywhere. (See Chapters 2 and 10.) However, over a period the changes will an bring area with a population of nearly 400 million people (more than either the European Union or the North American Free Trade Area), previously confined within the rigid COMECON system, into the wider world market economy.

### China

China's economy used to be centrally controlled and effectively isolated from the rest of the world, but for more than a decade it has been moving towards a market basis in increasingly many sectors internally; and in recent years it has been increasingly opened out to the world, with rising exports and inward investment, mainly in the form of joint ventures with foreign companies in a position to provide capital, management expertise, modern technology and overseas market outlets. It seems likely that in the course of the coming decades it will become increasingly a part of the wider world market system.

China's population of 1.2 billion makes it potentially both a very large producer and an enormous market. Hitherto, its size has been largely offset by its very low average GDP per head of $370 on an exchange rate basis, but nearer $3000 on a purchasing power parity basis[254]. However, it can be calculated that if GDP per head of the Chinese in China were as great as that of the Chinese in Hong Kong, the Chinese economy would be nearly as large as the United States, Japan and the European Union combined[254,275]. Moreover, this possibility may not be as remote as it might seem, since the Chinese economy has been growing very fast recently, by an average of 9 per cent a year in the 1980s and by about 13 per cent in each of 1992 and 1993[276].

## *The Uruguay Round*
The GATT Uruguay round, finally concluded in December 1993 after seven years of negotiations, constitutes a further major move towards a world-wide free market system:

- industrial tariffs to be cut, on average, by a further third:

- quotas on imports to the industrialised countries of textiles and garments under the Multi-Fibre Arrangement (MFA) to be dismantled over ten years from 1995 and replaced by tariffs, and the tariffs to be reduced;

- domestic farm supports to be reduced by 20 per cent, agricultural export subsidies to be cut by 36 per cent in value and 21 per cent in volume, and food import bans and quotas to be replaced by tariffs;

- fair trade principles to be applied also to international trade in services (but with arrangements for financial, telecommunications and media to be settled in further talks in 1994 and 1995);

- intellectual property rights to be internationally protected;

- government procurement to be opened to international competition;

- new, clearer rules to clarify permissible technical standards, subsidies and anti-dumping measures, and to facilitate settlement of disputes; and

- a new, permanent World Trade Organisation to implement the agreement.

The tariff cuts, the outlawing of non-tariff barriers, the winding up of the MFA and the opening up of government procurement are expected to bring a further expansion of world trade in manufactures. The reduction in agricultural support is expected to bring something much nearer a free market in world food products. The extension of free-trade principles to a wide range of services is expected to boost international trade in services. The protection for intellectual property rights and new rules for technical standards are expected to promote technology transfer. And the new World Trade Organisation may be expected to help ensure that the agreed changes are implemented and to result in continuing pressure for further liberalisation of world trade.

## The global market system

Developments within the European Union are bringing a single European economy; and the wider developments are bringing an increasingly global market system. The changes which have come about already are considerable.

### International finance

Financial markets are becoming increasingly international, with savings of people in one country channelled through financial institutions for investment in other countries around the world.

In 1991 UK mutual funds were estimated to have 39 per cent of their assets invested abroad, and UK pension funds 20 per cent[277]. Total foreign investments of the mutual and pension funds of the five leading countries amounted to more than $6,000 billion[277], equivalent to more than thirteen times the total foreign exchange reserves of these countries[278].

Shares in leading companies are traded in stockmarkets around the world and these are closely linked by modern telecommunications. In consequence, movements in one market, whether following material developments or changes in `sentiment', are quickly reflected in changes in other markets around the world - most notably on `Black Monday', 19

October 1987, when within hours the dramatic collapse in share prices spread to all the markets round the world.

International currency movements have risen even more spectacularly. Funds are switched by companies needing currency for their increasing international trading and investment operations, by companies wanting forward currency as a hedge to cover future operations, and by companies, financial institutions and individuals hoping to make a profit from speculation. The total foreign exchange market turnover in the three leading centres (London, New York and Tokyo) trebled in six years between 1986 and 1992[277], when it was equivalent to more than eighty times the value of the total merchandise trade of Britain, the United States and Japan[278], with turnover *each day* equivalent to more than three times these countries' total foreign exchange reserves. Global net foreign exchange market turnover is currently in the region of $1,000 billion a day[277,279], equivalent to more than thirty times the total daily value of world merchandise trade and more than ten times world GDP[278].

### International trade

Over the period 1961-94 the trade of the European Union countries has grown nearly twice as fast as their output[280]. And in the world as a whole over the whole period 1950-91 the volume of total exports has grown twice as fast as world output[281]. Over the same period the volume of exports of manufactures has grown nearly three times as fast as output. International trade in services is currently estimated to be worth about $900 billion[273], equivalent to more than a quarter of world exports of merchandise[278]. Consequently, international trade is accounting for a steadily increasing proportion of the economy of almost all countries, and the degree of interdependence between national economies is becoming correspondingly greater.

### International investment

While international trade is expanding twice as fast as GDP, international investment is expanding no less than four times as fast[282].

### International production

It is not only international trade, investment and finance, but also production itself which is becoming an increasingly global operation. Capital is raised in international markets; staff are recruited internationally; production equipment, components and materials, technologies and specialist services are imported from foreign sources; marketing is planned and sales are made in a world market; and profits are declared and taxes are paid in countries other than where they originate. Many of the more complex products are sourced from and sold in a large number of different countries as part of an operation that is truly global.

Much production of goods, and rather more provision of services, is still undertaken on a local or national basis; but a steadily increasing proportion is undertaken on an international, even global, basis. And it is the large multinational companies which are best placed to make use of the opportunities for international operations; and accordingly it is they which are accounting for a steadily increasing proportion of total business, and taking a growing proportion of economic decisions.

## Potential benefits of a single market

The construction of a Single European Market and, beyond that, the development of a single global market system, potentially should bring a number of important benefits. With a broader basis for competition, more efficient producers should grow faster than less efficient ones; resources should be allocated more advantageously; costs should be lower; output and incomes should grow faster; and consumers should have wider choice and lower prices.

Because the potential gains are so general and diffuse it is difficult to put figures to their likely size; but some attempts at quantifying the likely benefits have been made.

### Single European Market
A major study set up by the European Commission[279] has estimated that economies of scale, common technical standards and keener competition as a result of the Single European Market will bring a 4.5 per cent gain in gross domestic product (GDP) by 2002 and lead to the creation of about two million more jobs. Other analysts have estimated a gain in GDP of as little as one per cent and forecast a net *decline* in jobs. The first year of

the Single Market has made little noticeable impact, with half of British exporters interviewed in a survey saying they had felt no benefit from it[284]. However, the first year coincided with a period of recession in most of the member countries of the Union, and its longer-term impact is anyway hard to estimate because of the simultaneous impact of other factors and the difficulty of quantifying dynamic effects - for example the effects on business confidence.

## *Uruguay Round*

A number of exercises have been undertaken to quantify the consequences of the Uruguay Round, the most solidly based of which is probably a study made by the GATT Secretariat in November 1993 [285], based on the actual offers made in the negotiations. It foresees an annual growth in world exports of one per cent a year higher than in the absence of an agreement (five per cent a year as against four per cent), bringing a net gain of $230 billion a year by 2005 - roughly equivalent to half the GDP in China, or about three-quarters of one per cent of expected total world GDP in 2005[286].

The main increases in trade are expected to come in textiles and clothing (due to removal of quota barriers and lower tariffs) and in food (due to cuts in farm support and export subsidies). At present agricultural support in the European Union takes about half of the entire Union budget and provides subsidies of more than 50 per cent on cereals, oil seeds, sugar, beef, mutton and dairy products[286]; there are also high farm subsidies in the United States; and in Japan there is a ban on imported rice. It is estimated that in 1992 the average consumer paid $450 for agricultural protection in the European Union, $360 in the United States and $600 in Japan[286]. The OECD estimates that consumers in the European Union will get about 26 per cent of the total benefit from the deal[287].

## Potential problems with a single market

It seems likely that the process of globalisation will continue to bring problems as well as benefits. Any market system, to give the best results, needs to work within a suitable regulatory framework. And while national market economies work under the jurisdiction of national governments which set rules to regulate their operation, the emerging global market system has no comparable global authority to regulate it. There are three kinds of problems which this is likely to give rise to:

## Competition

The main instrument for achieving the potential gains is wider, keener, more effective competition. But if competition is to be more effective it will bring changes, as a result of which there will be gainers but also, by definition, losers and potential casualties. Firms will have expanding opportunities to sell in world markets; but they will also have to face keener competition in their home markets. Producers will be able to benefit from access to much more of the world for their finance, recruitment and training, R&D, equipment and systems, materials and components, business services, and their sales; but so also will their overseas competitors. Those which are more successful in competition will benefit and grow stronger; but those which are not will be in trouble.

When competition bites and some firms seen as strategically important get into difficulties there will be calls for help. In a humane and civilized society it may be necessary in some cases to make provision to cushion the shocks and alleviate the hardships - although this will inevitably to some extent weaken the impact of the competition and reduce the size of the gains from improved efficiency. And in so far as the casualties arise as a result of competition within the European Union, it is to the institutions of the Union that people will look to provide mechanisms and resources for taking some of the pain out of the changes - for example, by providing for the retraining of people displaced from newly uncompetitive firms.

## Location of economic activity

Another aspect of the operation of the new market system, which may give cause for concern, is the location of future economic activity. Companies will increasingly take decisions, without much regard for national boundaries or national government policies, on where to locate their investment, R&D, production and other facilities. They will normally take their decisions on the location of their new investments, understandably, on the basis of what they consider to be most advantageous to the company. This can be expected to bring the benefits associated with a free market in the form of economies arising from specialisation and efficient production with lowest costs.

However, the companies' pursuit of the most cost-effective locations may put pressures on national governments to make their countries attractive in ways which may be detrimental to other objectives. For example:

- Pressures to keep taxes low may restrict the scope for provision of public services and other activities requiring expenditure from government funds.

- Pressures to keep marginal rates of income and corporation taxes as low as possible may force undue dependence on indirect taxes.

- Pressures to keep labour costs low may inhibit making arrangements for ensuring good labour market and working conditions.

- Pressures to minimise government interference may limit the feasibility of imposing regulations for company law, for health and safety standards, for consumer protection, and for preservation of the environment.

There is thus a danger that, as choice of location becomes wider, there will be increasing international competition to attract vital inward investment, and that this will lead to the erosion of standards in many areas where the maintenance of high standards is necessary for a good quality of life.

Accordingly there will be a growing need for standards to be set to regulate the working of the market and ensure the preservation of things considered vital for a high quality society. And since national governments will be increasingly powerless to control the operations of multinational companies, the regulatory role in Europe will increasingly be seen as having to be fulfilled on a common Union-wide basis by the institutions of the Union itself.

## *Macroeconomic policy*

A third aspect which is likely to command increasing attention is the diminishing powers over their economies which national governments are able to exercise in the conditions of a single market system. In the first two decades after the war, governments in most of the industrialised countries had a fair measure of success in using macroeconomic policy measures to ensure full employment and economic growth.

In more recent years macroeconomic policy measures have not achieved such gratifying results, partly because some governments have been reluctant to use them, but also, more fundamentally, because the increasing interdependence of modern market economies has made the traditional economic control measures much less effective when operated by any one country on its own.

When imports account for a high proportion of consumption, and an even higher proportion of *increases* in consumption, some of the effects of macroeconomic policy measures taken by a government in one country tend to spill over into the economies of its international trading partners. For example, if a government seeks to accelerate growth or reduce unemployment through expansionary fiscal or monetary policies, this tends to suck in greater volumes of imports, thereby diluting the expansionary impact on the home economy and at the same time giving an unintended boost to other economies by providing an additional stimulus to their exports.

This has the consequence that when countries follow policies which are more expansionary than those of their neighbours (as did France in the early 1980s and Britain a few years later) they tend to run into balance-of-payments difficulties and pressures on the foreign exchange rate. Conversely if, in order to combat inflationary pressures, countries adopt macroeconomic policies more deflationary than those of their trading partners, they tend to experience an unintended build-up of payments surpluses and an appreciation of the exchange rate.

An area of particular difficulty is control of the exchange rate against attack from speculators. The removal of currency controls, changes in the structure of financial institutions, and improvements in technology have combined to produce extremely large international currency movements. Current turnover on the London market, for instance, is estimated to be in the region of $300 billion a day[277], with about 80 per cent of it in the hands of foreign institutions[288] and between 90 and 95 per cent of it representing purely speculative transactions[289,290,291]. On `Black Wednesday', 16 September 1992, the day when, under speculative pressure, the pound crashed, forcing Britain to leave the European Exchange Rate Mechanism (ERM), it is believed that turnover on the London market rose to about 50 per cent above the average, to somewhere in the region of $450 billion[288]. Thus in a single day turnover was greater than the value of total imports and exports over the whole *year*, and more than ten times as great as the total value of the foreign exchange reserves[277].

The result was that despite a series of strong statements of its determination to uphold the parity of sterling, and despite selling $15 billion or more from the foreign exchange reserves[288,292], and getting support from other central banks, raising base rate to 15 per cent and short-term rates to 100 per cent, the government was unable to prevent sterling from being forced out of the ERM.

It can be argued that politicians are often irresponsible in economic management and that market forces can play a useful role in correcting their mistakes; more specifically, it can be argued, with justification, that the Government entered the ERM at too high a rate, that at the time of the crash Sterling was manifestly over-valued relative to the Deutschmark, that the Government had unwisely rebuffed earlier offers of a managed realignment of exchange rates, and that the devaluation, even if forced, was appropriate, perhaps inevitable, and anyway a return to reality which would be good for Britain's exports and help the recovery from recession.

However, the same could not be said of the attack on the French Franc a year later. By common consent the Franc was *not* over-valued relative to the Deutschmark, inflation in France was *lower* than in Germany, and there was no economic rationale for a devaluation. Yet, despite the determined commitment of considerable reserves by the central banks in France and Germany, speculation against the Franc brought pressures so great that they ended in the disruption of the whole ERM system. What was involved was not the wisdom of the market being imposed on irresponsible governments, but irresponsible speculators speculating on the speculations of other speculators - on sufficiently massive a scale to overturn a central element of policy of the elected governments of two major countries. It is an aspect of the emerging global market system which brings no apparent benefits and obvious potential dangers.

If governments nowadays are no longer in a position to operate fully effective macroeconomic policies on their own, the European Union countries will have to find ways of doing collectively what they cannot do separately - for example by adopting jointly packages of macroeconomic policies designed to stimulate emergence from recession. And if individual governments, faced with the massive scale of daily financial movements, are no longer in a position to withstand speculative attacks on national currencies, the adoption of a single common currency would, at a stroke, end the possibility of speculation on future changes in the parities of separate European currencies. However, it would also give rise to a number of difficult issues with far-reaching implications. These are considered in Chapter 9.

## Key Points for Europe          The Economy

Real GDP per head in Britain doubled between 1950 and 1992, but other EU countries performed better, and Britain slipped from being the richest of the present EU countries to the ninth richest.

Over the period 1971-92 Britain's exports of manufactures rose only half as fast as imports, but since the departure from the ERM a weaker pound has gone with a stronger export performance.

The European Union's share of world exports of manufactures has fallen from 29 per cent of the total in 1980 to 24 per cent in 1992, and there is widespread concern to improve international competitiveness - for example by improving skill levels, increasing investment and making fuller use of new technologies.

In the past two decades the rate of growth in capital stock has been higher in other EU countries than in Britain - but higher still in the United States and much higher still in Japan.

Where Britain has been more successful than other EU countries is in attracting more investment from the United States and Japan - partly because it can provide a manufacturing base *within* the Union.

No EU country on its own has R&D spending on a scale to compete with that in the United States or Japan, but *together* their R&D is of comparable size - hence the importance of the measures being taken to bring European countries' R&D together.

The Single European Market will bring bigger sales for exporters, better value for consumers, but tougher times in home markets for any producers which are not competitive.

In an increasingly global economic system, competition to attract investment threatens to undermine national standards, and governments are losing control of national economies, but there is still scope for control through joint action at European Union level.

The most spectacular loss of national government control is in the financial markets. Currency speculation would be stopped at a stroke by the adoption of a single currency, but this would have far-reaching implications.

# Part II

## The Future of the European Union and Britain

Given the longer-term future developments foreseen in Britain and other EU countries, what are the implications for the future shape of the European Union? Are the various forces at work likely to favour expansion to take in new members; or to effectively confine it to its present size? Will the emergence of common problems and the need for a common response to them, draw the member countries together in a closer kind of union; or will differences in situation, interest and attitude keep them apart in a more limited kind of association?

The following chapters bring together the implications of the six previous ones for the future shape of the European Union, consider further the implications of monetary union and enlargement, and suggest the ways in which the Union is likely to develop in the longer term - and in the light of this the options for the future of Britain.

# 8  Shaping Factors

The issues considered in the preceding six chapters have implications for the future shape of the European Union, some favouring movement towards a closer union, some not, with the balance and form of the effects varying in each of the different areas.

## Security

The ending of the Cold War has brought fundamental changes not just to the scale, but also to the *kind* of security issues which need to be addressed. The break-up of the Warsaw Pact and the collapse of Communism have removed the mortal threat that originally brought the western countries together in NATO; but the increasing withdrawal of the United States from Europe is bringing new pressures on the EU countries to combine more closely for their defence against any new threats which may materialise in the future. At the same time the Bosnian tragedy has provided a reminder that the end of the Cold War has brought instability and increased potential for new wars within Europe, and the Gulf War a reminder that there is still the potential for wars in other parts of the world; and both have underlined the importance of integrated forces for effective action.

Also the increasingly high cost of modern high-tech weapons systems is making it prohibitively expensive for any medium-size country to be self-sufficient in its sources of supply, and the most practical alternative to buying mainly from America is for European countries to pool their arms procurement arrangements.

And just as a joint defence system would help make possible a quick, decisive response to any military threat, so also a joint *foreign policy* would help ensure that any military response was appropriate to the circumstances or, preferably, would avoid the circumstances being allowed to arise where military force was necessary in the first place.

However, the fact that common defence arrangements and a common foreign policy would have strong advantages is not a sufficient reason for them necessarily to be brought into being; if it were, the

Soviet threat in the late 1940s would have brought a United Europe instead of a NATO based on collaboration between separate nation states. Defence and foreign policy are highly emotive areas, mixed up with feelings about separate national identity and state sovereignty. These feelings are still strong today - not least in Britain - and are unlikely to disappear quickly. Hence close unity in defence and foreign policy, whatever the apparent advantages, is more likely to *follow* closer unity in other areas than to *precede* it.

It is significant that the Maastricht Treaty envisages closer unity in this area being achieved through its own separate `pillar', independent of the Commission, and operated through co-operation between the separate national states; that the integrated multinational military formations are still small and untested; and that, despite protestations of plans for more joint procurement, several national governments maintain defence industries of a scale and diversity which could not be justified on economic grounds alone.

What seems likely to happen is that there will be closer liaison in foreign policy and in defence planning, an increasing proportion of joint procurement, and a growth in the number and size of joint military formations - possibly in time becoming a joint `European Army', but co-existing with separate national armies and growing in importance relative to them only as fast as its usefulness is demonstrated and the fears associated with it are dissipated. And for many years to come NATO, although no longer needed for its original role, is likely to be kept going as a stand-by facility, in order to maintain American commitment in the remote eventuality of some new mortal threat arising.

But while security considerations (barring the eruption of some dramatic new threat) are unlikely to be a driving force for a *deeper* European Union, they may well be a major factor in bringing into being a *wider* one. For the countries of Central and Eastern Europe, memories of Russian occupation are still fresh; and the troubles of former Yugoslavia are a continuing reminder of the dangerous nationalist sentiments which the end of the Cold War has released in other countries also. Accordingly, they are concerned for security against attack by a resurgent Russia or by neighbouring countries with which they have a history of conflict. Many of them would like to join NATO, but the Partnership for Peace plan stops short of security guarantees and full membership is being opposed by Russia.

Accordingly, membership of the European Union, which is desired anyway on economic grounds, is also seen as carrying at least *implicit* guarantees against external attack, as well as providing a context of greater stability to make local tensions less likely to erupt into war.

For the existing member countries of the European Union their joining would bring risks: the taking on of commitments to countries some of which have unresolved difficulties with Russia and some of which have troubles with neighbours or with internal minorities. However, there would also be security advantages: it would bring a further layer of protection against the possibility of attack from Russia if it became expansionist again; and by bringing greater stability to a potentially turbulent area, it would help to resolve disputes before they got out of hand, and thus reduce the risk of the EU being pulled into a succession of Yugoslavias. Stability in Eastern Europe is a vital interest for Western Europe too.

Hence security considerations on both sides are likely to be a factor favouring the enlargement of the European Union to include another ten countries in Central and Eastern Europe. (See Chapter 10.)

## The Developing World

Developments in the developing World are liable to have a major impact on all countries in the European Union in the longer term in the form of resource scarcities and environmental difficulties as a result of continuing increases in population. However the impact of these developments is likely to be more on the *condition* of the European Union than on its *shape*.

In so far as the way things go, the Third World will be materially affected by investment, trade and aid from the industrial countries, and the European Union countries are important in all three. It follows that if investment is encouraged, trade is liberalised and aid is better directed,

Third-World problems will be mitigated and hence their impact on Europe reduced. And the activities of EU countries are likely to be more effective if they are well co-ordinated. But even if it may be the case that it would be in Europe's interests to act in unison in its relations with the Third World, it does not seem very likely that the pressures to actually do so will turn out to be a major factor in European unification.

To the extent that problems in the Third World worsen, one consequence will be continued pressures for immigration to Western Europe (in addition to possible pressures from Eastern Europe). Under the open-frontiers policy, given expression in the Schengen agreement, anyone given admission to any of the EU countries (except, at least for the time being, Britain, Ireland and Denmark) can move freely to any of the others. It follows that there is a need for the EU countries to have common procedures and policies for people arriving at the Union's external frontiers, and also for their treatment after their arrival.

This imperative will give an immediate boost for unification of policies in this particular area. However, *failure* to achieve the degree of common practice required may put strains on an important unifying measure already in place - the agreement to open internal frontiers. France, for example, delayed putting into effect its participation in the Schengen arrangements because of lack of confidence that entry controls in other EU countries were sufficiently effective to prevent an unacceptable flow of immigrants via other member countries. Thus there is the possibility that concern about Third-World immigration may have the effect of impeding the removal of restraints to free movement of EU citizens between member countries.

All in all, while in the longer term developments in the Third World may have a very important impact on the wellbeing of all the countries in the Union, it seems that their impact on the future development of the Union as an entity is unlikely to be great.

## Population and social change

Although there are important differences in detail and degree, the most striking thing about expected future developments in this area is the *similarity* of the EU countries, *all* of which expect populations stable in total size but with a markedly older age distribution, and all of which are experiencing changing social patterns, particularly in the structure and behaviour of families. There is also great similarity across all EU countries in the problems arising from these changes: demographic changes are putting pressure on the economics of the welfare state, and social changes are bringing pressures to adapt the *form* of the welfare state to take account of new patterns of need.

But, although all the countries have similar problems, there is in general neither need nor inclination to *solve* the common problems in the same way, or together. For the patterns of provision for health, welfare and social security, and the methods of financing them, have grown up in very different ways in different member countries, and it would be a very complex and difficult business to try to harmonise them in a common form. Moreover the changes needed in one country to meet changing future needs will often be quite different from those needed in another.

Also this is an area where local and national circumstances and needs vary greatly, as do also local and national attitudes towards the form and scale of provisions for meeting them. Accordingly, any attempt to bring about a standard Europe-wide pattern of provision would be not only very difficult, but also very strongly opposed.

Hence, except in the area of employment, where Europe-wide minimum labour standards have been instituted, there has been little attempt to harmonise the social-protection provisions of different countries. And social policy is likely to remain an area in which, in general, the principle of *subsidiarity* is maintained, and even if different countries face strikingly similar problems, they are likely to deal with them in markedly different ways. It is therefore not an area likely to generate pressures for a closer union.

## The environment

Some environmental issues, for example in town and country planning, are essentially local or regional, and there is no need for concerted international action, although there are many examples (for instance on ways of dealing with traffic problems in towns) where experience in one country may provide useful ideas for dealing with similar problems in other countries. There are many other environmental issues, however, which can *only* be dealt with adequately through joint action at an international level, and the need to deal with these will provide growing pressures for closer European union.

The Channel Tunnel and the high-speed rail and motorway links beyond it, and also the new high-capacity telecommunications networks in preparation, will improve Europe's competitiveness and bring countries effectively closer together, in ways which minimise environmental damage. However, the trunk networks are essentially continental and cannot be planned in separate national compartments. A single vision will be needed, together with the means for putting it into effect.

Water pollution from agricultural and industrial chemicals is a local problem, but can become an international one too when rivers cross national boundaries, or flow into shallow seas, or when waste is dumped at sea. Accordingly it has been found necessary to set quality standards for drinking water and agree international standards for sewage treatment, discharges of effluent into rivers and dumping at sea.

Disposal of solid waste is usually mainly a local problem (although regulation is needed of the growing practice of exporting toxic waste to countries with less demanding disposal standards), but international co-operation is needed to secure higher proportions of salvage and recycling.

Air pollution from cars is mainly a local problem, but some of the measures needed for dealing with it cannot be applied at local level; because the vehicle industry and the transport industry are international, it is necessary to set vehicle-emission standards internationally so as not to distort competition and impair efficiency.

Air pollution from factories and power stations tends to blow over longer distances and across national boundaries; only international agreement can bring stricter emissions standards in one country in order to prevent acid rain falling in neighbouring ones.

A consideration of importance is that in an increasingly inter-dependent global market system, competitive pressures can be inimical to environmental standards - firms claim they cannot afford to follow best environmental practice if competitors in other countries can undercut them by following cheaper but environmentally-damaging courses, and governments are under pressure to allow lower environmental standards in order maintain international competitiveness. But if high environmental standards are set throughout the European Union, and the bulk of most member countries' trade is with other countries within the Union, then firms know that their main competitors have to accept the same standards, and they will not be placed at a competitive disadvantage by keeping to them. Thus it is feasible, at a European level, to set standards higher than would be thought safe at national level.

Ozone depletion is essentially a *global* problem, but concerted action at a European level helped galvanise the rest of the world into action and ensured that CFC production in Europe was phased out sooner than in most other areas.

Climate change is also a *global* problem, but the initiatives and example of the European Union have put pressure on other countries to agree to set targets for lower greenhouse gas emissions and to take steps to achieve them. Measures to promote renewable energy sources and conserve energy, and proposals for energy and carbon taxes, have made a direct contribution, and also an indirect one in helping achieve a global response.

There are already many environmental issues which cannot adequately be dealt with at local or national level. With some of them action at European level is what is needed. For others, even a European-level response will not be sufficient on its own - but it will be a useful step towards getting the global action that is needed. The growing number and importance of the environmental issues which need a concerted European response means that this is an area in which pressures for closer European Union will grow steadily stronger.

## Employment

Over a long period, employment in the more highly-skilled occupations has been increasing, and the demand for unskilled labour has been declining, and this trend is expected to continue. Accordingly, in all EU countries there is seen to be a need to improve education and training in order to equip more people with the levels of skill required but, in general, this is not likely to need much joint action at European level.

The operation of the Single Market requires free movement of labour across national frontiers, and this is something which has already been largely achieved - the main barriers now are cultural and linguistic rather than administrative. It also envisages firms being able to compete on a level playing field, and one of the requirements for this is seen to be the establishment of common labour standards. Accordingly, the Commission has sent out a number of directives setting out standards for such things as maximum hours of work, dismissal procedures, representation on works councils, maternity and paternity rights, rights of women, young people and part-time workers, and so on. These provide for basic *minimum* standards to apply everywhere, so that firms cannot compete at their workers' expense by undercutting them, but they do not seek to regulate the extent firms go above the basic standards, or to interfere in wages.

To the extent that this succeeds in bringing common standards, and that it makes the Single Market work more effectively, it may be expected to be a factor making for closer European union. However, in Britain, where the Government has negotiated a derogation from the Social Chapter in the Maastricht Treaty, and has thereby prevented some of the common standards being applied, it has become a matter of controversy, seen by opponents as a reason for wanting to keep away from closer union, and by supporters as the kind of benefit to be gained from closer union.

At present all the EU countries are suffering from high levels of unemployment, and it will be a major concern to reduce them in the future. Whether or not this will lead to pressures for closer European union will depend on which measures are adopted for achieving this aim. One policy approach, which would not require European-level action is deregulation of labour markets so that less skilled workers can price themselves back into work. This approach has brought a greater increase in employment in the United States, but at the cost of the new jobs being largely part-time, insecure and low paid, a widening of earnings differentials, and an increase in poverty among people in work. For these reasons it is an approach unlikely to find favour in most countries in Europe.

Other approaches include lowering average working hours, shifting from social charges and taxes on labour to environmental taxes, increasing the level of productive investment, and raising the average level of demand. All of these, particularly the last of them, will be easier to adopt and have more chance of success if undertaken across Europe rather than in individual countries separately. With this in mind the Commission has put forward proposals for a package of measures designed to promote employment, growth and competitiveness, all at the same time, and through concerted action by the member countries together.

In so far as unemployment is likely to continue to be seen as a problem of central importance, and in so far as many of the proposals for reducing it involve joint European action, this is likely to be an area generating powerful forces for closer union.

## The economy

In an increasingly global world-market system economic growth is dependent on international competitiveness. Three requirements have been identified as particularly important for improving competitiveness: a more highly educated and trained labour force; effective exploitation of new technologies; and higher levels of productive investment.

Exploitation of new technologies depends largely on well directed and well diffused R&D. European countries are at a disadvantage relative to the United States and Japan in that, on their own, none of them can support R&D efforts of anywhere near the same size; but *together*, their combined R&D efforts are on a comparable scale. However, it is on only if separate national efforts can be pooled that Europe will be able to compete with the two giants on level terms.

For higher investment, one of the requirements is stable conditions with low inflation. And one of the ways proposed for achieving this is the adoption of a single currency and monetary policy. There are many difficulties in the way of bringing this about; and others which would follow afterwards; and in consequence the present plans may never be put into effect. But if they are, they are likely to have very far-reaching effects, not just for monetary affairs, but for economic and political union also.

Finally, if the European Union is joined by other countries in Central and Eastern Europe, it will change not only the size but also the characteristics of the Single market, forcing changes in, among other things, the CAP and the budget, and making closer union in some ways more desirable but in other ways more difficult.

## Conclusions

The longer-term developments likely to have the greatest impact on Britain and on other countries in Western Europe vary greatly in the impact they are likely to have on the future of the European Union itself.

- Changing security and foreign policy needs will make closer European co-operation desirable - but likely to be given only limited expression in view of the extreme national sensitivities in these areas. However, security considerations in Eastern Europe are likely to be a major factor affecting the Union's enlargement.

- Third-World problems are likely to have an impact on all EU countries - but will be only a marginal influence on closer union.

- Population and social changes will give rise to similar problems in all EU countries - but will mostly be dealt with separately at national level.

- Environmental issues, on the other hand, will become increasingly important and will increasingly require Europe-wide action if they are to be addressed effectively.

- The desire to get back to full employment also seems increasingly likely to require concerted measures at a European level.

- And the perceived need for greater economic competitiveness is likely to bring a need for closer integration of R&D efforts and economic policies - and may also involve the far-reaching step of monetary union.

All in all it would seem that likely longer-term developments will generate powerful underlying pressures for closer union in particular areas - while maintaining pressures for continuing separate national decision-taking in others.

Two possible developments seem likely to be of particular importance in determining the future shape of the European Union: one is the proposal for monetary union; and the other is the proposal for enlargement to include the countries of Central and eastern Europe. These are considered further in Chapters 9 and 10 respectively.

# 9  Monetary Union

The Maastricht treaty provides that, if a majority of member countries agree in the course of the 1996 intergovernmental conference, monetary union will be established from the beginning of 1997 for all member countries which meet the specified convergence criteria; and, failing that, monetary union will go ahead *automatically* from the beginning of 1999 for all countries which by then meet the criteria - except for Britain and Denmark which have kept the option to stay out.  If European Monetary Union (EMU) is indeed established within the next few years, it will be a development of exceptional importance in shaping the future of the European Union.

## Advantages and disadvantages

Monetary union is seen as following after customs union and the Single European Market as the next step towards closer European Union. It offers the possibility of a number of practical advantages. First, it will remove the transaction costs involved in transfers between the fifteen different currencies, which are estimated by the European Commission to amount to the equivalent of 0.5 per cent of EU GDP[293]. And second, it will finally put an end to speculation and fluctuations between the currencies merged in the union, thus removing uncertainty about the future. It will also strengthen the new currency relative to other currencies, reduce the size of the exchange reserves needed, simplify accounting and ensure transparency of prices. The combined effect is seen as likely to reduce costs, sharpen competition, stimulate intra-union trade and investment, and provide dynamic gains in faster growth and improved efficiency. Also the measures introduced for achieving convergence before monetary union, and the mechanisms for maintaining it after union, are seen as important means for controlling inflation.

The main drawbacks are seen as the irreversibility of the step, after which countries suffering from high unemployment or other economic difficulties will no longer be able to use interest rates or foreign exchange depreciation to try to adjust internal imbalances or improve their international competitiveness.

Underlying the technical and economic arguments are a number of powerful symbolic and emotional issues. Advocates of monetary union see it, favourably, as a symbol of a more general European union likely to lead to closer economic and political integration; while opponents view it *unfavourably* for the same reasons[294].

National currencies arouse particularly strong sensitivities. Opponents see the giving up of national currencies as involving an unacceptable loss of national sovereignty. On the other side, it is argued that for those of the smaller countries whose currencies already closely follow the Deutschmark, sovereignty is already more notional than real, and what will be involved will be exchanging control by the Bundesbank, which by statute is committed to pursue only German interests, for control by the new European Central Bank, which will be committed to act in the interests of Europe as a whole; while for the larger countries, in a world of massive speculative currency flows, monetary sovereignty is at best severely limited, and national interests will in practice be better served by pooling sovereignty in a stronger European Monetary Union. So what will be involved is not so much giving away some sovereignty as claiming back some of what has already been given away to the currency speculators.

But against this, in turn, it is argued that what will in reality be involved is not *pooling* sovereignty between the governments of the union, but *handing it over* to a new central bank which will be effectively independent of control by national governments or parliaments, or by the Council or the Commission of the European Union either.

Attitudes to the prospect of currency union vary greatly between countries. In some of the countries with weaker economies, which may have difficulty in meeting the convergence criteria, a single currency is favourably regarded, as bringing hope of greater financial stability; while in Germany the Deutschmark is much liked as a symbol of sound money (in contrast to the bad experience of hyperinflation between the wars) and there is concern lest with a single currency the probity of the Deutschmark would be diluted by association with other countries whose currencies have a less impressive record for holding their value.

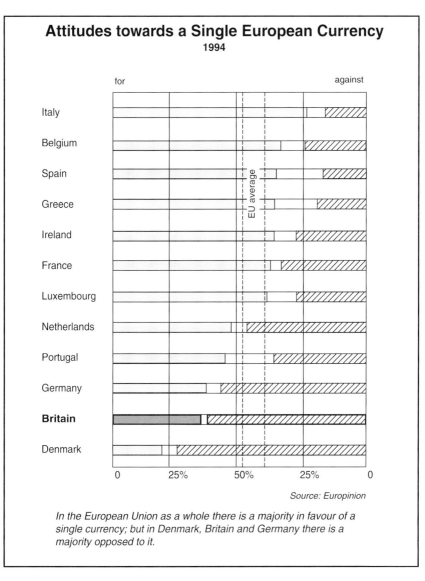

# Attitudes towards a Single European Currency
## 1994

for                                                against

Italy

Belgium

Spain

Greece

Ireland

France

Luxembourg

Netherlands

Portugal

Germany

**Britain**

Denmark

0          25%          50%          25%          0

*Source: Europinion*

*In the European Union as a whole there is a majority in favour of a single currency; but in Denmark, Britain and Germany there is a majority opposed to it.*

In Britain there has been a majority of nearly two-to-one opposed to a single currency, partly because a separate currency is widely perceived as a symbol of sovereign independence, and there is sentiment in favour of retention of the sovereign's head and other national symbols on coins and banknotes.

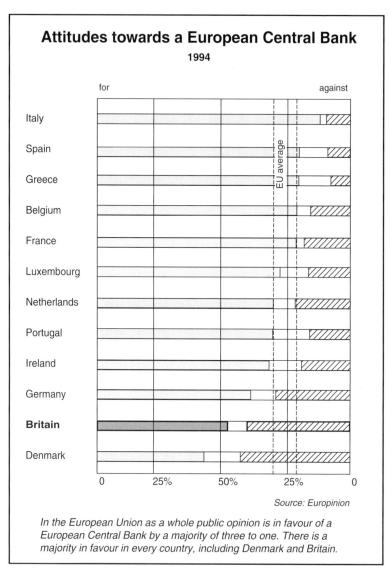

## Attitudes towards a European Central Bank
### 1994

*Source: Europinion*

*In the European Union as a whole public opinion is in favour of a European Central Bank by a majority of three to one. There is a majority in favour in every country, including Denmark and Britain.*

Even the name of the proposed new unit of currency has become a subject of controversy. For example, in recent opinion polls[295] in Germany 40 per cent of people accepted the `ECU' (European Currency Unit) as the name for the new currency unit, while 40 per cent preferred the Deutschmark or Euromark, while in Britain only 30 per cent favoured the `ECU' and 45 per cent preferred the pound or Europound.

In addition to the problems of sentiment there will also be significant practical difficulties in making the transition - changing all the coins and banknotes, changing the cash machines, ending machines and parking metres which use them, and changing the accounting systems and computer programmes associated with them. The European Banking Federation has estimated (296) that for the banks alone the cost of the change will amount to ECU8-19bn (£6.3-7.9bn). However, it points out that these are the once-and-for-all costs of transition; banks in countries outside the system will be disadvantaged by *continuing* higher costs in their business use of separate currencies.

## Convergence criteria

The Maastricht treaty specified five criteria as indicators of sufficient convergence in national economies to make them ready for monetary union:

1. the maintenance of the currency within the normal bands of fluctuation of the Exchange Rate Mechanism (ERM) for at least two years;

2. a rate of inflation close to that of the three best performing states;

3. convergence of long-term interest rates;

4. a budget deficit not greater than 3 per cent of GDP; and

5. total public debt not greater than 60 per cent of GDP.

In addition, politicians in Britain have suggested further criteria to be satisfied, such as convergence of the `real' economy as indicated by rates of unemployment, growth and competitiveness.

The signing of the Maastricht treaty was followed by poor referendum results in Denmark and France, difficulties in securing ratification in Britain and Germany, the enforced departure from the ERM of the pound and the lira in September 1992, the enforced widening of the ERM bands from 2.25 per cent to 15 per cent in August 1993, the further currency speculation subsequently, and the economic difficulties encountered in several countries during the recession.

Accordingly, it tended to be assumed for a while that the goal of currency union had receded far into the distance.

More recently, however, improving economic performance after the end of the recession has made the convergence criteria look less unattainable in a number of member countries and brought the issue back as one of the key items on the agenda for the intergovernmental conference in 1996.

For the first condition, the `normal' bands of fluctuation within the ERM were assumed to be 2.25 per cent. However, the heavy speculation in August 1993 forced the widening of the `normal' bands to 15 per cent, and it is very possible that most of the currencies in the ERM will be able to keep within these wider bands. Even the pound and the lira, although floating outside the ERM, could end up not fluctuating by more than 15 per cent. Thus although exchange rate fluctuations have been far greater than originally envisaged, it is possible that, in a formal sense at least, this Maastricht criterion will in the event be met by most of the currencies concerned.

The second condition - annual inflation of not more than 1.5 per cent above the average of the three best performing countries - is currently met by ten of the fifteen member countries. Of the other five, Britain is only marginally above it, and Portugal, Italy and Spain and Portugal are within two percentage points; Greece, however, is still very greatly above it [297].

The third condition - long-term interest rates not more than two per cent above the average of the three countries with the lowest rates - thanks partly to the currency realignments of recent years, is also currently met by ten of the fifteen countries; and of the others, Italy, Sweden and Portugal are within three percentage points of it [297].

With the fourth condition - a budget deficit not greater than three per cent of GDP - the gap is far wider. Currently only four countries come within the target range; eight others come fairly close; but the remaining three (Italy, Sweden and Greece) are far above it.

With the final condition - public sector debt not greater than 60 per cent of GDP - only four countries (Luxembourg, France, Britain and Germany) come within the limit. While several other countries are within striking distance of the limit, three countries (Greece, Italy and Belgium) have debt equivalent to more than 100 per cent of GDP, and so have little early prospect of getting below the limit. And among the

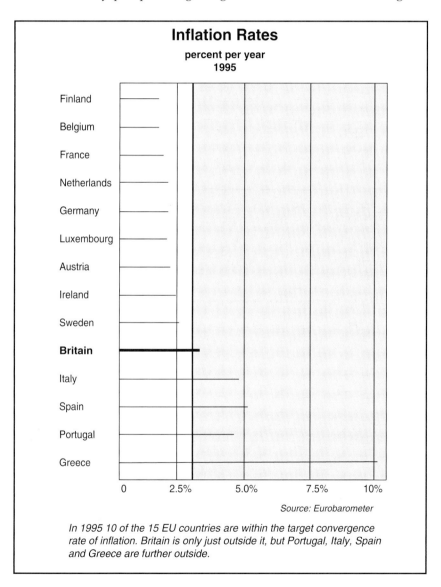

**Inflation Rates**
percent per year
1995

*Source: Eurobarometer*

*In 1995 10 of the 15 EU countries are within the target convergence rate of inflation. Britain is only just outside it, but Portugal, Italy, Spain and Greece are further outside.*

countries currently above the limit are Austria, the Netherlands and Belgium which are usually thought of as core members of a potential currency union.

Thus currently, Germany and Luxembourg are the only countries which formally meet all of the convergence criteria, although the Netherlands, France and Britain come very close; others may meet all the criteria by 1997, and still others by 1999; but, Italy, Spain, Portugal and Greece still have a long way to go.

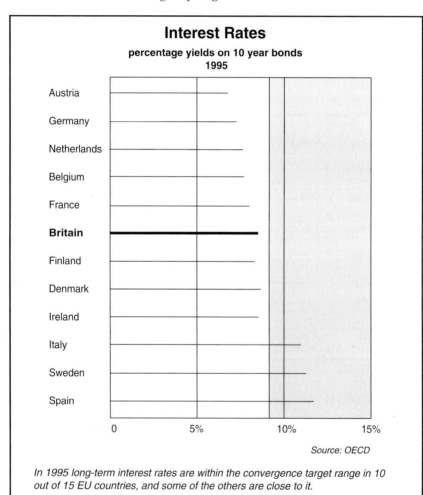

**Interest Rates**

percentage yields on 10 year bonds
1995

|  | |
|---|---|
| Austria | |
| Germany | |
| Netherlands | |
| Belgium | |
| France | |
| **Britain** | |
| Finland | |
| Denmark | |
| Ireland | |
| Italy | |
| Sweden | |
| Spain | |

0    5%    10%    15%

*Source: OECD*

*In 1995 long-term interest rates are within the convergence target range in 10 out of 15 EU countries, and some of the others are close to it.*

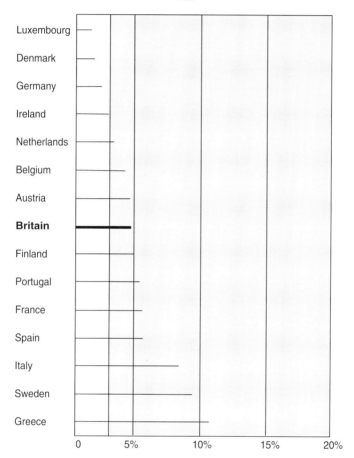

# Budget deficit
## as a percentage of GDP
## 1995

| | | | |
|---|---|---|---|
| Luxembourg | | | |
| Denmark | | | |
| Germany | | | |
| Ireland | | | |
| Netherlands | | | |
| Belgium | | | |
| Austria | | | |
| **Britain** | | | |
| Finland | | | |
| Portugal | | | |
| France | | | |
| Spain | | | |
| Italy | | | |
| Sweden | | | |
| Greece | | | |

0    5%    10%    15%    20%

*Source: European Commission*

*In 1995 only four EU countries, Luxembourg, Denmark, Germany and Ireland, have budget deficits within the 3 per cent converence target limit; but in 1996 Britain, Finland and the Netherlands are expected to meet it, and several other countries are expected to come near it.*

247

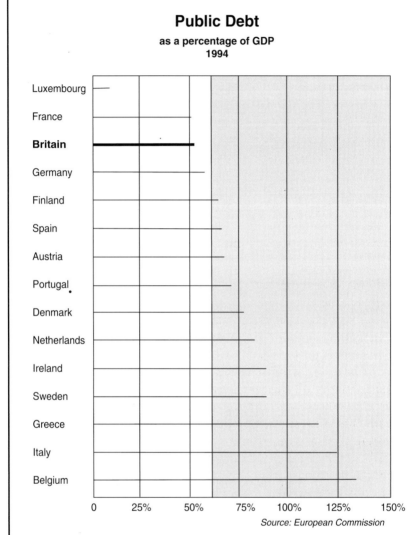

# Public Debt
### as a percentage of GDP
### 1994

| | | |
|---|---|---|
| Luxembourg | | |
| France | | |
| **Britain** | | |
| Germany | | |
| Finland | | |
| Spain | | |
| Austria | | |
| Portugal | | |
| Denmark | | |
| Netherlands | | |
| Ireland | | |
| Sweden | | |
| Greece | | |
| Italy | | |
| Belgium | | |

0    25%    50%    75%    100%    125%    150%

*Source: European Commission*

*In 1995 only four EU countries, Luxembourg, France, Britain and Germany are within the convergence target of public debt no greater than 60 per cent of GDP; but in 1996 several other countries are expected to come near it.*

However, the way the convergence criteria are defined leaves open the possibility of some flexibility in their interpretation. The `normal' ERM bands are now the 15 per cent ones. A rate of inflation `close to' the three best countries need not necessarily be taken to be as close as 1.5 per cent. A `convergence' of interest rates need not necessarily be taken to mean near identical ones. And budget deficits beyond the 3 per cent and 60 per cent criteria need not be regarded as `excessive' if they have `declined substantially' or are `temporary' or `approaching the reference criteria at a satisfactory pace'. And the interpretation of the criteria will be in the hands of the Commission; and the decision of the Council will be by qualified majority vote. There is thus sufficient latitude for the final decision to be taken not wholly on the basis of a mechanistic formula, but at least partly on political grounds.

## Prospects of monetary union

Given the difficulties in meeting the convergence criteria, it is quite possible that EMU will never be achieved. It seems more probable, however, that at some point it *will* be; because, quite apart from the hoped-for economic benefits, there are a number of political forces pushing in that direction. In most of the member countries there is popular support for the idea; in Germany monetary union is seen as a means of bringing about closer *political* union; in France it will be needed to justify all the sacrifices made already to try to meet the convergence criteria; and in most countries, including Germany, it will be seen as preferable to the alternative - the increasing *de facto* establishment of a Deutschmark zone in which other countries are tied to the German currency and interest rates, but have no say in the decisions of the Bundesbank which are taken on the basis of the interests of Germany alone rather than those of the Union as a whole. The German economy is already the largest and strongest in Europe, and the establishment of a common European currency is seen as a way of containing it within a wider European framework.

There are three possible ways in which monetary union may be established. The first is not in the orderly way envisaged in the Maastricht treaty but suddenly, in the course of a crisis (as it is rumoured was considered in the 1993 crisis) with a Franco-German summit producing a declaration of instant merger of the franc and mark, joined soon after by a few other core currencies. Such a forced crisis union would bring so many difficulties that it would not be undertaken unless it was thought that there was no other way of putting an end to excessive speculative pressures. However, the possibility cannot be entirely ruled out, given the strength of speculative forces in recent years and the consideration that, in the period approaching an expected currency union, currency markets are likely to become particularly volatile as speculators take positions on possible last-minute re-alignments before currencies are permanently locked together.

The second possibility is that, as envisaged in the Maastricht treaty, in the course of the intergovernmental conference in 1966 a majority of countries will be deemed to have met the convergence criteria and they will agree to proceed to monetary union between them from the beginning of 1997. However, it has been looking increasingly unlikely that a majority of member countries will have met all the convergence criteria by then; and, in Germany, the Bundesbank has made it clear that it will insist on a strict fulfilment of the convergence criteria, and the Constitutional Court has ruled that two-thirds majorities will be needed in both the Bundesrat and the Bundestag before Germany can give up the Deutschmark.

There is also the practical difficulty that the European Banking Federation has warned[298] that the printing, minting and distribution of the new money and other arrangements for its introduction, such as altering cash machines and computer software, will take a period of five years - *after* a decision has been taken to go ahead and agreement has been reached on the style and denominations of the new notes and coins. Since agreement has not yet been reached even on the *name* for the new currency unit, there would clearly be immense practical difficulties in having everything ready in time for 1997.

Accordingly, at the Cannes summit in June 1995 the heads of state tacitly recognised that 1997 was no longer a feasible date; but none the less reaffirmed their intention of going ahead on the third date envisaged in the Maastricht treaty - 1999[299]. The treaty specifies that all the countries which meet the convergence criteria by then, whether or not they constitute a majority of EU members (and with the exception of

Denmark and Britain if they exercise their opt-outs) will *automatically* proceed to currency union at the beginning of 1999.

By 1999 it is likely that several countries will have met all the convergence criteria, and several others will be very close to meeting them. It has already been suggested that an exception might be made for Ireland's public debt, in view of the progress made in reducing it, and even the Bundesbank is reported to have wondered whether Belgium also (despite its much larger public debt) should be treated as a special case in order not to keep out what has long been considered one of the `core' currencies of the Union[300]. And if concessions are made for some countries, there will be pressures for them to be made for other countries also, so that several countries which do not quite meet all the criteria may well be allowed to join the currency union if they wish to. And others, such as Britain and Denmark, even if initially they do not *wish* to join the Union, may be eligible to do so and may choose to join later.

The main opposition is likely to come from Italy and Spain, two major countries, one a founder member of the Union, both of which are very keen to join a monetary union, and both of which have made great efforts to meet the criteria, but neither of which seems likely to meet them in full, even by 1999, and neither of which, in view of their past records, is likely to be received with enthusiasm by the German Bundesbank.

If it turns out that Italy and Spain are unable to join, and Britain is unwilling to join, it is possible that France will be reluctant to enter a currency union without any of the other three larger countries. In that event it is possible some delay will be agreed, or some concessions made, to enable them to qualify. But it seems unlikely that even opposition from them - and Portugal and Greece, which are likely to be even further from meeting the criteria - will be enough to prevent currency union going ahead within a few years of 1999 for the countries which wish to proceed and feel ready to do so.

There will remain the practical difficulties of getting the money ready in time, but these can probably be overcome, for a 1999 date, by starting making the arrangements in 1996 or 1997, by accepting a period of currencies locked together before the full merger, or by putting more resources into speeding up the change-over.

Thus it seems probable that by around the turn of the century Germany, France, Austria, the Netherlands, Belgium and Luxembourg will have a common currency; that then or soon after some or all of Ireland, Finland, Sweden, Denmark and Britain will also join; and that later on there may be others as well. The establishment of a European Monetary Union, even if it does not include all the existing members of the Union, will be a development of very great importance for the future shape of Europe.

## Implications of monetary union

In Germany the prospect of monetary union is not popular, because people fear that the stability provided by the Deutschmark may be impaired by a merger with other weaker currencies. German politicians and officials have repeatedly stressed that, if it is to be successful, monetary union must imply further *economic* and *political* union. For example, Hans Tietmeyer, President of the Bundesbank told the German-British Chamber of Commerce in London[301]:

> In the long-run, any monetary union which lacks extensive political underpinning is likely to remain a fragile construction.

And Karl Lamers, the foreign policy spokesman of the Christian Democratic Union parliamentary group in Bonn, wrote in the *Financial Times*[302]:

> For a country to transfer power over its currency to an independent European central bank represents a most far-reaching form of European integration, not least because the central bank's decisions would affect governmental decisions in many other fields of economic and social policy.

> The European states linked by monetary union will need to show solidarity in many other spheres . . . Once the fundamental link between monetary and political union is recognised . . . European Union members that form the core of

monetary union will also be, for the foreseeable future, at the core of political union.

Those who cling to national sovereignty are seeking solace in an empty shell.

There are three considerations which seem likely to be particularly important in causing monetary union to lead to closer economic and political union: *monetary accountability, national convergence,* and *regional imbalance.*

### Accountability

It is intended that the new single currency will be managed by a new European Central Bank (ECB). Unlike the Federal Reserve Bank in the United States or the Bundesbank in Germany, which are ultimately subject to democratic authority, the new ECB will be fully independent both of national governments and parliaments and also of the EU Council and Parliament. It will work through a network of national central banks which, in their turn, will also be entirely independent of their national governments and parliaments.

Thus the new European Central Bank will have exclusive control over monetary policy which it will operate with the `primary objective' of ensuring price stability - an objective which cannot be changed except by unanimous agreement of the Council. It will thus have unrestricted power in a key area of economic policy which it will be expected to use in single-minded pursuit of the central objective of price stability.

Nobody disputes the importance of price stability. But there are also other possible objectives of public policy, for example: growth, competitiveness, full employment, environmental protection, social equity. Normally the reconciliation of different objectives, which can often be in competition, is a matter of economic and political debate and complex assessment of where the best balance of advantage may lie. A system which *automatically* gives *overriding* priority to only one objective - price stability - may be acceptable at a time when everyone happens to be in agreement that this is indeed the objective of overwhelming importance to which everything else should be sacrificed. But if the time comes when significant numbers of people think that other policy objectives ought to be given greater salience, then there is likely to be increasing dissatisfaction with a system which gives a built-in, permanent and absolute priority to only the one objective, and provides no form of democratic accountability in an area of manifest importance.

Even strong supporters of price stability and an independent central bank argue that the bank should be accountable at least for the *implementation* of its policies[303]; and increasingly many are arguing that accountability should be extended to cover the balance between different *policy objectives*[304,305,306], and expressing concern that otherwise `monetary policy will determine the rest of macroeconomic policy and Europe will be run by an unaccountable committee of governors of central banks'[307].

It is unavoidable that the new bank's power will be great; and when it is exercised in ways which are perceived to be detrimental to other policy objectives, there are likely to be increasing pressures for the power to be made more accountable. At present it is assumed that it will be balanced to some extent by ministers of national governments who will retain control of national fiscal policies. However, in any conflict of objectives, fifteen ministers, responsible to national governments, divided, and meeting only every six months, are unlikely to be a match for the bank's single team of full-time permanent experts operating from a clear mandate within entrenched powers. Any mechanism for greater accountability, therefore, is likely to involve more structured economic coordination and closer political union.

### National non-convergence

When monetary union goes ahead it will be on the basis of the prior achievement of convergence in terms of the five specified criteria of the various countries taking part. However, as the President of the Bundesbank has frequently stressed[301], for the system to work it is necessary for convergence to be achieved, not just on the day it starts, but *all the time*. To the extent that convergence is reached on the starting date, it will be something which has been achieved over a period of years and, in some cases, only with great difficulty and cost. There is no automatic mechanism which will ensure that the convergence is maintained subsequently; indeed, there are built-in pressures which will tend to make for *de*-convergence.

In a world of separate economies, if a government overspends and runs a deficit, it is likely to result in inflation and, if this is at a greater rate than in other countries, to a weakening in the balance of payments and to pressure on the foreign exchange rate and, at some point, devaluation to restore the balance. But with EMU there will be no longer any possibility of separate exchange rate depreciation, so that a budget deficit in any one country will bring inflationary pressure on the system as a whole. Thus, there will be a temptation for the government of any country to run a deficit in the knowledge that the ensuing problems will largely be passed on to the other partner countries. Hence there will be a need for the Union as a whole to prevent this happening.

However, at present it is envisaged that each national government will still retain responsibility for its own fiscal affairs, and there will be no mechanism in place to preserve the overall fiscal balance. It is true that there are the Maastricht convergence guidelines; but there is no formal arrangement to ensure *continuing* adherence to them; and, anyway, some flexibility will be needed. The particular figures of budget deficits not greater than 3 per cent of GDP and public debt not greater than 60 per cent of GDP have no scientific significance as the ultimate indicators of fiscal rectitude; they were merely adopted because they happened to be the EU average at the time of the Maastricht negotiations; and even if they *did* represent the optimal *average* levels, there would still be need for variations - for example, for *larger* deficits in a recession to help get out of it, and for *smaller* deficits, or surpluses, in a boom to help prevent it getting out of hand. Or, if the national budgets were to be kept permanently in balance, it would be desirable for the budget of the European Union itself to be varied to take on the counter-cyclical role commonly given to central institutions in federal systems[308].

In order to prevent national governments behaving irresponsibly in their national fiscal policies, and causing the whole system to break down, it will therefore be essential, at the least, to agree on a system of sanctions on governments which stray from the agreed guidelines; but, preferably, to set up a system to act in advance to *prevent* breakdowns by *co-ordinating* national fiscal policies in order to achieve a single effective macroeconomic management for the Union as a whole.

But macroeconomic policy is of such political importance in every country - particularly the fiscal balance, often the issue on which elections are won or lost - that there is no likelihood of its being allowed to slip beyond political control. Thus in order to make EMU work it will be necessary to set up mechanisms for bringing macroeconomic policies together and for keeping political control of them.

*Regional imbalance*
The third consideration why EMU is likely to lead to closer economic and political union is the need to prevent imbalances between different countries and regions in the Union. If some external shock hits some countries or regions more severely than others, it may make them less competitive and bring slower growth, unemployment and depression. Even in the absence of specific external shocks, it is likely that the working of the Single European Market will result in some regions or countries with a competitive advantage getting ahead, while others run into difficulties.

Gaps in GDP per head between *countries* have been tending to narrow a little, with the four poorest countries (Greece, Portugal, Spain and Ireland) improving their GDP per head from 64 per cent of the EU average in 1986 to 70 per cent in 1993[309]. Gaps between *regions*, on the other hand, are larger and have actually *widened*. In 1980 the ten weakest regions in the Union had an average GDP per head only 30 per cent as great as the ten strongest regions; and by 1991 it was down to only 27.5 per cent[309]. Similarly, in 1983 the twenty-five weakest regions had unemployment 3.2 times as high as in the twenty-five strongest ones; and in 1993, 5.1 times as high[309].

In separate national economies, one way that this problem can be met is by exchange-rate depreciation to improve the competitiveness of weaker areas; but with monetary union this will no longer be possible.

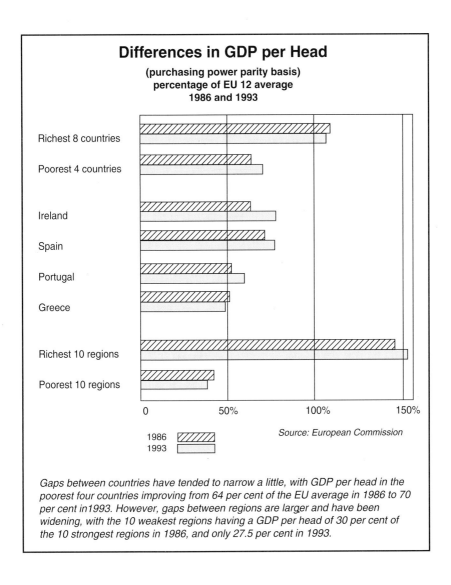

## Differences in GDP per Head

**(purchasing power parity basis)**
**percentage of EU 12 average**
**1986 and 1993**

Richest 8 countries

Poorest 4 countries

Ireland

Spain

Portugal

Greece

Richest 10 regions

Poorest 10 regions

0   50%   100%   150%

1986
1993

*Source: European Commission*

*Gaps between countries have tended to narrow a little, with GDP per head in the poorest four countries improving from 64 per cent of the EU average in 1986 to 70 per cent in1993. However, gaps between regions are larger and have been widening, with the 10 weakest regions having a GDP per head of 30 per cent of the 10 strongest regions in 1986, and only 27.5 per cent in 1993.*

Within some national economies regional disparities are adjusted by lower prices and wages in weaker areas to make them more competitive. However, in most of the countries of the European Union it appears that structural rigidities prevent sufficient price flexibility to achieve this [310];

while wage flexibility is also too little - it is estimated that on average a 10 per cent increase in unemployment tends to reduce wages by only 0.5 - 1.5 per cent[309].

Another way in which regional adjustment can be made within a single monetary area is by workers moving from the depressed region to seek work in other regions offering better prospects - as often happens, for example, in the United States. However, in Europe, despite the removal of formal barriers to movement of labour within the Union, the differences in language, culture, customs and social security arrangements mean that cross-border migration in search of work is on a much smaller scale than in the United States[310,311].

Within most national economies the most important way in which regional disparities are mitigated is by fiscal transfers. This may take the form of direct help for disadvantaged regions, for example through incentives for investment or provision of infrastructure. Usually much more important, however, are the transfers which happen automatically, and usually largely unnoticed, through the operation of the fiscal system. On the tax side, VAT and excise duties take more from richer areas where spending is higher, and income taxes in addition are on progressive scales which take disproportionately more from the particularly rich; and on the spending side, many kinds of benefits, such as health and education services, defence and pensions tend to be provided at a more or less standard level, to rich and poor areas alike, while some payments, such as for income support and unemployment benefits go disproportionately to the areas with the greatest problems.

The effect, then, is for the fiscal system in a country to result in a considerable evening out of differences between regions. It is estimated, for example, that between 10 and 28 per cent of a given change in regional income is automatically offset through the federal budget in the United States, and between 33 and 42 per cent in EU countries[312].

However, with a *European* currency union it will not be possible to make adjustments in national exchange rates; and with retention of *national* fiscal systems there will be no automatic fiscal transfers between countries or between regions in different countries. If large and growing disparities between richer and poorer countries and regions are to be avoided it will therefore be necessary to arrange for fiscal transfers by the European Union itself.

The need for major transfers following EMU was recognised by the Commission as far back as 1977[313], and in advance of EMU arrangements have been made for payments from structural funds to help regions with special difficulties and from cohesion funds to help the four poorest countries in the Union. These payments totalled ECU21bn in 1993 - about 31 per cent of the total EU budget. By 1999 it is planned to increase them to ECU30bn, representing 36 per cent of a larger budget[309].

However, even the larger payments envisaged for 1999 will represent less than half of one per cent of total EU GDP - a very small amount compared with the massive sums involved in automatic national fiscal transfers. Present plans envisage increasing the total EU budget to 1.29 per cent of EU GDP by 1999; this also is very modest compared with the 5 per cent or more envisaged in the MacDougall report two decades ago, or with the 20-25 per cent of GDP commonly taken by national budgets in federal states, or the 40-50 per cent of GDP commonly taken by national budgets in unitary states. It seems likely that, to avoid the development of excessive disparities between countries and regions in a single currency area, it will be necessary to increase very greatly the size of the structural and cohesion funds, or other kinds of transfer, and for this it will be necessary to increase greatly the size of the EU budget.

A much larger budget, including new kinds of expenditure, and possibly also including new sources of revenue and a more progressive tax base[314], will give the Union a bigger economic role than previously; and increased EU taxation and expenditure may be expected to be acceptable only if there is better political control over it. Hence the need to offset national and regional disparities within a single currency area may be expected to lead to closer economic and political union.

The various implications of monetary union will of course be much affected by expansion of the Union to include new members, some of them with different backgrounds and levels of development. The issues associated with enlargement are considered in Chapter 10, which follows.

And the establishment of monetary union will also have implications for the future development of the institutions of the Union. These are considered in Chapter 11.

# 10 Enlargement

The other longer-term development which is likely to have a particularly great impact on the future development of the European Union is the enlargement of its membership to include further new members. There is considerable uncertainty as to which new countries will join, and when, but there is little doubt that in due course a substantial number of additional countries *will* join, and that this will have a major impact, not only on the *size*, but also on the *character* of the Union.

## Past enlargements

From the beginning, the founder members of the European Community were concerned that it should be outward-looking and ready to welcome suitable further members. In the early days the constraint was that other eligible countries, including Britain, were sceptical of its prospects, or doubtful whether it suited their aims and situations; and several of them set up the looser European Free Trade Association (EFTA) as an alternative.

Later when Britain changed its position and wanted to join, it was blocked by de Gaulle who had a somewhat different view of the function of the Community and of France's role in it. Hence it was only in 1973, sixteen years after the signature of the Treaty of Rome, that Britain, together, with Ireland and Denmark, finally became members. They were followed by Greece in 1981 and by Spain and Portugal in 1986. These enlargements were preceded by long and difficult negotiations, and by transition periods to allow time for the necessary adjustments. The effect was to double the membership and size of the Community and to incorporate various modifications to accommodate the different circumstances of the new members - while holding fast to the fundamentals of past achievements and future objectives.

The European Community also established free trade links with a number of other countries, but after the establishment of the Single European Market in 1993, the seven EFTA countries - Austria, Sweden, Finland, Norway, Iceland, Switzerland and Liechtenstein - sought closer links. Negotiations led to the establishment of the European Economic Area (EEA) in 1994, which effectively brought the EFTA countries into the Single European Market, with the benefits and obligations of membership. Four of them - Austria, Sweden, Finland and Norway - went on to seek full membership of the European Union. Norway's application was withdrawn when it was defeated in a referendum in November 1994, but the other three became full members from the beginning of 1995.

Under the post-war settlement, Austria and Finland had been committed to neutrality, and Soviet opposition precluded their joining the European Community; and in Sweden there has been a long tradition of neutrality. After the collapse of the Soviet bloc, however, Austria and Finland were no longer prevented from seeking membership of the Union; and in Sweden the need for neutrality seemed less persuasive than before. There were also more positive reasons. All three countries are in geographically exposed positions relative to Russia, and they saw advantages in being integrated into a European structure as a safeguard against the possibility of some future Russian régime having aggressive designs at a time when the Americans might have departed from Europe.

However, the central motive for joining was economic. Their trade is predominantly with the Union and they are closely bound by the various economic measures taken by the Union. If they could not escape being greatly affected by the Union, and were in an economic sense virtually part of it already, they felt they might as well join it formally in order to at least have some say in the decisions which affected them.

From the point of view of existing members of the Union, their accession presented few problems and offered clear benefits. They are all small in population, rich, and successful, with strong economies, stable democratic political systems and high social standards. The richer northern countries felt at home with their attitudes; and the poorer southern countries hoped to benefit from their contributions to the central budget - estimated at a net gain of more than £2bn a year[300] So, given the deals that were negotiated to look after their special agricultural, regional and transport interests, their joining presented few difficulties for either new or existing members.

## Prospective further enlargement

In principle, membership of the European Union has always been open to other countries which meet the basic conditions: a European identity, securely established democratic government and respect for human rights, and a willingness and ability to accept the obligations of membership set out in the various treaties and the arrangements for giving effect to them. This last condition has been taken to require a functioning market economy and a compatible level of economic and social development. There is also the implied condition that the prospective new member should not be so large or so different as to be incapable of being accommodated by the existing members.

In the event, applications for membership were made by Turkey in 1987, by Malta and Cyprus in 1990, and by Switzerland in 1992 - the latter implicitly withdrawn when a referendum in December 1992 rejected the proposed membership of the EEA, but the Swiss Government maintains that membership is still a long-term goal. With the collapse of the Soviet bloc there has been interest in potential membership in most of the countries of Eastern Europe, and even in some of the republics of the CIS and in Russia itself.

In the face of so many possible new applicants, it was decided during the Maastricht Treaty negotiations to proceed as follows: first to consider during 1994 the applications of the four EEA countries; second, at the Intergovernmental Conference in 1996, to consider the changes needed to `deepen' the Union and prepare it for further expansion; and third, only after that was complete, to consider the applications of possible further new members - preferably, as with the EEA applicants, in groups, so as to allow the enlargement process to take the form of an orderly series of stages.

Meanwhile, it has been recognised that many of the Eastern European countries, attempting fundamental restructuring of political, economic and social systems, would benefit from interim economic links and assistance to help prepare them for membership. Accordingly, `Europe Agreements' have been concluded with the Czech Republic, Slovakia, Hungary, Poland, Bulgaria and Romania, to be followed by Slovenia, Lithuania, Latvia and Estonia. The aim of the agreements is to promote political and social co-operation and, in particular, to help the process of economic restructuring - by encouraging private investment, by dismantling customs and quantitative restrictions on exports, and by providing economic and technical assistance through the PHARE programme[315] and the European Investment Bank and the European Bank for Reconstruction and Development.

Attitudes in the twelve existing member countries towards the membership of the four EFTA countries was overwhelmingly favourable, with more than six people in favour for every one against. Attitudes towards the next wave of applicants in Central and Eastern Europe are also favourable, although less overwhelmingly so, ranging from three-to-one in favour of Hungary to rather less than two-to-one in favour of Slovenia[316]. Attitudes towards the Southern applicants are more varied, with two-to-one in favour of Malta, three-to-two in favour of Cyprus, but a small majority *against* the membership of Turkey[317].

There are differences in attitude between different countries with, for example, opinion in Spain and France particularly sympathetic to membership of the Eastern countries, opinion in Spain, Ireland and Britain particularly sympathetic to the Southern ones, and opinion in Greece overwhelmingly keen on Cyprus and hostile to Turkey; but in general the picture is broadly similar across all the member countries.

While the general climate of opinion is favourable to further enlargement, the prospects of particular countries are likely to vary considerably, depending on their individual circumstances and histories.

## The Southern countries

These countries have been seeking closer links over a long period, but their interest has not been rewarded by a reciprocal degree of enthusiasm on the part of the Union.

### Malta

Malta has had a series of association agreements starting as far back as 1970. In 1990 it formally applied for full membership. There are no serious economic obstacles - three-quarters of its trade is already with the EU, unemployment and inflation are low, and income per head is not greatly

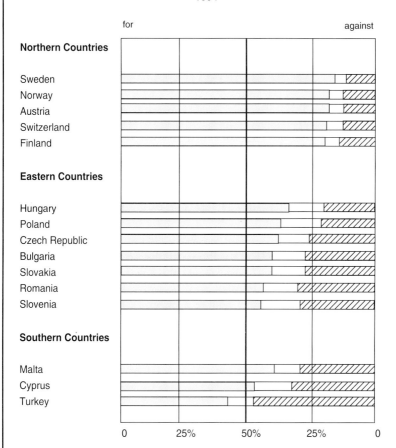

## Attitudes to Potential New Members
### European Union (12)
### 1994

Source: Europinion

*Attitudes in the 12 existing EU member countries to potential new members have varied from six to one in favour of the EFTA countries, through between three to one and two to one in favour of the Central and East European countries and Malta, to a rather smaller majority in favour of Cyprus and a smaller majority against Turkey.*

different from Portugal and Greece. The difficulties have been more political - the close ties with Libya, the objection of the main opposition party to full membership of the EU, and the small size of the country. In the past doubts have been raised whether a country with a population of less than 400,000 could take on the administrative burdens of full membership - for example the tasks associated with the Presidency. And if an exception were made, with some kind of less demanding status, whether this would imply a similar status for Luxembourg, a founder member of the Union, which has a population of similar size. While in the past it has not seemed worth reconsidering the Union's institutional arrangements for the sake of one new `micro-state' on its own, it is now expected that Malta will be included as part of a wider enlargement in the next round of negotiations[318].

### Cyprus
Cyprus negotiated its first association agreement as far back as 1972, and in 1990 applied for full membership. In 1993 the EU's Opinion[319] was that:

> Cyprus's geographical position, the deep-lying bonds which, for two thousand years have located the island at the very fount of European culture and civilization, the intensity of the European influence apparent in the values shared by the people . . . the wealth of contacts of every kind with the Community, all these confer on Cyprus, beyond all doubt, its European identity and character and confirm its vocation to belong to the Community.

However, Cyprus's relations with the Union have been bedeviled by the Turkish invasion of 1974 and the continuing bitter division of the island subsequently. Thus the 1993 Opinion expressed hope of early membership, but on the basis that the negotiations then under way would be successful -which they were not. Even so, it is now envisaged[318] that Cyprus, like Malta, will be included in the next phase of enlargement.

### Turkey
For Turkey, acceptance as a European state and membership of European organisations have been central national aspirations since the Ataturk revolution nearly a century ago; and after serving for half a century as the eastern anchor of NATO, and after several decades of sending many of

their young men to work in Western Europe, many Turks feel the time has come for their full acceptance into membership of.the European Union. Already in 1963 the principle of eventual eligibility was conceded, and in 1987 a formal application for membership was presented.

However, to many in Western Europe Turkey still seems more Asian than European, its democracy seems less than secure, and its treatment of the Kurds and other minorities seems less than liberal. There is also the perennial hostility of Greece, currently inflamed by controversies over Cyprus and the Aegean. And when these difficulties are out of the way, there will remain a more fundamental obstacles: while Malta and Cyprus may be difficult to accommodate because they are so *small*, Turkey has the opposite difficulty that it is so *large*. Its 1995 population of sixty-two million is three times that of the combined populations of the three new members which joined in 1995; and, unlike existing members, its population is growing rapidly - by 2025 it is projected to total ninety-three million, equivalent to 24 per cent of the population of the present fifteen members. Since average income per head in Turkey is less than a third of the average in existing member countries, Turkish membership would imply considerable additional burdens on the Union's structural funds and the possibility of substantial migration to countries with higher income levels. There would also be problems in accommodating Turkey's large agricultural sector.

Accordingly, in its Opinion in 1989, the Commission concluded that neither Turkey nor the Community were yet ready for Turkey's full membership. Hence, while in 1995 a customs union was negotiated to replace the association agreement, full Turkish membership of the European Union still looks remote.

## The EFTA countries

*Norway*

Norway is in the unique position of having twice applied for membership of the European Community, having twice been accepted, but having twice rejected the proposed union in a referendum - by a narrow 53 per cent - 47 per cent majority in 1972 and by an even narrower 52 percent - 48 per cent majority in 1994. On both occasions the country was deeply divided, with majorities in Oslo, the towns and industry favouring union, and majorities in coastal and northern areas, fishing and agriculture rejecting it.

The rejection reflected concerns about the future of fishing and agriculture within a European Union framework, and concern for preservation of national cohesion and traditional ways of life through regional policies to support people living in remote areas. Underlying these specific worries were a general suspicion of foreign entanglements - the result of nearly 500 years' subordination to Denmark and Sweden prior to independence in 1905 - and doubts about perceived bureaucracy, secretiveness and lack of direct democratic control in EU institutions - which were reinforced by the initial rejection of Maastricht in the first Danish referendum.

Norway has grown prosperous and is in a position to pursue an independent economic policy as a result of its large oil and gas industry which accounts for 16 per cent of GDP - slightly more than manufacturing industry. And its manufacturing exports, the great majority of which go to the EU, have the benefit of a free trade agreement. However, in the longer term the economic position is expected to deteriorate as a result of declining petroleum reserves, falling inward investment and a growing tendency of Norwegian industries to invest for future production in EU countries with lower costs. Norway will not be in the Single European Market, and now that Denmark, Sweden and Finland are all in the European Union and only Iceland, Switzerland and Liechtenstein remain as partners in EFTA, will be increasingly isolated in economic negotiations.

Accordingly, while no third application for membership is in immediate prospect, it seems likely that at some point the balance of opinion will tilt towards joining the European Union, particularly if the experience of Norway's Nordic neighbours within it proves to be encouraging.

### Iceland
Iceland is in a situation similar to Malta's in that its small size presents problems for fitting into EU institutions and implies that acceptance of

its membership will be more easily arranged as part of a restructuring encompassing a number of other countries also; and it is in a situation similar to Norway's in that it is jealous of its independence, acquired only in 1944, and is particularly concerned about fishing - indeed, Iceland's economy predominantly *is* fishing.

Hitherto, its international interests were believed best served by membership of NATO and EFTA. However, with diminished American involvement in NATO in Europe (and the potentially increased importance of the EU's Western European Union), and with the departure from EFTA of Sweden, Finland and Austria, Iceland will feel more isolated, and possible membership of the European Union is likely to become a more serious item on the agenda. Key factors in the decision are likely to be what special arrangements can be made for fishing, and whether Norway decides to join.

## Switzerland

Switzerland's position is anomalous: geographically `at the heart of Europe', entirely surrounded by EU member countries, and conducting the great majority of its trade with the European Union, it is none the less the only country in Western Europe (apart from Norway) which is not a member of the Union. The main factors which have kept Switzerland out of the Union have been its 700 years attachment to the concept of neutrality and to a political system based on direct democracy and federal devolution to the cantons. There have also been specific difficulties with agriculture, transport and movement of people.

Switzerland was a founder member of EFTA and signed a bilateral trade agreement with the European Community in 1972. When the Single European Market was being introduced, Switzerland saw exclusion from it as a serious disadvantage, and joined with other EFTA countries in the negotiations for the European Economic Area. However, the agreement that emerged was not seen as favourable and was rejected in a referendum in 1992.

The Swiss economy is efficient, the Swiss franc is strong, and Swiss living standards are among the highest in the world. It is therefore feasible to go-it-alone - at least for the time being. However, Swiss exporters and the national airline are at a disadvantage as a result of their exclusion from the European Single Market, and the obstacles to joining the European Union are being re-examined to see whether they are permanent and insuperable.

A group of the Federal Council has reconsidered the traditional view of neutrality and proposed a more restricted, military interpretation, which would be compatible with EU membership - provided the EU's defence `pillar' is not extended unduly. While some political powers would have to be pooled in the Union, the competencies concerned are mainly federal ones in Switzerland, and would not seriously impinge on cantonal rights -provided the principle of subsidiarity is fully applied in EU institutions. The problem of transport (in the form of the EU's wish for unimpeded trans-alpine links) has already been partly solved by the Swiss £15bn plan for two new rail tunnels. Agriculture is less likely to be a problem if the Common Agricultural Policy is radically reformed - as it will need to be anyway to make possible the accession of other new members. Free movement of people is likely, however, to remain a contentious issue in a country which is a powerful magnet to migrants and in which already one-resident-in-five is non-Swiss[320].

Thus the disadvantages of isolation are tending to grow, and the obstacles to joining are tending to diminish. Since 1992 it has been official federal government policy to seek EU membership, and it seems likely that at some time (probably not very soon) the balance will shift sufficiently for Switzerland to take its `natural' place at the centre of the European Union.

### Liechtenstein
Finally, for Liechtenstein, the other remaining EFTA member, the problems of size would appear to be insuperable. With a population of only 29,000 - only 8 per cent of that of Luxembourg - there is no conceivable way it could take on the full responsibilities of an EU member state. If it is to join, it will presumably need to be on some special basis, possibly in association with one of its neighbours.

## Central and Eastern Europe

With the collapse of the Soviet Union and the Warsaw Pact, the countries of Central and Eastern Europe have once again become free to shape their own political and economic policies, and many of them have expressed a wish to join the European Union - in the hope of achieving a degree of military security in case of any later resurgence of Russian expansionism, with a view to sharing in the perceived economic success of Western Europe, and as an expression of cultural identification with Europe as a whole. However individual countries vary greatly in the strength of their wish to join and in the difficulties they face in trying to do so.

*The Czech Republic, Slovakia, Poland and Hungary*
All of the `Visegrad-4' countries have concluded trade and co-operation agreements with the European Union, followed by Europe Agreements; and all have been pressing for full membership at the earliest opportunity. The Copenhagen Summit in June 1993 explicitly recognised the eventual goal of membership[318], and it is expected that negotiations will begin after the Intergovernmental Conference in 1996. Their applications have the approval, with varying degrees of enthusiasm, of all the EU governments.

Emerging from decades of Soviet occupation, and conscious of long histories of earlier troubles, all four countries would like to join NATO as a guarantee of their independence in the event of a threat from some future Russian imperialist. Since the Partnership for Peace plan stops short (deliberately) of offering security guarantees, they hope to enter NATO by the back door by joining the European Union, assuming that this will bring at least an implied assurance that other member countries would come to their defence if the need arose.

They also seek membership of the Union for its own sake, in the belief that they are part of Europe and have a fair claim to be a part of the developing economic and political union - from which they hope to derive great benefit. They can reasonably argue that they will 'fit in', that their history, culture, religion and attitudes are more Central European than East European; three of them before the First World War were part of the Austro-Hungarian Empire; two of them between the wars were part of a stable social democracy; and all of them have set up democratic political structures.

They have also set about converting their economies to a market basis and have made more progress in this than most of the other countries in Central and Eastern Europe. In this they have been helped by assistance under the PHARE programme and the Europe Agreements.

However, in all four countries there were setbacks in the early years of economic restructuring, which have not yet been fully recovered from. In consequence, in all of them GDP is still *lower* than it was before the reforms[321]. The Europe Agreements have stimulated investment from the West, which has amounted to a total of $10.8bn in the two-and-a-half years from the beginning of 1992, over half of it going to Hungary, but only 3 per cent to Slovakia[322]. The Europe Agreements have also helped bring a great increase in exports of manufactures to the European Union[323], but they have included restrictions on `sensitive' items and on agricultural products - the very areas offering them the best prospects. They have thus been unable to balance their trade with the European Union, and the deficit of Poland alone has been estimated as representing exporting unemployment of 200,000 jobs[324].

Slovakia has problems in its dependence on declining heavy industries; Hungary and Poland both have major agricultural sectors; and all four countries have income-levels far below the average of existing members of the Union[325,326]. An independent study estimates that entry of the Visegrad-4 would more than double the cost of the Common Agricultural Policy in its present form[327]; while a study for the Commission itself estimates that the four countries would more than double the cost of the EU structural funds[328].

Despite these difficulties, it seems likely that all four of the `Visegrad' countries will secure membership of the European Union by the turn of the century or soon after. However, accession is likely to require a long transition period and will be on a basis which excludes them from the open-ended support provided by the CAP in its present form.

*Bulgaria and Romania*

Bulgaria and Romania have also secured Europe Agreements, help under the PHARE programme and recognition at the Copenhagen Summit of their claims to eventual membership. However, for Bulgaria, and even more for Romania, the accession process looks like taking far longer than for the `Visegrad-4'.

In neither country are democratic institutions yet securely established and in Romania the rights of the large Hungarian minority are not yet safeguarded. In both countries economic reform is less advanced than in the Visegrad-4 and economic dislocation is still severe - in 1994 GDP was still 30 per cent below 1989[321]. Inward investment has been low, equivalent in 1993 to only $17 a head in Bulgaria and $9 a head in Romania[322]. While there is little doubt that in due course membership will be achieved, there is equally little doubt that many changes over many years will be needed before they are ready for it.

*Lithuania, Latvia and Estonia*

The three Baltic republics, which were independent states before the Second World War, since breaking away from the Soviet Union in 1991, have been pressing for membership of the European Union - with support from their Nordic neighbours across the Baltic. Their objectives are to avoid risk of reannexation by Russia, to link their economies to the West, and to assert their European identity.

They already have free trade agreements with the European Union and will shortly have Europe Agreements with the long-term aim of preparing them for accession.

They have already established vigorous democracies, but full civil rights have not been extended to the Russian minorities which comprise a quarter of the population of Estonia and a third of the population of Latvia.  Until a satisfactory resolution of these problems is achieved there is a risk that they will provoke the very Russian intervention it is desired to avoid.

The economies of the Baltic States were particularly closely integrated with the economy of the rest of the Soviet Union, and the friction accompanying their breakaway has brought severe economic disruption. For example, Estonia's trade with the Soviet Union fell from 95 per cent in 1990 to only 15 per cent in 1993, while its trade with EU and EFTA countries rose from 3 per cent to 56 per cent of the total[324]. In each of the Baltic states GDP in 1994 was only about half the 1989 level[321].

## Slovenia

Of all the republics of former Yugoslavia, Slovenia is the one that has emerged best from the break-up, without economic sanctions, significant fighting, disaffected minorities or major dislocations. Its economy, although still not recovered to 1989 levels, has suffered less disruption than those of the other former Yugoslav republics, and income per head is higher than in any of the other former Communist countries[325], roughly similar to that in Greece[326]. Like the Czech Republic, Hungary and Poland, before the First World War it was part of Austria-Hungary, and still retains some affinities with Austria. It has recently secured a Europe Agreement and seems likely to be ready to join the European Union at the same time as the `Visegrad-4'.

## Serbia, Croatia, Bosnia, Macedonia and Albania

Albania has always been one of the poorest countries of Europe, and has suffered from a Communist r_gime which was particularly rigid and slow to give up power. Macedonia, also one of the poorest countries in Europe, has been troubled by ethnic divisions and hostile neighbours - in particular Greece, which suspects it of having designs on Greek Macedonia. Serbia has yet to establish democracy and respect for human rights and has an economy crippled by economic sanctions. And Croatia and Serbia have suffered the ravages of civil wars of great ferocity and destructiveness. It will take many years to repair the damage and many more to heal the bitterness.

None of these countries looks like being ready for membership of the European Union for many years to come. However, they are undoubtedly European, and are surrounded by other countries which are already members of the Union or are aspiring to become members. At some distant date, therefore, they too may be expected to be included in the Union - indeed, once that goal is accepted, it is likely that the efforts to prepare for membership, and the help given them in this by the EU, may contribute significantly to the solution of their many problems.

## The former Soviet Union

In the euphoria following the collapse of Soviet Communism and the end of the Cold War, there were some who envisaged that even Russia might some day join the European Union. However, it soon became clear that, even were there a wish for union on both sides, and even if solutions could be found for Russia's daunting political and economic problems, there was no way the European Union could incorporate a superpower, albeit one of much diminished strength, without fundamentally changing its character. Russia, with its population of 150 million and numerous different ethnic groups, would simply be too large to be absorbed. And although part of Russia is in Europe, it extends also across a further 4,500 miles to the eastern extremities of Asia - Vladisvostok is almost as far from Brussels as Los Angeles is. Thus with Russia, as indeed with the United States, it will be important to establish improved economic links; but there will not be much point in trying to include Kamchatka, any more than Alaska, within a `European' entity.

With the European republics of the CIS - Ukraine, Belarus and Moldova -it may be noted that before the war Moldova used to be part of Romania; and in the Ukraine, ever since the country lost its independence to Russia in 1654, there have been Ukrainian nationalists resentful of past Russian dominance and keen to minimise links with Russia in the future[329]. However, the economies of all three countries (which, like Russia's, are in severe difficulties) are still oriented strongly towards Russia's; and their shared history has given them strong cultural and institutional ties with Russia. A recent opinion poll in Belarus showed 71 per cent of people seeing their future as being with Russia, compared with only 7 per cent seeing their future being with Europe, while in the Ukraine the ratio was 48 per cent to 12 per cent [325]. Thus the likelihood would seem to be that, despite current differences between Russia and the other republics, in the longer term many of the CIS republics will join with Russia in an economic area which will be adjacent to, and in some ways complementary to, but not part of, the European Union.

## North Africa

It is often argued, particularly in Spain and France, that the European Union should direct more of its attention towards the countries on the southern and eastern shores of the Mediterranean and the Middle East. Morocco, Algeria, Tunisia, Libya and Egypt, the five countries along the African shore of the Mediterranean, have insecure governments, resurgent militant Islamic movements, massive development problems and populations expected to increase to over 200 million by 2025[330]. Developments in these countries are likely to be important to Europe in the decades ahead - not least in the form of increasing migration pressures.

The European Commission has proposed arrangements somewhat similar to the EEA free-trade zone to cover, not only the North African countries, but Lebanon, Syria, Jordan, and Israel as well[331]. It is envisaged that the European Union will provide ECU5bn of aid to these countries over the period 1995-1999[331] - but on the understanding that they will help control illegal immigration and illicit drugs. However, it is not likely that these countries will actually *join* the European Union, even in the longer term, on account of the lack of democratic institutions in many of them, their ethnic and cultural differences, the size of their populations and their problems, and the basic objection that they are not in Europe and cannot be regarded as having a `European identity'.

Possibly, in the longer term, they will form some kind of association among themselves; in which case, it will clearly be important for the European Union to establish effective economic links and friendly political relations with the new grouping on the southern and eastern shores of the Mediterranean, just as with the CIS countries to the East.

## The enlarged European Union

While there must remain great uncertainty about the future position of any one particular country, the broad shape of future enlargement of the Union as a whole is becoming clearer.

It is expected that the 1996 intergovernmental conference will be followed by negotiations with the next wave of prospective new members. By the turn of the century, or soon after, this is likely to result in membership for Malta, Cyprus, the Czech republic and Hungary, and also, at the same time or a few years after, for Poland, Slovakia and Slovenia.

In the course of the coming decade it is possible that Norway will reverse its decision to stay out, and that this will result in Iceland deciding to join also. Similarly in Switzerland it is possible that the balance of opinion will swing in favour of membership. Bulgaria and Romania are already seeking membership, but their more difficult problems make it unlikely that they will be included in the first wave of further negotiations. However, they are likely to be included in subsequent rounds, and it is possible that by 2005 they will be deemed ready for membership - albeit with major derogations and long transition periods.

Thus the European Union, which started with only six members in 1957, and has already grown to fifteen members in 1995, is likely to be further enlarged to at least twenty-two members, and possibly as many as twenty-seven, by the year 2005.

However, the process of enlargement is unlikely to stop at the stage reached by 2005. In the course of the following two decades, Norway, Iceland and Switzerland, if they have not already done so, are likely to decide to join. Bulgaria and Romania, if not already in membership by 2005, are likely to be accepted some years later. And the three Baltic states, already eager to join, are also likely to have been accepted into membership.

For Albania and the four republics from former Yugoslavia the current situation and immediate prospects are bleak. However, in three decades time their situation may be much better; and, if they seek membership of the Union, their European identity cannot be denied. For Turkey, on the other hand, it is its essential European identity - or doubts about it - which is likely to prove the most enduring obstacle to membership. Even so, after three decades, it is possible that Turkey too will have become accepted as a full member of the European Union.

## 1970

**Members**    **6**
West Germany
France
Italy
Netherlands
Belgium
Luxembourg

**Languages**   4

**Population**   1.88
'00 millions

**Gross Domestic Product**    2.315
'000 bn ECUs at 1995 prices

**1995**

**Members    15**

| | |
|---|---|
| West Germany | Britain |
| France | Denmark |
| Italy | Ireland |
| Netherlands | Spain |
| Belgium | Portugal |
| Luxembourg | Greece |
| | Austria |
| | Finland |
| | Sweden |

**Languages    11**

**Population    3.49**
'00 millions

**Gross Domestic Product    6.238**
'000 bn ECUs at 1995 prices

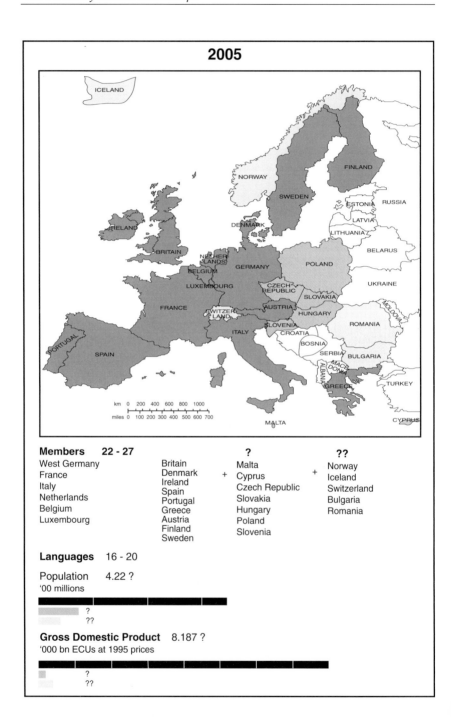

# 2005

**Members** **22 - 27**

| | | | ? | | ?? |
|---|---|---|---|---|---|
| West Germany<br>France<br>Italy<br>Netherlands<br>Belgium<br>Luxembourg | Britain<br>Denmark<br>Ireland<br>Spain<br>Portugal<br>Greece<br>Austria<br>Finland<br>Sweden | + | Malta<br>Cyprus<br>Czech Republic<br>Slovakia<br>Hungary<br>Poland<br>Slovenia | + | Norway<br>Iceland<br>Switzerland<br>Bulgaria<br>Romania |

**Languages** 16 - 20

Population 4.22 ?
'00 millions

?
??

**Gross Domestic Product** 8.187 ?
'000 bn ECUs at 1995 prices

?
??

# 2025

**Members** 30 - 36

| | | ? | ?? |
|---|---|---|---|
| Germany | Britain | Malta | Albania |
| France | Denmark | Cyprus | Macedonia |
| Italy | Ireland | Czech Republic | Croatia |
| Netherlands | Spain + | Slovakia + | Serbia |
| Belgium | Portugal | Hungary | Bosnia |
| Luxembourg | Greece | Poland | Turkey |
| | Austria | Slovenia | |
| | Finland | Norway | |
| | Sweden | Iceland | |
| | | Switzerland | |

**Languages** 23 - 25

**Population** 4.91 ?
'00 millions

?
??

**Gross Domestic Product** 14.110 ?
'000 bn ECUs at 1995 prices

?
??

Bulgaria
Romania
Lithuania
Latvia
Estonia

Thus it is probable that by the year 2025 the European Union will have grown to embrace thirty member countries - double the present number - and possibly as many as thirty-six.

## The implications of enlargement

The importance of the likely enlargement of the Union lies not only in the expected increase in the number of member countries, but also in the implied changes in the *character* of the Union.

### Population

Because most of the new member countries are small or very small, the increase in the Union's total population will be much less than in proportion to the increase in the number of member countries. By 2005 the seven probable new member countries will add about 20 per cent to the total population of the existing fifteen EU countries, and the five possible ones perhaps a further 13 per cent.

By 2025 the population of the fifteen existing member countries is projected to increase by only 3 per cent. The projected future populations of the fifteen probable new member countries will increase the total by about 37 per cent. If the remaining Balkan countries join it will increase the total by a further 8 per cent. And if Turkey joins it will increase the total by a further 26 per cent - equivalent to more than two-thirds of the combined total of all fifteen of the probable new members.

Thus in a Union of thirty countries the new members will account for only a little over a quarter of the total population. Even so, the enlargement will result in a significant shift in the balance of the Union from the North and West to the East and South. With a still larger Union of thirty-six countries, the new members are likely to account for more than 40 per cent of the total population by 2025, and in terms of population Turkey will replace Germany as the largest single country. In such a larger Union the balance may be expected to tilt still more strongly to the East and South.

With fifteen or more new members, most of them much poorer than the existing members of the Union, enlargement may be expected to result in increased migration flows from the new member countries to the old. Of the four poorest of the existing members, about 1.4 per cent of Spaniards, 4 per cent of Greeks, 9 per cent of Portuguese and 15 per cent of Irish people are now resident in other counties of the Union. It is difficult to know how many people from the prospective new member countries would, given the chance, choose to move to other EU countries. One estimate[332] suggests perhaps three-to-six million people might migrate from the four Visegrad countries alone. This would represent less than 2 per cent of the present population of the Union of fifteen, and would be much smaller than some of the population movements which have been accommodated in the past. It would be spread over a number of years and some of the people, it must be remembered, would probably make the move anyway, even in the absence of enlargement. However, if the numbers from other new member countries were much larger, and if the migrants tended to concentrate in a few centres (which is likely), the migration could be large enough to give rise to problems.

*Economy*
Already the European Union has a total GDP slightly larger than that of the United States and much larger than that of Japan - $7,500bn against $7,200bn and $4,700bn in 1995[333] - and the enlargement in prospect will make the economy of the Union larger still. But because the prospective new-member countries are mostly small and less economically developed than the existing ones, the increase they will bring to the Union's aggregate GDP will be relatively modest.

Between 1995 and 2025 the total GDP of the European Union is likely to more than double, but the overwhelming bulk of the increase will be due to the continuing expansion of the fifteen existing members. If their economies grow at an average of 2.5 per cent a year, the total cumulative increase will be 110 per cent. If the economies of the fifteen probable new members grow at the same rate, they will add only a further 8 per cent to the 2025 total; and the economies of the six other possible new members, if they come in, will add only a further 2 per cent.

Far more important than the new members' impact on the *size* of the Union's total economy will be their impact on its *structure*. The economies of the countries in Central and Eastern Europe were in the past closely integrated with the COMECON bloc; but with membership of the Union their economies will become increasingly oriented towards the West to take advantage of the complementarity that potentially exists, with the more advanced economies in the West providing investment and advanced products, and the lower-cost economies of the East providing more basic products and food.

Already Western investment has been stimulated by the Europe Agreements, and between 1985 and 1992 EU imports of manufactures from eastern countries doubled, and could, it is estimated, increase by five times in the short to medium term[323]. Thus, when present restrictions are removed after membership of the Union, industries in Western Europe will face stronger competition from the low-wage countries in Eastern Europe; but as these countries' economies advance and their export earnings increase, industries in Western Europe will have access to expanding new markets in Eastern Europe. In the longer term the outcome should be mutually advantageous; but in the shorter term there may be serious problems of adjustment.

Poland and Hungary and some of the other Eastern countries have large agricultural sectors and could become major suppliers of food to Western Europe if present discriminations were removed. Indeed, it is in this area that they probably have the greatest competitive advantage. If they become full members of the Union, it will not be acceptable to exclude their food exports or to keep them out of the Common Agricultural Policy; but nor will it be *possible* to include them in the CAP in its present form.

In the European Union at present, agriculture accounts for only about 3 per cent of total GDP (although far more in some countries such as Ireland and Greece.) In the countries of Central and Eastern Europe agriculture is far more important, accounting for 5-24 per cent of GDP[321]. The cost of supporting their agriculture on the same basis as in the present CAP would be prohibitively high.

It therefore seems inevitable that, if the accession of the new members involves the incorporation of their agriculture within the Union economy, it will only be possible on the basis of a radical overhaul of the Common Agricultural Policy; and this in turn is likely to result in a restructuring and scaling down of agriculture in some western countries, in a redistribution of food sources from West to East, and in some reduction in food prices for consumers.

A further impact of enlargement is likely to be some shift in the relative position of the economies of existing members. Enlargement to

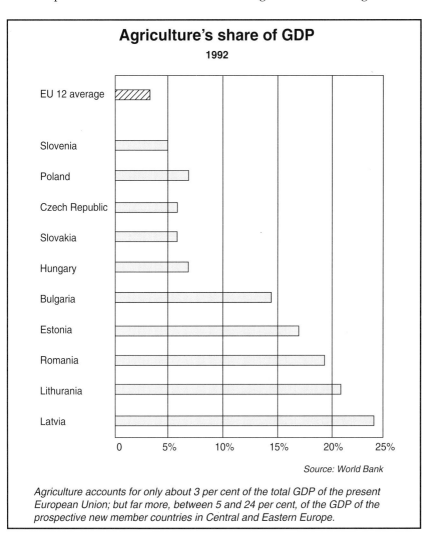

**Agriculture's share of GDP**

**1992**

*Source: World Bank*

*Agriculture accounts for only about 3 per cent of the total GDP of the present European Union; but far more, between 5 and 24 per cent, of the GDP of the prospective new member countries in Central and Eastern Europe.*

the East will put Germany in a more central position in the Union and make it well placed to take advantage of the new opportunities. Already in the period 1990-93 German direct investment in the Visegrad countries was more than twice as high as that of any other European country[334]; and in 1993 German exports to the Visegrad countries and Russia were four times as great as any other European country's and accounted for over half the EU total[334].

The German economy is already the largest in the Union, half as large again as the second largest[326]. If as a result of enlargement it becomes even more pre-eminent, this may be expected to give rise to fears of German economic domination and lead to increased concern, not least in Germany itself, for German strength to be harnessed to wider European ends through closer economic and political union.

### Stability

Enlargement to the East will involve incorporating areas of potential instability. Most of the Union's fifteen existing members have enjoyed a long period of economic growth and social and political stability. The prospective new member countries in Central and Eastern Europe have had a less happy experience - more than four decades of foreign domination, followed, after a brief euphoria, by many difficulties and disappointments.

All the countries of Central and Eastern Europe have been attempting to change their economies to more market-based systems. In the absence of clear plans, experienced staff, suitable institutions or large-scale external assistance, all of them have run into considerable difficulties; and while the economies of the EU countries have continued their expansion, with no worse than a 0.5 per cent dip in 1993[326], the countries of Central and Eastern Europe have seen a *fall* in GDP of anything from 15 to 50 per cent[321]. World Bank analyses[335] have shown that real wages have fallen heavily, for example by 28 per cent in Poland and 45 per cent in Latvia; unemployment has risen greatly, for example to 13 per cent in Hungary and 16 per cent in Poland; and income inequality has risen significantly.

There has been argument as to whether the changes attempted were too great or too little, too fast or too slow, misconceived or merely incompetently executed; and there is hope (supported by better performance in 1994) that the troubles are transitional and temporary, and that the restructured economies will perform much better in the future.  Meanwhile, general living standards have fallen, with much hardship for more vulnerable sections of the population. An EU survey in 1994 of the ten Central and East European countries likely to join the Union, found that in *all* of them more people thought their household financial situation had worsened in the past twelve months than thought it had got better; and in five of the ten more expected things to get worse in the next twelve months than expected them to get better[325].

It is therefore not entirely surprising that the earlier overwhelming belief in the merits of the market economy has in most countries fallen sharply, although in seven of the ten countries there is still a majority in favour of it.

Economic disappointment, coupled with other factors, such as the rise of corruption and organised crime, erratic and capricious changes in income distribution, and the resurgence of nationalism and intolerance towards minorities, have led to a wider disillusion and pessimism. The same EU poll in 1994[325] found that in six of the ten Central and East European countries more people thought their country was going in the wrong direction than in the right one; in seven of them, a majority of people felt there was not much respect for human rights; and in all then of them a majority of people - in some a very big majority - were dissatisfied with the development of democracy in their country.

There seems little doubt that many of the prospective new-member countries are not experiencing the degree of social cohesion and contentment that is taken for granted in most of the existing member countries, and unless their situation improves considerably they will bring the risk of political instability, possibly even of a violent kind. To exclude them from membership on that account would not prevent them at some point possibly becoming a threat to the welfare and security of the existing Union; indeed, bringing them into membership could help improve their situation and reduce the risks both for the Union and for the countries concerned. The prospect and actuality of

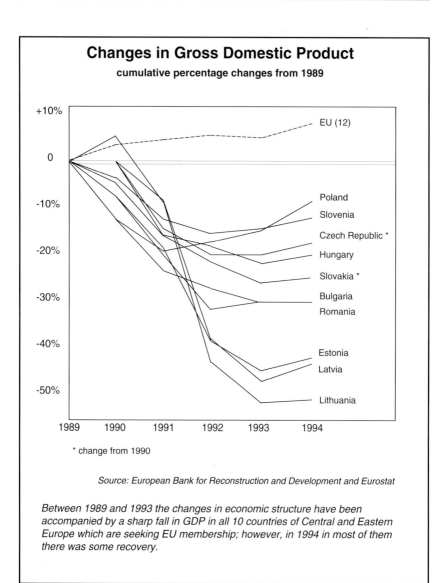

**Changes in Gross Domestic Product**

cumulative percentage changes from 1989

* change from 1990

Source: European Bank for Reconstruction and Development and Eurostat

Between 1989 and 1993 the changes in economic structure have been accompanied by a sharp fall in GDP in all 10 countries of Central and Eastern Europe which are seeking EU membership; however, in 1994 in most of them there was some recovery.

Community membership was a significant factor helping to restore and maintain democracy in Spain, Portugal and Greece. However, the relatively lower level of stability in some of the prospective members will imply a need for the Union to take a number of measures (some of them expensive) to help them achieve improved stability in the future.

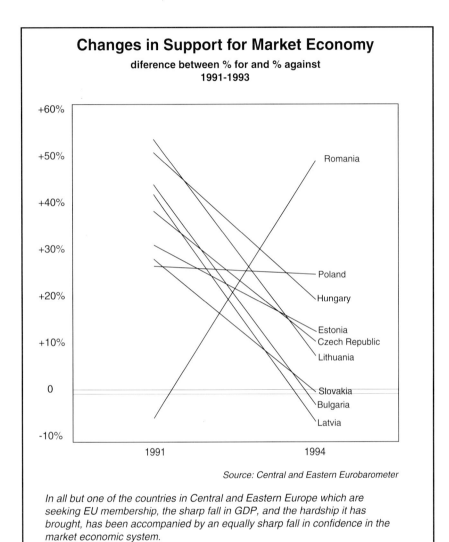

## Changes in Support for Market Economy
diference between % for and % against
1991-1993

Romania

Poland

Hungary

Estonia
Czech Republic

Lithuania

Slovakia
Bulgaria

Latvia

1991                    1994

*Source: Central and Eastern Eurobarometer*

*In all but one of the countries in Central and Eastern Europe which are seeking EU membership, the sharp fall in GDP, and the hardship it has brought, has been accompanied by an equally sharp fall in confidence in the market economic system.*

### Diversity

The fifteen existing member countries of the European Union encompass a wide range of differences in culture and customs and in economic, social, legal and political arrangements and institutions. This diversity can and should be a source of enrichment and strength rather than discord and difficulty; but it *does* give rise to tensions and disputes

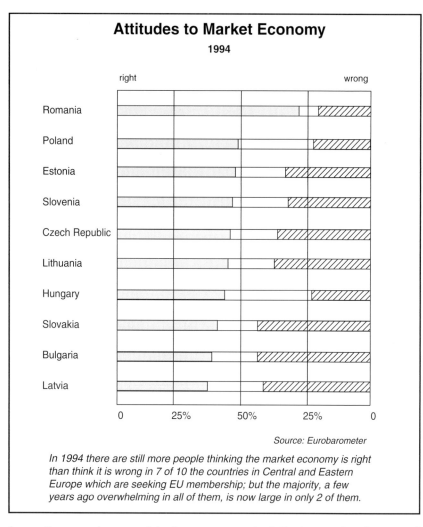

## Attitudes to Market Economy
### 1994

right         wrong

Romania

Poland

Estonia

Slovenia

Czech Republic

Lithuania

Hungary

Slovakia

Bulgaria

Latvia

0     25%     50%     25%     0

*Source: Eurobarometer*

*In 1994 there are still more people thinking the market economy is right than think it is wrong in 7 of 10 the countries in Central and Eastern Europe which are seeking EU membership; but the majority, a few years ago overwhelming in all of them, is now large in only 2 of them.*

from time to time, and it *does* set practical limits to the degree of integration that can realistically be expected in any foreseeable period.

Enlargement of the Union will extend considerably the range of this diversity, bringing in countries with very different political and economic backgrounds, and with an even wider range of cultural differences. For example, the present European Union of fifteen countries already has eleven different languages; a Union of thirty countries will have no less than twenty-three.

Where existing differences are particularly great it will make it particularly difficult for prospective new member countries to accept the Union's `acquis' - the aims and contents of the treaties and the institutional arrangements, legislation, court decisions, declarations and agreements which have subsequently given effect to them. In the past, full acceptance of the `acquis' has been a key condition of acceptance into membership. The greater diversity in the circumstances of potential future members will certainly require extensive derogations and long transition periods, and it may even require some reconsideration of the basic principle itself [336].

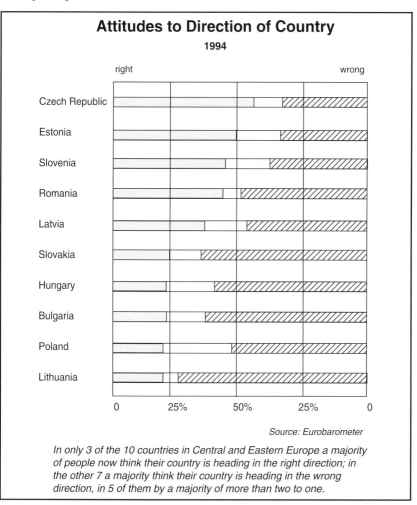

**Attitudes to Direction of Country**

1994

right · wrong

Czech Republic
Estonia
Slovenia
Romania
Latvia
Slovakia
Hungary
Bulgaria
Poland
Lithuania

0 · 25% · 50% · 25% · 0

*Source: Eurobarometer*

*In only 3 of the 10 countries in Central and Eastern Europe a majority of people now think their country is heading in the right direction; in the other 7 a majority think their country is heading in the wrong direction, in 5 of them by a majority of more than two to one.*

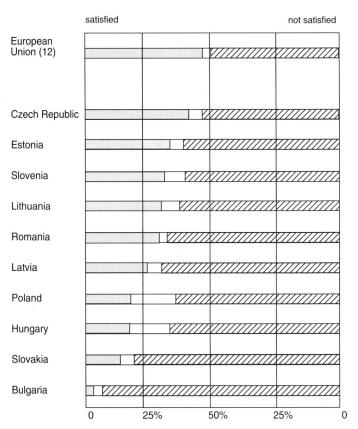

## Satisfaction with Democracy in Own Country
### 1994

satisfied                  not satisfied

European Union (12)

Czech Republic

Estonia

Slovenia

Lithuania

Romania

Latvia

Poland

Hungary

Slovakia

Bulgaria

0       25%      50%      25%       0

*Source: Eurobarometer*

*In the existing member countries of the European Union about half the people are satisfied with democracy in their own country, and about half are not. In all the countries of Central and Eastern Europe a majority, in most a very large majority, are not satisfied.*

One area of diversity which may give rise to particular difficulties is differences in income levels. There were no problems on this account with the three recent new members of the Union, each of which had an income level above the average of the Union as a whole; and the same will apply to Switzerland, Norway and Iceland. All the other prospective new members, however, have an average GDP per head well below the average of the existing members. Slovenia, which has the highest, has a GDP per head (on the purchasing power parity basis) about the same as that of Greece - which is about half the average of the Union as a whole. The others have a GDP per head far lower, several of them less than a quarter of the average of the existing members [325,326].

Such large differences are not wholly without precedent. Portugal, at the time of its accession, had a GDP per head equivalent to only 23 per cent of the average of the existing members, and to only 62 per cent of the poorest member[337]. The ten prospective new members in Central and Eastern Europe have an average GDP per head a little above 23 per cent of the average of the present members and not very different from 62 per cent of the poorest member. The crucial difference, however, is that whereas Portugal's accession increased the Community's population by only about 4 per cent, the ten Central and East European countries will increase it by about 30 per cent. To absorb, close together, the poorer countries with such a large population will present much greater problems than the accession of Portugal.

These large differences in income levels imply conflicts of interest which could give rise to serious tensions between poor new members expecting solidarity in the form of assistance from the Union, and existing poor members fearing that the assistance they already receive will be diverted to the new, much poorer, members; and the net contributors to Union budgets, fearing unlimited demands on them for ever larger transfers. And these conflicts of interest will be worked out in a context where the poorer countries will command a much higher proportion of votes than hitherto, and so will be in a stronger position to press for larger transfers from rich to poor.

Moreover, if monetary union leads (as discussed in the previous chapter) to a need for greatly increased transfers from better-off

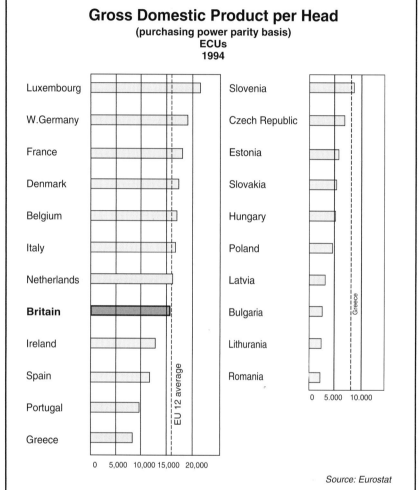

# Gross Domestic Product per Head
## (purchasing power parity basis)
### ECUs
### 1994

Source: Eurostat

*There are differences in income levels between existing members of the European Union - GDP per head in Greece is about half the EU average. With the prospective new members in Central and Eastern Europe the differences are much greater - all but one have a GDP per head lower than Greece and their average GDP per head is only about one quarter of that of existing members.*

countries, regions and groups to worse off ones, then enlargement to include a number of much poorer countries may be expected to amplify the scale of the needed transfers much further. And since many of the new-member countries are anyway most unlikely to be able to satisfy the current convergence criteria in the foreseeable future, enlargement may be expected to make it much more difficult to achieve a common currency for the Union as a whole. Hence it will make it more likely that monetary union will be introduced in a limited number of countries only, thereby institutionalising a division between the stronger and the weaker economies in the Union.

## *Institutions*
Some modification of the institutions of the Union will anyway be needed to take account of the increases in population and the changes in economic structure which will result from enlargement. Far more important, however, is likely to be the increase in the *number* of member countries. Institutions which were originally designed for a Community of only six members, and which are proving seriously unwieldy for a Union of fifteen, are highly unlikely to be manageable for a Union of thirty or more.

One implication of the increase in numbers is that unanimity will be much more difficult to obtain and, if total paralysis is to be avoided, it will be necessary to take more decisions in the Council by qualified majority vote. However, the Council Secretariat has made calculations[338] which show that, if the current voting formula were applied in a Council of twenty-eight members (including all those countries listed as `probable' except for Iceland and Switzerland), the new members would have enough votes to constitute a blocking minority and so, in theory, would be in a position to veto the decisions of existing members. It would also be possible, in theory, to make up a qualified majority in the Council on the basis of the votes of countries accounting for less than half the total population of the Union.

Also, the greatly increased diversity of attitudes, interests and circumstances that will result from the accession of the new members, together with the instability of some of them, will put further strains on the Union's institutions and necessitate further modifications in them.

The longer-term pressures on the Union's institutions as a result of enlargement, monetary union and other developments, and the changes likely to result from them, are considered further in the chapter which follows.

# 11 The Future of Europe

There are powerful longer-term forces making for a closer Europe; and there are powerful forces making for a larger Europe. In a number of important ways they are likely to be in conflict. The choice is likely to be between attempting deepening and widening at the same time, despite the considerable difficulties; or adopting a variable geometry solution - which will seem easier in the short term but is likely to bring difficulties of its own in the longer term. Either way, major changes are likely to be needed in the Union's institutions.

## Forces for deepening EU

As discussed in Chapters 2-9, there are a number of longer-term forces which are tending towards a more closely integrated Europe.

There are some areas - such as education, culture, the media, land use, health, social security and social services - where for reasons of national identity, local responsiveness or administrative effectiveness it is likely that arrangements will continue to be made at national, regional or local level. But there are increasingly many areas where future developments will bring a need for closer European co-operation.

In the post-Cold War world, the diminishing American presence in Europe, the instability following Soviet withdrawal from Eastern Europe, and the high cost of modern defence systems will all bring a need for closer European military integration. The problems of the Third World will bring a need for co-ordination of trade and development aid initiatives and for a joint response to mounting migration pressures. The cross-border movement of pollution and the global scale of other environmental threats mean that pan-European measures will increasingly be needed for environmental protection. The growing interdependence of economies will mean that joint macroeconomic measures will be needed to reduce unemployment. In an increasingly globalised economy joint R&D programmes and infrastructure improvements will be needed to help ensure European competitiveness. Finally, the proposed move to monetary union will give a powerful impetus to closer economic and political union.

These forces making for closer union are longer-term ones, and there is nothing inevitable about their outcome. However, a momentum has built up behind them as a result of the expectations engendered by a succession of treaties and declarations, and the underlying popular attitudes to European union.

In the European Union as a whole the proportion of people seeing their country's membership as a `good thing' outnumbers those seeing it as a `bad thing' by more than three-to-one, although the degree of enthusiasm varies greatly, from 76 to 8 per cent in the Netherlands and Ireland to 45 to 26 per cent in Denmark and 36 to 27 per cent in Britain[338]. The proportion of people seeing EU membership as beneficial to their own country is conspicuously smaller (51 per cent beneficial against 36 per cent not), with a majority in France, Spain and Britain seeing it as *not* beneficial to their countries[338].

But while there is clearly less than universal enthusiasm for the European Union *as it now is* - with widespread dissatisfaction with its perceived bureaucracy, secrecy and inadequate democratic accountability - this does not appear to be incompatible with a desire for closer European unity in the future. In a succession of opinion polls large majorities of people have declared themselves in favour of the unification of Europe. And when asked about the speed of unification in Europe, 48 per cent think it is going ahead slowly, and only 17 per cent think it is going ahead rapidly; when asked at what speed they *would like* unification to go, only 16 per cent say slowly and 60 per cent say rapidly[339].

There are also clear indications of the areas in which further unification is desired: there are large majorities in favour of joint European decision- taking in Third World co-operation, scientific research and development, environmental protection, the fight against drugs and control of immigration; but majorities *against* joint decision-taking in areas such as culture, education, health and social welfare[339]. There are large majorities in favour of common defence and foreign policies, a European Central Bank and a European government; but

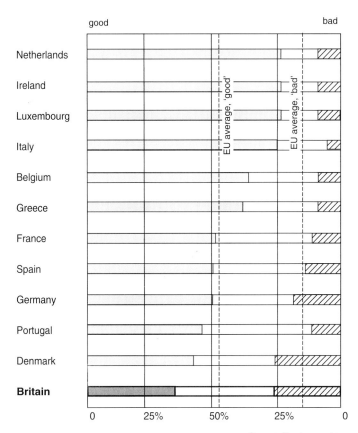

**Attitudes to EU Membership** *

**1994**

good                                                                 bad

| | |
Netherlands
Ireland
Luxembourg
Italy
Belgium
Greece
France
Spain
Germany
Portugal
Denmark
**Britain**

0        25%        50%        25%        0

*Source: Eurobarometer*

*In the European Union as a whole the proportion of people seeing their country's membership as a 'good thing' outnumbers those seeing it as a 'bad thing' by more than three to one; but the majorities in Denmark (45 - 36 per cent) and Britain (36 -27 per cent) are much slimmer than in the other countries.*

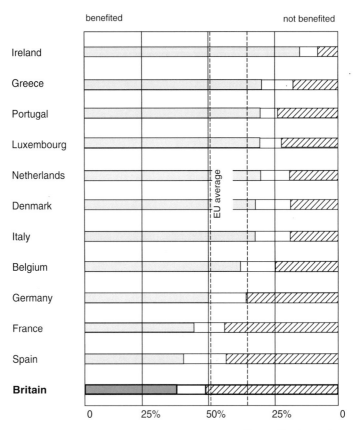

# Perception of Benefits for Own Country of EU Membership

**1994**

benefited                           not benefited

Ireland

Greece

Portugal

Luxembourg

Netherlands

EU average

Denmark

Italy

Belgium

Germany

France

Spain

**Britain**

0        25%        50%        25%        0

*Source: Eurobarometer*

*The proportions seeing EU membership as beneficial to their own country are much smaller than the proportions seeing it as a 'good thing'; in France, Spain and Britain there is a majority seeing it as not beneficial.*

smaller majorities in favour of a single currency and a more powerful European Parliament[339].

It is of course true that public attitudes, as measured in opinion polls, tend to fluctuate substantially from one time to another, depending on the political and media salience of current events. Attitudes to European union tend to be weaker in times of recession and more positive in times of prosperity. It may be noted that opinion polls in 1992-94 were taken in a period of recession; and the crucial intergovernmental conference in 1996 may well take place in a context of recovery and restored confidence.

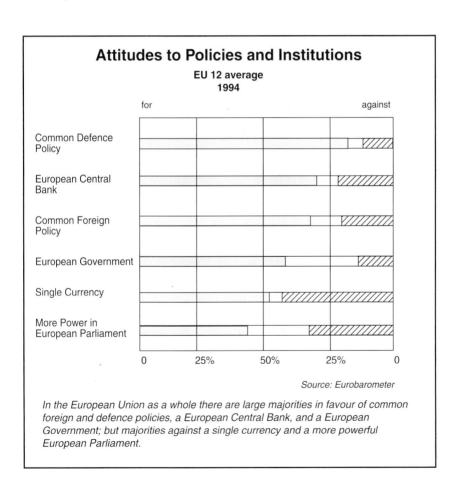

**Attitudes to Policies and Institutions**

EU 12 average
1994

Source: Eurobarometer

*In the European Union as a whole there are large majorities in favour of common foreign and defence policies, a European Central Bank, and a European Government; but majorities against a single currency and a more powerful European Parliament.*

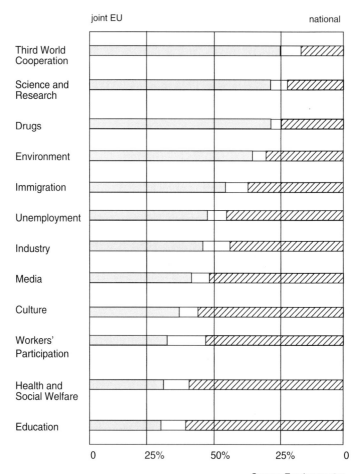

## Attitudes to Decision Taking

**whether decisions should be made on joint EU or national basis**
**EU 12**
**1994**

joint EU                                                                national

Third World Cooperation

Science and Research

Drugs

Environment

Immigration

Unemployment

Industry

Media

Culture

Workers' Participation

Health and Social Welfare

Education

0            25%            50%            25%            0

*Source: Eurobarometer*

*In the European Union as a whole there are large majorities in favour of decision taking at European, as opposed to national, level in third world cooperation, scientific research and development, the fight against drugs, and control of imigration; but majorities against joint decision taking in areas such as culture, education, health and social welfare.*

## Forces for widening EU

There are also powerful longer-term forces (see Chapter 10) making for a *wider* European Union, with fifteen countries likely to join within the next few decades. Of these, Switzerland, Norway and Iceland are prosperous, stable and already closely linked to the Union, so their accession should present few problems; and two others, Malta and

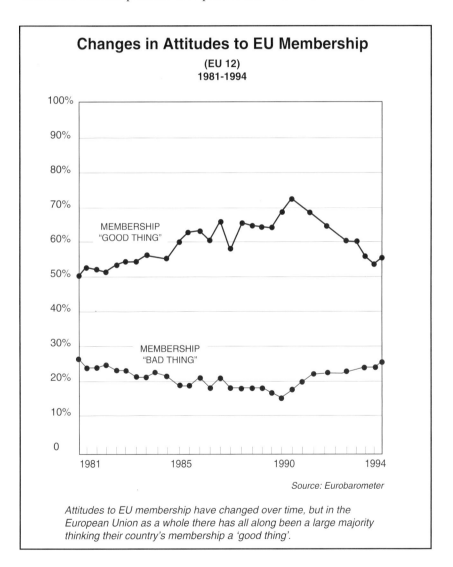

**Changes in Attitudes to EU Membership**
(EU 12)
1981-1994

Source: Eurobarometer

*Attitudes to EU membership have changed over time, but in the European Union as a whole there has all along been a large majority thinking their country's membership a 'good thing'.*

Cyprus, are small enough not to give rise to serious difficulties; attention is therefore likely to be focused mainly on the other ten countries from Central and Eastern Europe - the Czech Republic, Hungary, Poland, Slovakia, Slovenia, Bulgaria, Romania, Lithuania, Latvia and Estonia - which are more different from existing member countries and whose accession could prove more contentious.

The countries of Central and Eastern Europe see strong reasons for joining the Union. They wish to assert their European identity. They see membership as offering security against future attack from a resurgent Russia or, in some cases, from one another. They see membership as also providing support for political stability, reinforcing fragile democratic institutions, guaranteeing basic human rights and safeguarding the position of minorities. And they see integration with the more strongly established economies of Western Europe as likely to help their conversion to a market economic system, provide export markets and inward investment, bring technical and financial assistance, and give hope of an early rise to affluence.

For its part, the European Union has always been ready *in principle* to welcome new members which are essentially European and which accept its aims and arrangements; *in practice*, applications from prospective new members have often met with delays, tough negotiations and long transition periods, but have almost always ended with acceptance. In the case of the applicants from Central and Eastern Europe, there are strong longer-term reasons for wanting then in the Union, in particular the prospective complementarity of their economies and the desire for their reunion with the rest of Europe after nearly half-a-century behind the Iron Curtain. And, perhaps more compelling, there are the reasons against *not* letting them join: the traumatic disappointment it would bring in the countries rejected, leading, very likely, to resentment, even hostility; the economic difficulties and hardship it would bring, leading, very likely, to political instability, the undermining of new democratic institutions and a resurgence of aggressive nationalism; and the risk of tensions leading to war within or between countries in Eastern Europe, or even the return of the Russians. It would clearly be highly dangerous for the countries of Western Europe to allow another Bosnia or a bigger Chechnya in Eastern Europe.

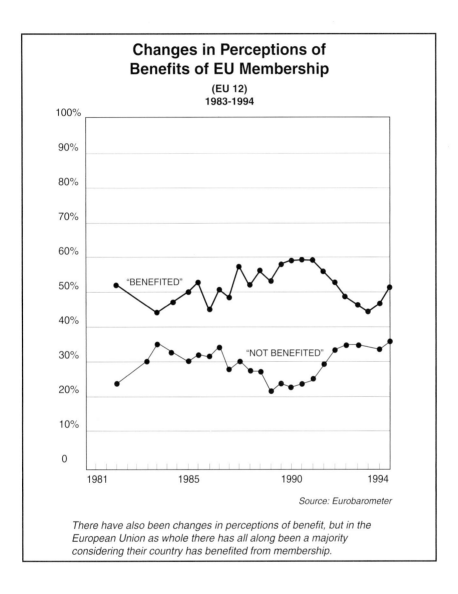

## Changes in Perceptions of
## Benefits of EU Membership
**(EU 12)**
**1983-1994**

"BENEFITED"

"NOT BENEFITED"

*Source: Eurobarometer*

*There have also been changes in perceptions of benefit, but in the European Union as whole there has all along been a majority considering their country has benefited from membership.*

Here too, the longer-term forces are reinforced by underlying public sentiment. In the countries of Central and Eastern Europe there is overwhelming popular support for joining the European Union[340] - although it is being eroded by delays and economic difficulties). And in the countries of the European Union public opinion is strongly in favour of accepting the new members[338] - although it is possible that popular approval will wilt once practical difficulties are encountered.

In the event, the European Union has already given varying degrees of assurance and commitment to the countries of Central and Eastern Europe that their claims to EU membership are accepted *in principle*; and it has given effect to this with a number of Europe Agreements and other anticipatory arrangements. And while there is no intention of starting formal negotiations until after the conclusion of the intergovernmental conference in 1996, the pressures for enlargement have acquired a momentum which cannot easily be stopped.

## Conflict between deepening and widening EU

Thus on the one hand there are powerful longer-term forces making for a deepening of the Union; and on the other hand there are powerful forces making for enlargement. In some senses these may be seen as pulling in the same direction. For instance, the prospect of major enlargement has given extra strength and urgency to recent moves towards closer union by those who wish to see the integration of existing members irrevocably secured before it is put under strain by the accession of further new members. However, there are a number of important ways in which the pressures for a *deeper* union is likely to come into conflict with the pressures for a *wider* one. And the conflict is likely to come to a head at the 1996 IGC, which will therefore be a crucial turning point in the further development of the Union.

The most far-reaching further step contemplated in the deepening of the Union is the adoption of a single currency and monetary union - probably in 1999 or soon after. The effect of this (see Chapter 9) is likely to be an important and early shift to closer economic integration and political union - *for the countries taking part*. However, it is most unlikely that all fifteen member countries *will* take part. A core group of Germany, France, Austria, the Netherlands, Belgium and Luxembourg seem likely to be ready to go ahead - on their own if necessary. A number of other countries may also meet the convergence criteria, some coming in from the start, others choosing to stay out initially, but possibly deciding to join later. And other countries may come near to meeting the criteria, and hope to join a few years later. However, there is likely also to be a fourth group of countries - Greece and Portugal and probably Spain and Italy - which are unable to meet the criteria in 1999, and are unlikely to do so in the following years either. They will therefore be left outside, at any rate at the start.

If EMU goes ahead with the core countries and some of the others, and if it achieves the benefits hoped for from it - such as lower inflation, stronger foreign exchange position, lower interest rates, increased internal and inward investment, nil transaction costs and a more effective single market - the EMU countries may be expected to enjoy a competitive advantage relative to the non-EMU countries, and to see the benefit of it in the form of faster growth and stronger economies. Thus, if at the time of the start of EMU there is a gap between the EMU economies and the others deemed not yet strong enough to take part, as time goes on the gap, far from closing, may be expected to *widen further*. Hence any countries not joining at the start or soon after may find themselves effectively excluded from the increasingly close and successful EMU group for a more or less indefinite period. The effect of EMU, then, may be, that while bringing the EMU countries *closer* to each other, it may at the same time take them *further apart* from the non-EMU ones.

It is possible, of course, that the non-EMU countries will redouble their efforts and, somehow succeed in catching up, despite any competitive disadvantage. And it is also possible that the EMU countries will make special provisions to *help* them to catch up. However, they will not be under any special pressure to do so because, under the Maastricht treaty provisions, they will have got agreement to go ahead on their own *unconditionally*. This marks a major departure from previous changes in the Union in which all countries proceeded *together;* and, if that presented difficulties for some members, special arrangements were negotiated for *helping* the weaker members as a *condition* of their agreement to *everyone* going ahead.

It is possible that, faced with the prospect of exclusion from the EMU group for an indefinite period, Italy and Spain will object so strongly that France and Germany will hesitate to go ahead without them, and will agree to a delay, or to special arrangements to enable them to join soon after. If, on the other hand, they proceed with EMU on the basis already agreed to at Maastricht, then the effect will be not an *enlargement*, but a *shrinking* of the heart of the Union to an inner group of countries able to meet the requirements of EMU.

The time when the ten prospective new members in Central and Eastern Europe are ready to join a monetary union would seem to be very remote; but even apart from EMU there are a number of formidable problems attached to their accession. The existing Union has been built up incrementaly, through free trade, the customs union, the single market, the European Court, the European Defence Union and a succession of treaties, laws and directives - over a long period. The prospective new members will be expected to take all this on board over a very much shorter period, together with any further developments agreed on in 1996, and to do so from a base when their economies are in the midst of a fundamental and difficult transition and still producing at substantially below earlier levels. It will mean undertaking four decades of change in a single giant leap.

In addition, there are five specific areas in which their accession will bring head-on conflict with powerful sectional interests in the existing member countries:

1. Their large agricultural sectors will transform EU food markets, making the CAP subsidies too expensive to continue - implying conflict with the protected farmers of Western Europe.

2. Their most competitive industrial exports will be in low-cost coal, steel, clothing and textiles - implying conflict with high-wage workers in EU industries.

3. With an average GDP per head only about a third of the average of existing members, they will qualify for a large share of EU structural funds - implying conflict with existing beneficiaries fearing they will get less, and with existing donors fearing they will have to pay more.

4. To avoid them having unacceptable voting power in qualified majority votes in the Council it will be necessary to reduce the

present over-weighting of smaller countries - implying conflict with existing smaller member countries reluctant to weaken their favourable position.

5. Free movement of labour will open the possibility of large-scale migration of workers to the West - implying conflict with people in likely receiving areas.

These specific issues, together with the number of the applicants and their greater difference from existing members, are likely to make their accession more difficult than previous ones; and the many problems involved in the enlargement may be expected to make more difficult, not only EMU, but most of the other forms of possible deepening of EU currently in prospect.

It is by no means clear how this conflict between deepening and widening EU can be resolved. To concentrate entirely on further *deepening,* and leave enlargement aside, would be a betrayal of original ideals and recent commitments and produce a situation in Eastern Europe which would be, not only very poor, but also highly dangerous to the countries in the existing Union. But to concentrate entirely on *enlargement*, and leave further deepening aside, would be to abandon original ideals in this area and to frustrate the widespread desire for closer union. And to give up in face of the difficulties, and do nothing much about either, would be likely to get the worst of both worlds, leading not only to stalemate and disillusion, but very possibly to the partial disintegration of much of what has been achieved already.

There would seem to be two possible ways of reconciling the conflicting pressures - neither of them easy.

## Deeper *and* wider EU

One way will be to proceed as fast as possible with both deepening *and* widening at the same time: sticking to the principle that it is a Union in which all have equal rights and all accept full responsibilities, and making maximum use of derogations, transition periods and special assistance to enable new members to be accepted and all to proceed together to further deepening.

EMU, even among relatively similar countries, implies a need for international fiscal integration and also for cross-border transfers to help weaker countries and regions - and hence the need for a larger central EU budget. If in the interests of following previous practice of all going ahead together, Italy and Spain, and even Portugal and Greece, are to be included in EMU at or near the start, this will imply the need for special arrangements to help them, and the likelihood of cross-border transfers considerably greater than otherwise - and a central EU budget larger still. And to bring in the countries of Central and Eastern Europe also at a reasonably early date will imply still greater transfers and a central EU budget even larger still - together with development of political processes for controlling it.

If they are not be given only *second class* membership, the new prospective members in Central and Eastern Europe will need to accept all the responsibilities of *full* membership. To prepare for this they will have to be allowed major derogations and long transition periods; and they will need to use them to good effect. They will have many changes to make in order to conform with EU requirements; and, probably even more important, they will need to achieve a rapid rate of economic development (and political and social progress) in order to reduce the gap between themselves and existing members, and with it the size of likely future transfers.

However, to achieve such a rapid rate of economic development will not be easy. It is likely to require very substantial help in the transition period - something of a vision and scale comparable with the Marshall Plan after the war - but paid for, not by the United States, but by the existing member countries of the European Union.

But even more important than outside aid will be the opportunity to *earn* their way to greater prosperity through increasing their exports of industrial products and, in particular, food. And this will require major adjustments by the existing members of the Union - accepting increased competition in sensitive industries and a fundamental review of agriculture. There is little scope for a middle way in agriculture - for example, even if the Central and East European farmers were not given the CAP subsidies, the sheer volume of their produce would so affect market prices that the cost of payments to *existing* EU farmers would make the CAP prohibitively expensive[341]. Hence the need - over a period - to phase out the present cumbersome and expensive arrangements, and go over to a new scheme more suited to future needs[342].

Such an approach will be ambitious, even heroic, but in the longer term is the one most likely to secure the best outcome - one Europe, secure, stable, equitable and prosperous. However, *in the short and medium term*, which is the time-frame in which most decisions tend to be made, politicians in EU-member countries, and perhaps even more their electorates, may be deterred by the need for making painful adjustments and substantial transfers, and may discount offsetting benefits such as additional export outlets, lower costs for food and industrial products, and the possibility of reduced defence expenditure with greater stability in Eastern Europe. It may be that their genuine enthusiasm for a closer, wider European Union falters at the perceived price tag.

## Variable geometry

It is therefore rather more probable that the leaders of the Union will go for a *variable geometry* approach. This is *not* a matter of Europe _ *la carte*, where each country picks and chooses, opting in for this and out for that - the resulting mixture would be legally complex, administratively unworkable and anyway politically unacceptable to most of the Union's existing members. What will therefore be involved is an acceptance of the proposition that different countries are in circumstances so different as to be incompatible with their all proceeding together in the same way and at the same speed; and that therefore they should proceed at different speeds, with different responsibilities and arrangements - but in an orderly, structured, agreed way.

Under this scheme of things the countries which meet the convergence criteria in 1999 will go ahead with EMU, and with the closer economic and political union likely to follow from it. They will form the inner group of the union.

The remainder of the present fifteen members will form the second, middle, group. They will continue to enjoy the benefits of the Single Market, will join with the first group in closer union in whatever areas seem useful and practicable, will continue to work towards meeting the convergence criteria and, hopefully, will join the first group in monetary union and whatever follows from it in due course.

The third, outer, group will consist of the new members from Central, Eastern and Southern Europe. In recognition of their more difficult circumstances, they will not be expected to take on all the responsibilities of full membership immediately. They will progress,

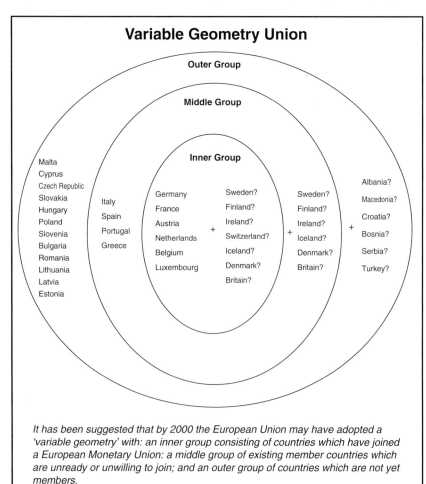

**Variable Geometry Union**

Outer Group

Middle Group

Inner Group

| | | | |
|---|---|---|---|
| Malta | | | Albania? |
| Cyprus | | | |
| Czech Republic | | Sweden? | Macedonia? |
| Slovakia | Italy | Germany | Sweden? | |
| Hungary | Spain | France | Finland? | Finland? | Croatia? |
| Poland | Portugal | Austria | Ireland? | Ireland? | |
| Slovenia | Greece | Netherlands | + Switzerland? | + Iceland? | + Bosnia? |
| Bulgaria | | Belgium | Iceland? | Denmark? | Serbia? |
| Romania | | Luxembourg | Denmark? | Britain? | |
| Lithuania | | | Britain? | | Turkey? |
| Latvia | | | | | |
| Estonia | | | | | |

*It has been suggested that by 2000 the European Union may have adopted a 'variable geometry' with: an inner group consisting of countries which have joined a European Monetary Union: a middle group of existing member countries which are unready or unwilling to join; and an outer group of countries which are not yet members.*

through free trade and customs union to full participation in the Single Market, and will also participate increasingly in other areas, such as environmental protection and defence. Hopefully, they too will eventually reach the stage where they are ready to join the others in EMU and closer economic and political union. Meanwhile, not having taken on the full responsibilities of membership, they will not expect the full rights either - hence they need not be given full voting rights or entitlement to CAP support.

Such a plan has obvious short-term attractions. Each country can proceed at its own pace, joining the group appropriate to its

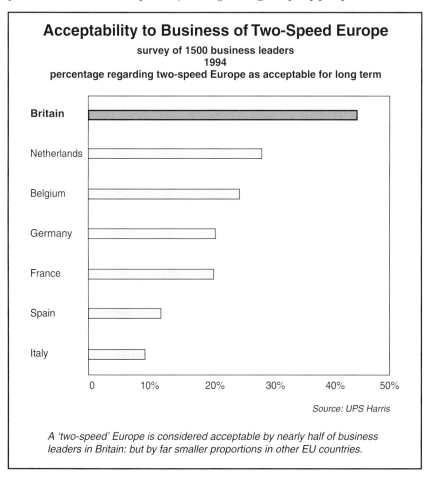

## Acceptability to Business of Two-Speed Europe
**survey of 1500 business leaders**
**1994**
**percentage regarding two-speed Europe as acceptable for long term**

*Source: UPS Harris*

*A 'two-speed' Europe is considered acceptable by nearly half of business leaders in Britain: but by far smaller proportions in other EU countries.*

circumstances. There is no need for some countries to risk getting into trouble by going faster than they are capable of, and all necessary adjustments can be made at a pace gentle enough to be accommodated by those affected. Deeper links can be forged without delay between those countries which are ready for them, while enlargement can still proceed by allowing a less demanding pace for the new members. In short: no abrupt shocks, no enormous bills; each country goes at its own pace, some take longer getting there, but we all arrive safely in the end.

Such a rosy scenario may come true - but it may turn out less problem-free than is hoped. The EMU group may indeed prosper - but so well that the second group never catches up with them, and comes to resent its perceived relegation to second-class status. Most of the countries in the third group may well come to feel that they have little chance of *ever* catching up with the others, that they have been *permanently* put in a third, outer group, which constitutes the lower, inferior tier, and is restricted to limited, third-class membership.

In particular, the countries in the East and South may come to feel that, despite all their acknowledged difficulties and weaknesses, it is *they* who are expected to make all the painful adjustments, while the better-off countries in Western Europe are not prepared to make changes which would offend even numerically-small interest groups. And, with all the rhetoric about free competition and market systems, they may believe that to make an exception solely for agriculture - the one area in which they are best placed to compete - is both unfeasible and unfair. The outcome could well be economic failure and popular disillusion - leading to dangerously unpredictable consequences.

Thus the variable geometry approach, while avoiding difficult early decisions, may end with a Europe more or less permanently divided into three, with very unequal situations and prospects, and constant scope for tensions between them. The attempt to get enlargement `on the cheap' in the short term, may bring high costs from instability or even hostility in the longer term.

In some ways the progress of the countries of the European Union can be likened to the progress of a group of ships, proceeding in convoy for mutual protection and support. As is the way with convoys, progress has been at the speed of the slowest ship, giving rise to frustration in some of the more powerful ships which would like to go faster, and the need for them to give some help to the slowest vessels to speed them up a bit. Now a group of even slower ships wishes to join them: so what should be done?

For the existing convoy to sail off, abandoning the new arrivals to their fate, would be callous - and invite retribution if they ever caught up. For the whole, enlarged, convoy to proceed at the much slower speed required by the new arrivals, would be disappointing for all. Accordingly, there appear to be two alternative strategies on offer. One is for the more powerful ships to use some of their power to help speed up the slower ships - and then all proceed as rapidly as possible in a single convoy. The other is for the convoy to split into three, each one going at the speed best suited to it, and come together again at the other end. This may seem the easy and obvious option - the only trouble is that the slow convoy may never make it to the reunion at the other end.

## The budget

Whether the strategy adopted is deeper and wider together, or variable geometry, or some messy mixture of the two, the need will remain for further evolution of the Union's institutions and for further enlargement of its budget.

The budget of the European Union amounted to ECUs73bn (about £60bn) in 1994. This represented an increase of more than a quarter compared with four years before, and further increases are planned in the coming years. But large as it is, the budget is small in comparison with the budgets of national governments - in 1994 it represented only 1.24 per cent of total EU GDP, compared with the 40-50 per cent of national GDP taken by the governments of member countries.

At present 51 per cent of EU revenue comes from VAT in member countries, 19 per cent from customs duties, 3 per cent from agricultural levies, and the remaining 27 per cent (the `fourth resource') on a formula related to each member country's GDP. The effect is to draw revenue from member countries roughly in proportion to the size of their GDPs.

315

The expenditure of the Union is dominated by agriculture. The CAP, despite the recent reforms, still takes about half the total budget. A further 30 per cent of the total is taken by the structural funds which are designed to help weaker countries and regions, mainly through investment in infrastructure projects.

In a fair budget system the richest countries would pay the largest net contributions and the poorest countries would gain from the largest net benefits; but because the  benefits of the CAP are distributed somewhat capriciously, the overall redistributive effect of the Union's central budget is bizarre.

It can be calculated[343,344,345] that Luxembourg, the richest country, gets the second largest net *gain* per head from the budget transfers, and Belgium and Denmark, the third and fourth richest countries, also get net *gains* from the budget. The four poorest countries also get net gains, but Ireland gets a net gain per head that is eight times as large as that of Spain, which is slightly poorer, and twice as large as that of Portugal which is much poorer, and half as large again as that of Greece, which is much poorer still.

On the revenue side of the budget Germany makes by far the largest net contribution - more than all the other countries combined. Germany's contribution per head is five times as large as that of Italy, and eight times as large as that of France, although Germany's GDP per head (after re-unification, on a purchasing-power parity basis) is actually *lower* than theirs; while Luxembourg, Belgium and Denmark, also richer than Germany, make no net contribution at all.

Despite its deficiencies, the present EU budget *does* have the effect of giving substantial help to some of the smaller, poorer countries - increasing the GDP of Ireland and Greece by 5 per cent, and of Portugal by nearly 3 per cent. At the same time it does not place excessive burdens on the larger net contributor countries - reducing Germany's GDP by less than 1 per cent and Britain's by only about 0.3 per cent.

However, with enlargement there will be need for more transfers to help new member countries, and with EMU there will be need for more

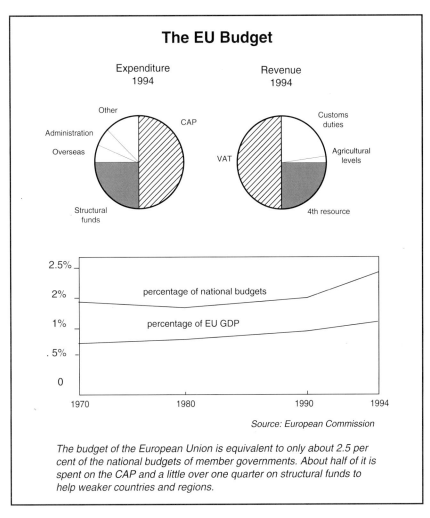

## The EU Budget

Expenditure
1994

Revenue
1994

Source: European Commission

*The budget of the European Union is equivalent to only about 2.5 per cent of the national budgets of member governments. About half of it is spent on the CAP and a little over one quarter on structural funds to help weaker countries and regions.*

transfers to help weaker areas within the system. Hence there will be need for a substantially larger budget, with the benefits dispensed more efficiently and the revenue raised more equitably.

If in the course of enlargement it is necessary to phase out the CAP, this will remove the worst of the present anomalies and release substantial funds for other purposes. However, even this is unlikely to allow all the new needs to be met, and if substantially larger revenues have to be raised it has been suggested[344] that it will be fairer and easier

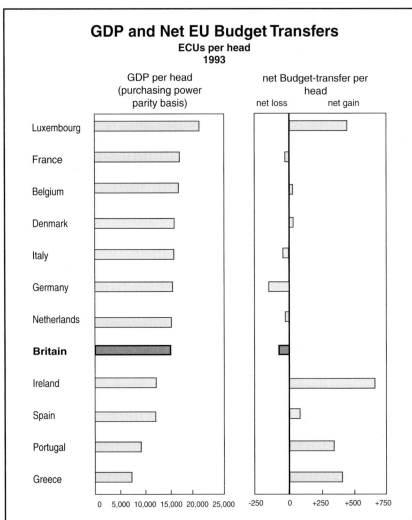

# GDP and Net EU Budget Transfers
### ECUs per head
### 1993

Source: Eurostat and EU Court of Auditors

*Because of the dominant part played by the CAP, the transfers resulting from the EU budget are capricious: Luxembourg, Denmark and Belgium, three of the four richest countries. all get net gains from the budget: and Britain, with a GDP per head slightly below the EU average, makes the second largest net contribution per head.*

to raise them on a more progressive basis, taking proportionately more from those richer and better placed to pay, in line with the normal practice in the personal tax structures of industrial countries.

A larger central EU budget will bring with it the need for improved administrative machinery to ensure that it is efficiently spent, and for improved political instruments to ensure that it is subject to proper control.

## The Commission

It is likely that in the future the European Commission will have, not only a larger budget, but also new responsibilities, for example in macroeconomic policy and in other areas such as the environment; and if a variable geometry pattern is adopted, its organisation will be complicated by the need for variable geometry administration, performing some functions for all member countries, and other functions for only some of them.

Up to now the Commission has managed to keep itself fairly slim, with total staff numbers far smaller than those of the civil services of most member-country governments. In the future its competencies will be extended more widely and it will be important to avoid a great growth in bureaucracy by confining its attentions to its areas of specific concern and, within them, keeping to the broad strategic issues and leaving details of implementation to be worked out in the member countries.

One problem which will need early attention is the way in which Commissioners are appointed to run the Commission. Countries like to feel that they have one of their nationals in a senior position on the Commission and the practice has grown up of each country nominating one of the Commissioners, and the five larger countries each nominating two. This has the effect that each time a new country joins a new Commissioner has to be appointed and a new Directorate has to be created for the new Commissioner to preside over. It also has the effect that the Commission has become unwieldy at the top, with twenty Commissioners; and will become even more so with the possibility of thirty-five Commissioners or more if all the likely prospective new-member countries actually join.

At some stage it will become necessary for the Commission to be restructured along functional lines, with the number and competencies of the Directorates based on the tasks they are to fulfil rather than on the number of Commissioners wanting a post; and with new Directorates set up when there are new functions to perform, rather than when new states join the Union. The Christian Democratic Union in Germany has suggested that ten Directorates might be a suitable number[346]; although, in addition to ten full Commissioners there could presumably also be a rather greater number of junior Commissioners, just as in a national government there are full Cabinet Ministers and also junior Ministers responsible for particular sub-areas within a government department. It will probably make for greater efficiency and better accountability if the Commissioners are appointed by, and held accountable to, the President of the Commission, in much the same way as Cabinet and junior Ministers are appointed by the head of government in a nation state. It may, however, be necessary to preserve the feeling that each country has a direct stake in the senior management of the Commission, by setting guidelines to ensure some balance between different sizes of country and regions of the Union.

## The Council

The Council, which embodies the intergovernmental aspects of the Union, used to operate on the basis of unanimity. However, what was more or less workable with only six members has become too restrictive in a Union of fifteen members and would lead to complete paralysis in a Union of thirty or more. Accordingly, it has been agreed that, for some issues not considered to involve vital national interests, decisions can be taken by a qualified majority vote, with a majority of at least 70 per cent of the weighted votes needed for a measure to be passed.

### Council Votes

| | | | | | |
|---|---|---|---|---|---|
| Germany | 10 | Greece | 5 | Sweden | 4 |
| Britain | 10 | Belgium | 5 | Denmark | 3 |
| France | 10 | Netherlands | 5 | Ireland | 3 |
| Italy | 10 | Portugal | 5 | Finland | 3 |
| Spain | 8 | Austria | 4 | Luxembourg | 2 |

With greater numbers of members it will become increasingly difficult to secure unanimity and, if repeated deadlock is to be avoided, it will be necessary to extend more widely the areas in which decision is taken by qualified majority vote. It may also be necessary to modify the weighting of the votes themselves. The present system is, deliberately, weighted heavily in favour of the smaller countries which on average have about three times as many votes per million population as the larger ones. However, with the accession of a large number of additional smaller countries, it has been calculated that with weighting on the current basis it would in theory be possible to gain a 70 per cent majority of the weighted votes on the basis of countries accounting for less than half the Union's total population; and it would, in theory, be possible also for the new member countries to muster a 30 per cent vote to block any proposals of the existing members[347]. To remove such anomalies it may become necessary to reduce slightly the extent of the over-weighting of the smaller countries.

If development takes the course of variable geometry, this will be likely to throw up contentious problems over who should be allowed to vote on what. For example, should issues arising from monetary union be decided only by those countries who are actual members of the EMU group? Or should other countries in the middle group, which may aspire to join later, and which may be affected by it even while outside it, be allowed a voice in the discussions? Or a vote too? And should the newly-joined countries in the outer group, if they are not in the CAP, none the less have a say in deciding the agricultural policy of the Union? Once the Union departs from the previous principle that all countries are equally in everything together (even if subject to transition periods) there is likely to be abundant scope for dispute over which countries should have a part in determining which issues.

## The European Parliament

When in an opinion poll[348] people were asked whether they thought citizens had sufficient democratic influence in EU decision-making, 71 per cent said No and only 14 per cent said Yes. There were substantial majorities saying No in all the member countries. It seems that a sense of bureaucratic remoteness and lack of direct democratic accountability are

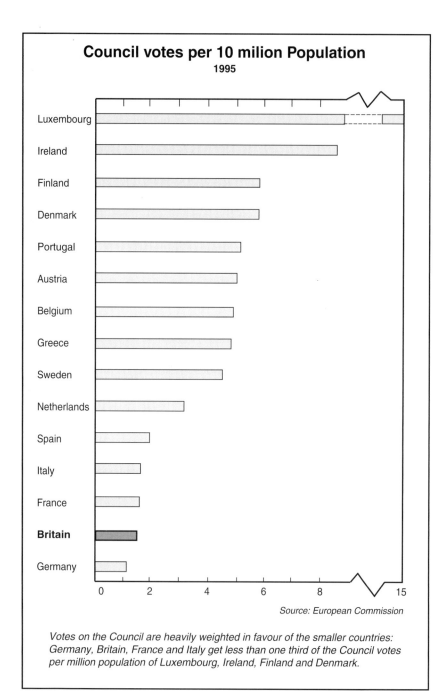

## Council votes per 10 milion Population
### 1995

| | |
|---|---|
| Luxembourg | |
| Ireland | |
| Finland | |
| Denmark | |
| Portugal | |
| Austria | |
| Belgium | |
| Greece | |
| Sweden | |
| Netherlands | |
| Spain | |
| Italy | |
| France | |
| **Britain** | |
| Germany | |

0   2   4   6   8   15

*Source: European Commission*

*Votes on the Council are heavily weighted in favour of the smaller countries:
Germany, Britain, France and Italy get less than one third of the Council votes
per million population of Luxembourg, Ireland, Finland and Denmark.*

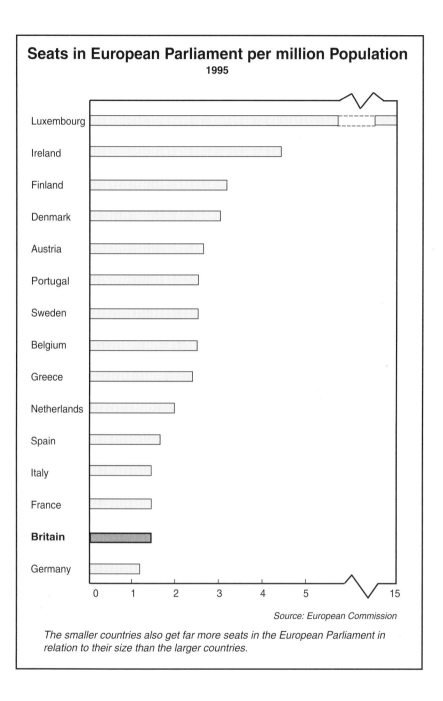

## Seats in European Parliament per million Population
### 1995

| | |
|---|---|
| Luxembourg | |
| Ireland | |
| Finland | |
| Denmark | |
| Austria | |
| Portugal | |
| Sweden | |
| Belgium | |
| Greece | |
| Netherlands | |
| Spain | |
| Italy | |
| France | |
| **Britain** | |
| Germany | |

0   1   2   3   4   5   15

*Source: European Commission*

*The smaller countries also get far more seats in the European Parliament in relation to their size than the larger countries.*

two of the main considerations associated with disenchantment, or even with hostility towards, the European union.

It is likely that national parliaments will seek to play a larger role in scrutinising European legislation and holding the Commission to account for its actions. However, national parliaments are inevitably too cumbersome, remote, separated from one another and focused on other things to be well placed for keeping quick, informed and effective control of the Commission; and even less are they in a position to take the initiative in putting forward legislation. At best they can examine, query and obstruct; they cannot be expected to act in a positive, constructive, initiating role.

If there is to be more democracy in Europe, the European Parliament is the obvious vehicle for it; MEPs are directly elected on a European mandate, address themselves exclusively to European issues, and are in close and regular contact with the Commission. Democracy at a European level is their job.

In the past the European Parliament had only modest impact and esteem because it was perceived as a decorative side-show, based in Luxembourg and Strasbourg, away from the action in Brussels, and with very limited powers.

Under the Maastricht treaty, however, the European Parliament now has increased rights of co-decision and consultation, and its elections are synchronised so that the new parliament is already in place at the time in the cycle when the new President of the Commission and Commissioners are chosen.

It is likely to be given further new powers by the intergovern-mental conference in 1996, and this could help significantly to make the Commission more democratically accountable and the Parliament more effective and more popular.

## European government

While the 1996 intergovernmental conference will be a key turning point, it is unlikely that the processes of change will come to a halt thereafter. On the contrary, it may be expected that the various EU institutions will continue to evolve and, influenced by the underlying longer-term factors, will tend to develop in ways which lead to a closer European Union.

As the European Parliament becomes more effective and more popular, it is likely to seek and get increasing powers, and to move to Brussels. It is also likely to operate in an increasingly European way. At present the majority of people vote in European parliamentary elections more on the basis of national issues than of European ones[339]. However, when the European Parliament is perceived as having real power to actually *do* things, people will be less inclined to treat European elections as indicators of support or disapproval for *national* governments, and more as a means of having a say in what is done in *Brussels*. And MEPs, elected on mandates for *European* issues, will tend to see themselves less as representatives of *national* interests and more as proponents of particular *political* objectives at a European level.

Already Christian Democrats, Socialists, Liberals, Greens and others are making transnational alliances in the European Parliament in pursuit of common objectives. Once there is real power at issue, it is likely that the European Parliament will become increasingly *politicised* in the sense that differences of political objective will be seen as more important than differences of national origin. And just as in national elections people are concerned not so much about the result in any particular area as about which political party wins *nationally*, so in European elections, the interest will shift from national perspectives to European ones: which coalition of political parties can win a majority *in the Union as a whole*, and so have an impact on outcomes in Brussels?

And as the European Parliament comes to have more say in the choice of the President of the Commission and the Commissioners, and more power to hold them to account, it may be expected that their relationship will in time come to be more like that between national prime ministers and ministers and their parliaments, and the Commission will come to take on more of the attributes of a European Government.

At the same time the Council also may be expected to evolve. It represents the separate *national* identities of the member countries - an aspect which is real, important and will not go away. It will therefore need to be given continued expression. However, this may in time come to be expressed less through *governments* and more through *individuals*. Just as in the United States the separate identities of the member states are represented through the elected members of the Senate, and in Germany the separate identities of the Länder through the members of the Bundesrat, so in Europe the Council may in time evolve into a second chamber for Europe, with the Parliament representing the individual citizens and the Council the member countries.

Thus, over a period, the present *federation of states* may evolve into a *federal state* - a European Government. Such a development will not necessarily prove unwelcome; indeed in a recent opinion poll[339] there was a majority of 4-1 in favour of a European Government in the Union as a whole, and a 5-2 majority in favour in Britain.

It is important to be clear that such a European Government will be very different from federal governments in countries such as Germany and the United States. Because national differences are much greater in Europe, and because national identities are cherished and people wish to preserve them, there will be no question of a federal government having powers covering areas as wide as those covered by the governments of Germany or the United States, still less those of unitary governments such as in Britain and France. On the contrary, in accordance with the principle of *subsidiarity*, its competencies will be restricted to those things which cannot be done as well, or at all, by governments at national, regional or local level. Its powers will be important, and will probably increase over time; but they will none the less be limited, and will leave the majority of things to be dealt with at lower levels.

Even so, a European government will constitute a major concentration of power, albeit one that is controlled by a democratic parliament. The danger will be that, if it is evolving, piecemeal, without any clear long-term plan, it will tend to go on growing of its

# Attitudes to a European Government
**1994**

for              against

| | |
|---|---|
| Netherlands | |
| Luxembourg | |
| Italy | |
| France | |
| Spain | |
| Belgium | |
| Germany | |
| Ireland | |
| Greece | |
| **Britain** | |
| Portugal | |
| Denmark | |

0     25%     50%     25%     0

*Source: Eurobarometer*

*There is a majority of at least two to one in favour of a European Government in each of the 12 EU member countries - except Denmark, where these is a majority against.*

own accord, and the guidelines of subsidiarity will become more rhetoric than reality.

It will therefore be necessary at some stage to come to a formal constitutional settlement, to clarify and define the roles, limits and procedures, to establish the specifics of a federal system. A codified constitution will be needed to legitimise what a European government is empowered to do; but also to delimit the boundaries of its domain and ensure that it does not encroach beyond it.

# 12 The Future of Britain and Europe

The 1996 intergovernmental conference is likely to decide on both further deepening and further widening of the European Union. What will be the effective options for Britain? Circumstances of history and geography have all along tended to result in attitudes in Britain being much less enthusiastic about European Union than in most of the other member countries - and also very volatile. Much will be at stake in the decisions taken in 1996, and it will be important for Britain's longer-term interests to be assessed correctly.

## Attitudes to the European Union

Almost every country in Europe has waged war against almost every other country within reach at some time in its history, in some cases on more than one occasion. In all countries in Europe this history of many centuries of wars leaves lingering hostilities with some people. And differences in language, culture and institutions are sufficient to give a strong sense of separate national identity and unease at the prospect of getting `submerged' in a broader European entity. In most of the member countries of the European Community, however, these feelings have been largely outweighed by the experiences of two world wars and the Cold War, and by perceptions of current and prospective benefits of closer European union.

In Britain, however, the sense of difference and separateness has remained stronger - even the word *Europe* itself is most commonly used to mean *continental* Europe, which is perceived as something Britain is separate from, not part of. These attitudes are partly a legacy of a different historical experience -  more than 900 years without successful invasion, enemy occupation, border changes or enforced population movement; and no experience of domestic revolution and violent overthrow of old institutions. The tendency has been to look for links less with European neighbours than in the wider world of the Empire, the Commonwealth and the United States.

Accordingly, attitudes have always been more equivocal in Britain than in most other member countries, both towards the Union in general and on most of the specific issues concerned with closer unification. In the referendum on joining the European Community in 1975 the vote was 67 per cent to 33 per cent in favour. Since then the evidence of opinion polls has varied, reflecting both apparent shifts in opinion and different responses to different ways of presenting questions.

The *Eurobarometer*[349,350] provides the most consistent series going back over a long period, and brings out the volatile changes in attitudes over time. While in 1975, consistently with the referendum, it showed a two-to-one majority (47-21) regarding membership of the European Community as a `good thing' rather than a `bad thing' for the country; by 1980, with the disputes about budget contributions, this had turned into a two-to-one majority against (21-55); by 1991 this was reversed with again a two-to-one majority (57-26) considering membership to be a `good thing' for the country; and most recently the gap has been narrowed again to only 36-27 in favour. The proportion in Britain seeing membership as a `good thing' has always been well below the EU average, and has often been the lowest of any of the member countries.

The proportion thinking Britain has actually *benefited* from membership has usually been substantially smaller than the proportion seeing membership as a `good thing', and for much of the time more people have thought Britain has *not* benefited than have thought it has. Most recently the ratio has been 51-38 thinking Britain has *not* benefited. Here too the proportion seeing Britain as having benefited is much lower than the proportion seeing benefit for their country in most of the other member countries.

A large majority (57-13) in Britain regard the Common Agricultural Policy as having bad results, but an even larger majority (64-13) regard the recent reform as a `good thing'. The Single Market is seen as a `good thing' rather than a `bad thing' by a majority (32-18) in Britain; and the Maastricht Treaty is seen in Britain as having positive rather than negative effects for Europe by a large majority (43-20), but as having positive rather than negative effects *for Britain* by a much smaller majority (36-31). Attitudes to both the Single Market and Maastricht are the least favourable of any country in the Union.

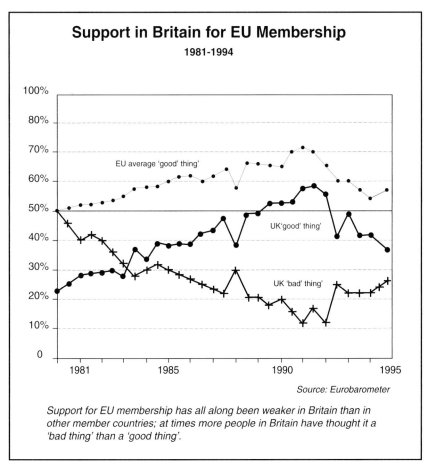

**Support in Britain for EU Membership**
**1981-1994**

EU average 'good' thing'

UK'good' thing'

UK 'bad' thing'

*Source: Eurobarometer*

*Support for EU membership has all along been weaker in Britain than in other member countries; at times more people in Britain have thought it a 'bad thing' than a 'good thing'.*

On the general question of further European integration as envisaged under Maastricht, opinion in the majority of EU countries is favourable, but in Britain, and also in Denmark and Germany, there is a majority preference for looser arrangements[351]. On the other hand, while in the Union as a whole there is a 60-16 majority in favour of unification proceeding rapidly rather than slowly, even in Britain there is a 52-20 majority for proceeding rapidly.

In Britain there is majority support for joint EU decision-taking on third world co-operation, the environment, and science and research, but not on other issues; and there is majority support for a common

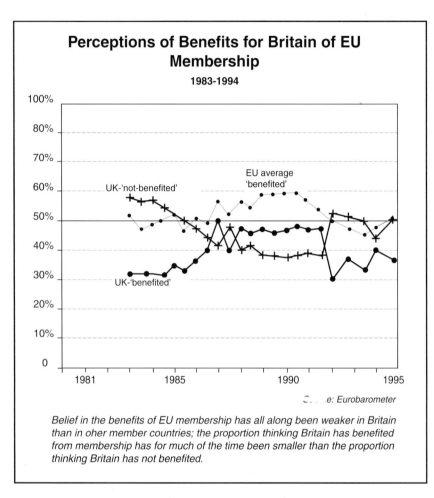

## Perceptions of Benefits for Britain of EU Membership

### 1983-1994

*Source: Eurobarometer*

*Belief in the benefits of EU membership has all along been weaker in Britain than in oher member countries; the proportion thinking Britain has benefited from membership has for much of the time been smaller than the proportion thinking Britain has not benefited.*

European defence policy, a common foreign policy, a European Cental Bank and for a European Government, but less support for a single currency or for a more powerful European Parliament. On all these issues, support for a European approach is less strong in Britain than in the Union as a whole, and on several issues support in Britain is the weakest of any member country.

While attitudes in Britain (and also Denmark) have all along been much more doubtful than in the other EU countries about most aspects of *deepening*, on *widening* British attitudes have been broadly in line with the

## Attitudes to Integration of Europe

percentage favouring a more integrated Europe
as envisaged under Maastricht and
percentage favouring a looser arrangement
between independent states
1994

In favour of more integration
In favour of looser arrangement

*Source: Harris Research*

*In the European Union as a whole there is more support for more integration than there is for a looser form of association: but there are majorities in favour of a looser association in Denmark, Britain and Gernamy.*

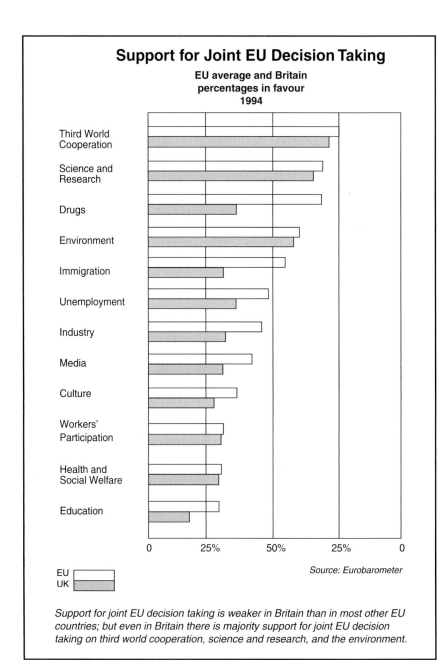

## Support for Joint EU Decision Taking

**EU average and Britain
percentages in favour
1994**

Third World Cooperation

Science and Research

Drugs

Environment

Immigration

Unemployment

Industry

Media

Culture

Workers' Participation

Health and Social Welfare

Education

0     25%     50%     25%     0

EU ☐
UK ▨

*Source: Eurobarometer*

*Support for joint EU decision taking is weaker in Britain than in most other EU countries; but even in Britain there is majority support for joint EU decision taking on third world cooperation, science and research, and the environment.*

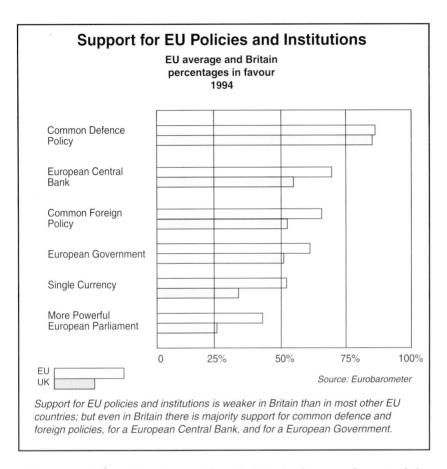

Support for EU policies and institutions is weaker in Britain than in most other EU countries; but even in Britain there is majority support for common defence and foreign policies, for a European Central Bank, and for a European Government.

other countries, with substantial majorities in favour of most of the countries of Central and Eastern Europe and of Malta and Cyprus.

On the question of perceived alternatives to Europe, attitudes in Britain have changed markedly over time. In 1969 far fewer people thought Europe was most important to Britain than thought the Commonwealth or the United States were (21-34-35); but by 1991 the balance had moved decisively to Europe (52-22-19).

To sum up, the evidence on public attitudes is imprecise and inconsistent, but suggests that the position is roughly as follows. Attitudes in Britain are sympathetic towards enlargement, and have moved over time towards seeing the future as lying with Europe, rather than elsewhere; but they have all along been less enthusiastic about European unification than in other EU countries, with less sense of a positive

European identity, and more opposition to many of the specific measures involved in closer union. National sovereignty is still an emotive issue and `federalism' tends to be perceived negatively in terms of giving up powers to Brussels rather than positively in terms of devolving powers to the lowest level feasible.

But alongside much chauvinism and nostalgia for the glories of the past, particularly among older people, there is also, particularly among younger people, a growing sense of `Europeanness', encouraged by increasingly easy and frequent travel to other countries. Even on unification itself, attitudes in Britain are far from consistently negative, with a majority of more than two-to-one saying they want unification to proceed rapidly rather than slowly, and a majority of no less than four-to-one expressing support for a European Government.

It appears that British attitudes to European Union are volatile and capable of moving sharply in either direction - away from Europe in times of recession when unpopular things can be blamed on Brussels, and towards Europe when media and politicians give a more positive lead. In these circumstances it may be expected that the underlying longer-term pressures will in the end prove decisive, and public attitudes will in time accommodate to them. The key issues for Britain are: what alternatives are there to Europe? And within Europe, what are the effective options available?

## Alternatives to the European Union

Before the Second World War Britain's world-view was founded on the Empire. After the war the Empire was dissolved, but the Commonwealth of independent nations which succeeded it won popular affection, and at the time of the early attempts to join the Common Market the Commonwealth was widely perceived as a viable alternative. The trading and political links between Britain and the Commonwealth were important to both.

After Britain joined the European Community, however, both the economic and political importance of the Commonwealth declined, and it now accounts for less than 10 per cent of Britain's trade[352]. Although it is still regarded as valuable by Britain and other members, it is no longer in any sense a viable economic or political alternative to the European Union.

The declining importance of the Commonwealth in the 1960s and 1970s was accompanied by an increasing interest in North Atlantic links. The `special relationship' with the United States was always asymmetrical, but was none the less rooted in bonds of common history, language, culture and institutions, and cemented by substantial trade and investment flows and by perceptions of common interest and mutual support in two world wars and the Cold War. There remains an important American cultural influence, for example in films, television, music, fashion and fast food -as, in varying degrees, there is also in other European countries.

However, the end of the Cold War seems certain to reduce American strategic interest in Europe, and in Britain as its oldest and staunchest ally; and, conversely, in Britain, it seems certain to weaken the belief that specially close ties with America are essential to Britain's security.

United States economic interest has been shifting from the Atlantic to the Pacific; and United States economic interest in Europe has shifted more towards Germany and the European Union as a whole. America's long-term economic objective is perceived as lying in the development of the North American Free Trade Area with Canada and Mexico - later to be extended to the rest of Latin America and possibly to the European Union also. There is relatively little interest in developing trade-and-investment links with Britain - except as an English-speaking member of the European Community. At present only about 12 per cent of Britain's trade is with the United States[352], and even this proportion would probably decline if Britain were no longer a full member of the European Union. So closer linkage with the United States is also not a practical alternative to Europe.

In 1958 there was a third alternative - the European Free Trade Area. However, all its former members except Norway, Switzerland, Iceland and Liechtenstein are now in the European Union. They have tried the wider free trade area idea and they are now joining the European Union - in the full knowledge that monetary union is in prospect. They have decided, after decades in a looser free trade area, that their future interests will best be served by coming into a closer union.

The alternative to the European Union, then, is not joining some other group of nations, but dropping out into economic and political isolation.

This appears to be feasible, if not in the long run profitable, for Norway with much oil and few people, and for Switzerland with its proverbially strong currency. And it might look attractive to tiny countries hoping to earn their way in the world with postage stamps, naval bases or money-laundering. It looks decidedly less hopeful for Britain, with a large but not outstandingly robust economy, which has been falling behind its partners to the extent that its GDP per head is now slightly below the EU average.

Sixty per cent of Britain's trade is now with the other fourteen members of the European Union[353]. Moreover, the other members are increasingly trading with one another, with inter-Union trade rising from 38 per cent of the total in 1961 to 62 per cent in 1991. There are also all the many other links that have been built up since Britain joined the Community more than two decades ago.

To choose to drop out of the European Union now, at a time when almost every other country in Europe is either determined to *stay in* or desperate to *come in*, and when all round the world most other countries are in the process of coming together in economic blocs, would be quixotic - and economically, politically and strategically disastrous. When even the United States feels the need for a wider union, it is bizarre to imagine that Britain could do better all alone in the world.

Thus whatever the alternatives to Europe may have been several decades ago, in the world today it is starkly clear - there *is* no alternative. The only real options for Britain are *within* Europe.

## Options in Europe

The European Union has changed greatly in the past few years, and further important changes are in prospect - a major enlargement of membership, increased use of majority-voting in the Council, greater powers for the European Parliament, monetary union and further economic and political union. Details of the form and timing are still very uncertain, but three things are already clear:

1.  There is now sufficient momentum that major changes *will* go ahead.

2.  Britain will *not* be in a position to stop the changes - if necessary the others will move on together, leaving Britain behind.

3.  Britain will not be allowed to pick and choose *à la carte* - the derogation from the Social Chapter is already being attacked as undermining the Single Market by permitting unfair competition through lowering standards. While some degree of variable geometry may be found unavoidable, there will be no question of accepting a complex patchwork of each country opting in or out, item by item.

In these circumstances there will be no gain for Britain in adopting an essentially negative posture, seeking at every point to cut back, slow down, opt out, or go into reverse. For the way the intergovernmental bargaining process works, is that each country presses its own interests, and in the final package-deal each country's most important needs are broadly met, and countries with particular difficulties normally get understanding and concessions as part of the basis for going ahead together - but on the assumption that they are all *wanting* to go ahead together.

If a country gives the impression of *not* really wanting to go ahead together anyway, it is likely to be isolated and friendless, to be unable to make fruitful alliances in the bargaining process, and to end up getting no sympathy, trade-offs or concessions. If, after looking into the abyss, it is clear that for Britain there *is* no alternative to the European Union, it follows that Britain will get the best deal from its partners if it joins positively in shaping the changes ahead, many of which appear to be very much in Britain's longer-term interest.

### Enlargement

It is very much in Britain's interest to secure stability, democracy and prosperity in the countries of Central and Eastern Europe through allowing them to join the Union. Their joining will open up new opportunities for exports and investment, but will also bring new import competition and the need for economic assistance.

### The Council

The need for Council unanimity already impedes decision-taking in many areas and threatens to bring complete paralysis after enlargement. It will therefore be necessary to extend more widely the taking of decisions by weighted majority vote. This pooling of sovereignty should be in Britain's interest in a number of important areas. It will be the only way of pushing through a radical overhaul of the CAP and releasing half of the Union's budget for other purposes; and of getting agreement on a fairer basis for national contributions to the EU budget; and for giving practical effect to a common foreign policy.

### Parliament
The limited accountability of the European Commission and the inadequate democratic participation in the working of the Union are a matter of frequent British complaint. Increased powers for the European Parliament will make the Commission more responsive to popular feelings and give British voters more sense of participation in European decision-taking - which should do much to increase interest in, and approval of, the European Union and its institutions.

### Monetary union
If monetary union goes ahead and Britain can achieve convergence in the monetary criteria, and also in the real economy, it will be in Britain's interest to join the currency union. Opting out would undermine the City of London's position as the leading financial market in Europe and put Britain at a competitive disadvantage relative to the countries within the monetary union. In particular, being perceived as outside the inner group of countries would put at risk the considerable inward investment coming to Britain - more from within the Union than any other country, and more than three times as much from outside the Union as any other EU country.

Moreover, Britain would be in a Second Division of countries outside the currency union, the other members of which were mostly outside not from choice, but from necessity. Unlike Britain, they would be actively trying to qualify to join, and at some stage might succeed in doing so - effectively relegating Britain to the Third Division of EU countries, the new members from Central and Eastern Europe. This would be likely to help continue Britain's slide in relative importance from top of the EU league (in terms of GDP per head) in 1950, to fourth place in 1973 and ninth place in 1992[354].

Whatever the problems with monetary union - and there are important ones - when it happens Britain cannot afford to be outside it.

*Economic and political union*
Monetary union is likely to be followed by closer economic union, which in turn will lead to closer political union. It can be argued that it would be more sensible for the three developments to happen in the opposite sequence. But if the fact of the matter is that monetary union is established first, and is followed by closer economic integration, Britain cannot fail to be affected by the decisions of the integrated group, and cannot afford to be left out if it is to remain one of the major economies of Europe. And if economic integration brings closer political union, Britain will not be able to keep out of that either - nor should it wish to. For macroeconomic policy is far too important to be left outside of political control. The need is to *share* sovereignty, not to *abdicate* it.

The progress of the European Union has been likened to a train heading for a destination called `European unity'. Although the train has recently been gathering speed, no-one is too sure how long the journey will take or what it will be like at the other end. Since we have the good fortune to be already on board, we are well placed to develop friendships with the other travellers, and discuss constructively with them about how best to make the journey successful - and how to ensure that our particular interests are satisfactorily met. This we can, and should do. What the other travellers have made clear is that they will *not* at this point accept any suggestion to head for some different destination, or to stop the train where it is, or even to put it into reverse. If we do not like the look of where we are all heading, of course we still have, in theory, the option of getting off and leaving the train altogether - but the train would then go on without us, and we would be left to make a long, slow, lonely walk to nowhere very inviting. Better, therefore, to stay on board and work constructively with the others.

## Unity and diversity in Europe

On balance, longer-term forces seem to be making for a larger European Union of thirty countries or more, and for closer union in a number of areas such as foreign policy, defence, the environment, technology and the economy. There appears to be sufficient momentum for greater EU involvement in these areas in the years ahead, and these are likely to result in the institutions of the Union evolving into something with many of the characteristics of a European Government. Provided it is efficient and democratic, this is a natural, pragmatic development which could bring important advantages to all the member countries, including Britain.

But it could also bring potential disadvantages. For there appear to be other areas, such as culture, education, health, social security and local services, where there will be benefit from preserving diversity and separate identities. There is a danger that central power, once established, tends to spread out into more and more areas, particularly if it grows piecemeal without the benefit of prior thought. It can thus encroach on areas where national or local autonomy is preferable, or even vital. Hence the importance of the principle of *subsidiarity* - devolving decisions to the lowest feasible level.

But subsidiarity will not be achieved just by talking abut it. If we want the things which are best done centrally to be done effectively, efficiently, openly, and with due democratic control - while also wanting the rest (including most of the detailed implementation) to be kept firmly at national, regional or local level - then we shall need to give attention to the mechanisms by which these things are to be achieved. It will not be enough to hope that an incremental jumble of disparate bits will somehow add up to a mechanism perfectly suited to our needs. At some point we shall have to face head-on the *federal* question, to arrive at a formal, codified constitutional settlement which sets out clearly the powers, functions and *limits* of central institutions, to ensure that what is best done centrally is done well, and what is not best done centrally is left alone.

Thus it seems that the underlying longer-term factors are making for a larger closer European Union; and that the only realistic future for Britain is within that union. The challenge will be to take a positive role in helping *shape* the future, so that we have a better Europe and a better place for Britain within it.

# References

## 1 Introduction

1.  Jim Northcott, *Britain in 2010*, Policy Studies Institute, London, 1991.

2.  Alexis Jacquemin and David Wright (Eds), *The European Challenges Post-1992: Shaping Factors, Shaping Actors*, Edward Elgar, Aldershot, 1993.

3.  R.Maldague, P.Leroux and A.Gilot, `Belgium: Shaping Factors', *The European Challenges Post-1992*, Edward Elgar, Aldershot, 1993.

4.  P.Nedergard and S.Thomsen, `Denmark: Shaping factors', *The European Challenges Post-1992*, Edward Elgar, Aldershot, 1993.

5.  Jean-Baptiste de Foucauld, Commissaire au Plan, *La France et L'Europe d'ici 2010: Facteurs et Acteurs décisifs*, Commissariat Général du Plan, La Documentation Française, Paris, 1993.

6.  Karl-Heinz Paqué, Rudiger Soldwedel et al, *Challenges Ahead: Long-Term Perspectives of the German Economy*, Institut für Weltwirtschaft, Kiel, 1993.

7.  G.Economu, N.Tsaveas, and P.Politis, `Greece: Shaping factors', *The European Challenges Post-1992*, Edward Elgar, Aldershot, 1993.

8.  Rory O'Donnell, *Ireland and Europe: Challenges for a New Century*, The Economic and Social Research Institute, Dublin, 1993.

9.  N.Delai and A.Mairate, `Italy: Shaping factors', *The European Challenges Post-1992*, Edward Elgar, Aldershot, 1993.

10. S.Allegrezza, `Luxembourg: Shaping Factors', *The European Challenges Post-1992*, Edward Elgar, Aldershot, 1993.

11. Frans Bletz, Willem Dercksen, Kees van Paridon, *Shaping Factors for the Business Environment in the Netherlands after 1992*, Netherlands Scientific Council for Government Policy, The Hague, 1993.

12. J.M.Gago et al, `Portugal: Shaping factors', *The European Challenges Post-1992*, Edward Elgar, Aldershot, 1993.

13. J.Segura Sanchez, `Spain: Shaping Factors', *The European Challenges Post-1992*, Edward Elgar, 1993.

14. Jim Northcott and Ian Christie, *Shaping Factors and Business Strategies in the Post-1992 European Community*, Policy Studies Institute, London, 1992.

## 2 Security

15. *Transition Report*, European Bank for Reconstruction and Development, London, October 1994.

16. Hannes Andomeit, `Russia as a great power in world affairs: images and reality', *Inernational Affairs*, Royal Institute of International Affairs, London, 1994.

17. Neil Melvin, *Forging the New Russian Nation*, Royal Institute of International Affairs, London, 1994.

18. Julian Cooper, *the Conversion of the Former Soviet Defence Industry*, Royal Institute of International Affairs, London, January 1994.

19. Trevor Taylor, `West European security and defence co-operation: Maastricht and beyond', *International Affairs*, Royal Institute of International Affairs, London, January 1994.

20. *Defending our Future: Statement on the Defence Estimates 1993*, HMSO, London, 1993.

21. Ruth Leger Sivard, *World Military and Social Expenditures 1993*, World Priorities, Washington DC, 1993.

22. Martin Fletcher, `Presidents speed dismantling of nuclear arsenals', *Times*, London, 29 September 1994.

23. *The Military balance 1993-1994*, International Institute of Strategic Studies, London, 1993.

24. Scott Sagan, *The Limits of Safety: Organisations, Accidents and Nuclear Weapons*, Princeton University Press, Princeton, 1993.

25. Michael McGwire, `Is there a future for nuclear weapons?', *International Affairs,* Royal Institute of International Affairs, London, April 1994.

26. William Walker, `Nuclear weapons in the former Soviet Republics', *International Affairs,* Royal Institute of International Affairs, London, October 1993.

27. Steve Crawshaw, `Alarm over Russia's nuclear bazaar', *Independent,* London, 16 August 1994.

28. `Nuclear experts blame Russian mafia for red mercury demand', *Times,* London, 26 July 1994.

29. John Burton, `North Korea has five nuclear bombs', *Financial Times,* London, 28 July 1994.

30. Richard Latter, *The Nuclear Threat to Global Security,* Wilton Park Paper 85, Wilton Park, Steyning, 1994.

31. Peter Rudolph, `Non-proliferation and international export controls', *Aussenpolitik, IV/91,* Hamburg, 1991.

32. John Simpson, `Nuclear non-proliferation in the post-Cold War era', *International Affairs,* Royal Institute of International Affairs, London, January 1994.

33. Peter van Ham, *Managing Non-Proliferation Régimes in the 1990s,* Pinter, for Royal Institute of International Affairs, London, 1993.

34. David Lascelles, `Thorp's order for phase 2 halved', *Financial Times,* London, 31 December 1994.

35. David White, `Europe undergoes change in defence identity', *Financial Times,* London, 12 January 1994.

36. Robert Hunter, US ambassador to NATO, quoted in `The defence of Europe: it can't be done alone', *Economist,* London, 25 February 1995.

37. Bernard Gray  and Bruce Clark, `The best lines of defence', *Financial Times,* London, 17 May 1994.

38.  William Walker and Susan Willett, `Restructuring the European Defence Base', *Defence Economics*, Harwood Academic, Switzerland, Volume 4, Number 2, August 1993.

39.  François Heisbourg, `The future direction of European security policy', *What is European Security after the Cold War?*, The Philip Morris Institute for Public Policy Research, Brussels, 1993.

40.  Manfred Wörner, Secretary General of NATO, `European security: political will plus military might', *What is European Security after the Cold War?*, The Philip Morris Institute for Public Policy Research, Brussels, 1993.

41.  Michael Lindemann, `Germans put forward EU defence plan', *Financial Times*, London, 8 June 1995.

42.  Perez de Cuéllar, UN Secretary General, in speech at the University of Bordeaux, quoted by Adam Roberts in `Humanitarian war: military intervention and human rights', *International Affairs*, Royal Institute of International Affairs, London, January 1991.

43.  Marrack Goulding, former UN Under-Secretary General for Peace-keeping Operations, `The Evolution of United Nations peacekeeping', *International Affairs*, Royal Institute of International Affairs, London, July 1991.

44.  Trevor Taylor and Ryukichi Imai (Eds), *The Defence Trade: demand, supply and control*, Royal Institute of International Affairs, London, 1994.

45.  *Human Development Report 1994*, United Nations Development Programme, New York, 1994.

46.  Bruce Clark, `World arms spending is still falling', *Financial Times*, London, 16 June 1995.

47.  Trevor Taylor (Ed), *Reshaping European Defence*, Royal Institute of International Affairs, London, 1994.

48.  *Stable Forces in a Strong Britain: Statement on the Defence Estimates 1995*, HMSO, London, 1995.

49.  *Financial Statement and Budget Report 1994-95*, HM Treasury, HMSO, London, 1994.

## 3 The Developing World

50. *Human Development Report 1994*, United Nations Development Programme, New York, 1994.

51. *Human Development Report 1992,* United Nations Development Programme, New York, 1992.

52. *Global Economic Prospects of the Developing Countries*, The International Bank for Reconstruction and Development, Washington DC, 1994.

53. Didier Blanchet, `Estimating the relationship between population growth and aggregate economic growth', *Consequences of Rapid Population Growth in Developing Countries*, Taylor and Francis, New York, 1991.

54. *Long-Range World Population Projections, 1950-2150*, Department of Economic and Social Affairs, United Nations, New York, 1992.

55. T.E.Malthus, *An Essay on the Principle of Population as it affects Future Improvement of Mankind*, 1798, reprinted Macmillan, London, 1926.

56. *World Development Report 1992: Development and the Environment*, The International Bank for Reconstruction and Development, Washington DC, 1992.

57. Michael Carley and Ian Christie, *Managing Sustainable Development*, Earthscan, London, 1992.

58. L.R.Oldeman, V.W.P. van Engelen and J.H.M.Pulles, `The extent of human-induced soil degradation', annex 5, L.R.Oldeman, R.T.A.Hackeling and W.G.Sombroek, *World Map of the Status of Human-Induced Soil Degradation: an Explanatory Note*, rev. 2nd ed., International Soil Reference and Information Centre, Wageningen, Netherlands, 1990.

59. *World Grain Database* (unpublished printouts), 1991, and *World Grain Situation and Outlook*, US Department of Agriculture, Washington DC, March 1993.

60. *Fertiliser Yearbook 1993*, United Nations Food and Agriculture Organisation, Rome, 1993, and earlier,

61. Gerald Barney, *Global 2000 Revisited*, The Millennium Institute, Arlington, Virginia, 1993.

62. UN FAO data quoted by Lester Brown, Hal Kane and Ed Ayres, *Vital Signs 1993-94*, Worldwatch Institute, Earthscan, London, 1993.

63. *Recent Developments in World Fisheries*, United Nations Food and Agriculture Organisation, Rome, 1991.

64. *World Resources 1992-93*, The World Resources Institute, New York, 1992.

65. *Water Development and Management*, Proceedings of UN conference, Mar del Plata, Argentina, 1977, Pergamon Press, Oxford.

66. Donella Meadows, Denis Meadows, Jorgen Randers, *Beyond the Limits*, Earthscan, London, 1992.

67. *Human Development Report 1993*, United Nations Development Programme, New York, 1993.

68. *The State of World Population 1993*, United Nations Population Fund, New York, 1993.

69. Sharon Russell and Michael Teitelbaum, *International Migration and International Trade*, International Bank for Reconstruction and Development, Washington DC, 1992.

70. Rouala Khalaf, `Politics mask N African population successes', *Financial Times*, London, 15 February 1995.

71. Richard Baldwin, *Towards an Integrated Europe*, Centre for Economic Policy Research, London, 1994.

72. *Financial Flows to Developing Countries in 1994*, Development Assistance Committee, Organisation for Economic Cooperation and Development, Paris, 28 June 1995.

73. *Global Economic Prospects and the Developing Countries 1993*, The International Bank for Reconstruction and Development, Washington DC, 1993.

74. *World Development Report 1993: Investing in Health*, The International Bank for Reconstruction and Development, Washington DC, 1993.

75. *World Development Report 1991: The Challenge of Development*, The International Bank for Reconstruction and Development, Washington, 1991.

76. Caroline Southey, `Seeking to aim aid at competitiveness', *Financial Times*, London, 15 February 1995.


## 4 Population and Social Change

77. Office of Population Censuses and Surveys, *1992-Based National Population Projections*, HMSO, London, 1995.

78. John Hills, *The Future of Welfare*, Joseph Rowntree Foundation, York, 1993.

79. Judy Jones, `Leading doctor urges legalising euthanasia', *Independent*, London, 14 November 1991.

80. Paul Abrahams, `Prescription costs rise by 87 per cent over 10 years', *Financial Times*, London, 17 May 1993.

81. Daniel Green, `Drug companies face cut in sales', *Financial Times*, London, 8 March 1994.

82. John Willman, `Welfare versus wealth of nations', *Financial Times*, London, 25 October 1993.

83. J.Haskey, `Current prospects for the proportion of marriages ending in divorce', *Population Trends 55*, HMSO, London, 1989.

84. P.Willmott and M.Young, *Family and Kinship in East London*, Routledge and Kegan Paul, London, 1957.

85. P.Willmott, *Social Networks, Informal Care and Public Policy*, PSI, London 1986.

86. Michael Willmott, *Planning for Social Change 1990*, Henley Centre for Forecasting, London, 1989.

87. Employment Department, quoted in *Social Trends 1995*, Central Statistical Office, HMSO, London, 1995.

88. Department of the Environment, quoted in *Social Trends 1995*, Central Statistical Office, HMSO, London, 1995.

89. David Utting, *Family and Parenthood*, Joseph Rowntree Foundation, York, 1995.

90. Antonio Golini, Bruno Cantalini and Agostino Lori, `Population Changes in Europe, Demographic and Social Prospects and Problems, *Labour Review of Economics and Industrial Relations*, vol. 5, no. 2, autumn 1991.

91. John Carvel, `EC urged to act as number of homeless reaches 2.5m', *Guardian*, London, 25 September 1993.

92. Interpol figures quoted by Terry Kirby in `British crime figures rise to highest in EC', *Independent*, London, 25 March 1992.

93. Council of Europe, quoted in *Social Trends 1995,* Central Statistical Office, HMSO, London, 1994.

94. Department of Employment, *New Earnings Survey 1994*, HMSO, London, 1994, and earlier.

95. *Employment Outlook 1993*, Organisation for Economic Cooperation and Development, Paris, 1993.

96. John Hills, *Changing Tax*, Child Poverty Action Group, London, 1988.

97. Institute for Fiscal Studies figures quoted by Robert Chote and Patricia Wynn Davies in `Tax changes have made the rich richer', *Independent*, London, 9 February 1994.

98. Lissa Goodman and Steven Webb, *For Richer for Poorer: the Changing Distribution of Income in the United Kingdom, 1961-1991*, Institute for Fiscal Studies, London, 1994.

99. *Households below Average Income: a Statistical Analysis, 1979-1992-93*, Department of Social Security, HMSO, London, 1995.

100. Lissa Goodman and Steven Webb, *The Distribution of UK Household Expenditure, 1917-1992*, Institute for Fiscal Studies, London, 1995.

101. Steven Webb, *Poverty Dynamics in Great Britain*, Institute for Fiscal Studies, London, 1995.

102 K.Gardiner, *A Survey of Income Inequality over the Last Twenty Years - How does the UK compare?*, London School of Economics, London, 1993.

103. John Hills, *Income and Wealth*, Volume 2 of Joseph Rowntree Foundation Inquiry into Income and Wealth chaired by Sir Peter Barclay, Jospeph Rowntree Foundation, York, 1995.

104. Ronald van de Krol, `Dutch parties cross swords over welfare', *Financial Times,* London, 29 April 1994.

105. Ariane Genillard, `German health spending winding down', *Financial Times*, London, 13 September 1993.

106. Quentin Peel, `Bonn seeks to patch up an ailing social state, *Financial Times*, London, 19 November 1993.

107. David Buchan, `French welfare in terminal state', *Financial Times*, London, 24 November 1993.

108. Robert Graham, `Rome reins in runaway state pension scheme', *Financial Times*, London, 31 December 1993.

109. Andrew Hill, `More funds in prospect for Italian pension plan', *Financial Times*, London, 7 April 1995.

110. International Labour Organisation figures quoted in `Ageing population must work longer to fund pensions', *Independent*, London, 26 April 1995.

111. Christopher Brown-Humes, `Sweden cuts benefits to curb deficit', *Financial Times*, London, 6 April 1995.

112. David Lipsey, `Do we really want more public spending?', in Roger Jowell, John Curtice, Lindsay Brook and Daphne Ahrendt (Eds), *British Social Attitudes: the 11th report*, Social and Community Planning Research, London, 1995.

113. Maurizio Ferrera, *EC Citizens and Social Protection*, report of a Eurobarometer survey, Commission of the European Communities, Brussels, 1993.

114. Julian Le Grand, `Can we afford the welfare state?', *British Medical Journal*, London, 23 October 1993.

115. Mark Kleinmann and David Piachaud, `Britain and European Social Policy', *Policy Studies*, PSI, London, autumn 1992.


## 5 Environment

116. R.Kershaw, *Long-Term Trends in the Distribution of the Population of England*, FACT/Department of the Environment, London, 1988.

117. *Digest of Environmental Statistics 1995*, Department of the Environment, HMSO, London, 1995.

118. Fred Pearce, `How green is your golf course?', *New Scientist*, London, 25 September 1993.

119. Chris Arnot, `City centres fall prey to march of malls', *Observer*, London, 16 October 1994.

120. Simon London, `A longer shopping list', *Financial Times*, London, 2 June 1995.

121. Stuart Hampson, *Planning for Shopping*, paper given at conference on Britain in 2010: Future Patterns in Shopping, held by Royal Society of Arts, London, 22 June 1989.

122. John Roberts, *The European Experience*, paper given at conference on Britain in 2010: Future Patterns in Shopping, held by Royal Society of Arts, London, 22 June 1989.

123. Vanessa Holden, `Shopping for a revival', *Financial Times,* London, 1 June 1994.

124. House of Commons Environment Committee, *Shopping Centres and their Future*, HMSO, 1994.

125. Neil Buckley and Simon London, `Back to where they once belonged', *Financial Times*, London, 15 May 1995.

126. Department of Transport, *Transport Statistics of Great Britain 1994*, HMSO, London, 1994.

127. Department of Transport, *London Traffic Monitoring Report 1994*, HMSO, London, 1994.

128. David Black, `London speeds up 3mph since 1912', *Independent*, London, 30 November 1989.

129. Terence Bendixson, `better a road toll than a death toll', *Observer*, London, 29 January 1989.

130. Christian Wolmar, `Roads report leak shows rising opposition', *Independent*, London, 8 November 1993.

131. Patrick Wintour, `Study admits more roads means more traffic', *Guardian*, 25 January 1994.

132. Report of Standing Advisory Committee on Trunk Road Assessment quoted by Charles Batchelor in `Report calls £2bn road-building programme into question', *Financial Times*, 20 December 1994.

133. Shyama Perera, `£1bn scheme to widen the M25 scorned as a wrong solution', *Guardian*, London, 2 March 1989.

134. Stephen Plowden and Mayer Hillman, *Danger on the Road: Needless Scourge*, PSI, London, 1984.

135. *Trends in the Transport Sector, 1970-1993*, ECMT, Paris, 1995.

136. `Copenhagen: bus lanes replace motorway schemes', *Independent*, London,25 March 1994.

137. Centraal Bureau voor de Statistiek, *De Mobiliteit van de Nederlandse Bevolking 1989*, the Hague, 1990.

138. David Pearce, *Blueprint 3: Measuring Sustainable Development*, Earthscan, London, 1993.

139. *Myths and Facts: Transport Trends and Transport Policies*, Transport 2000, London, 1994.

140. Mayer Hillman, `Influencing personal travel decisions: the role of public policy' in J.D.Carr (Ed) *Passenger Transport: Planning for Radical Change*, Gower, Aldershot, 1986.

141. Charles Batchelor, `M-way toll trials soon', *Financial Times*, London, 16 September 1994.

142. Hamilton Fazey, `Road tolls plan moves nearer', *Financial Times*, London, 21 September 1993.

143. Charles Batchelor, `Sharp cuts in road building programme', *Financial Times*, London, 30 November 1994.

144. Christian Wolmar, `Bicycle schemes to get higher profile', *Independent*, London, 8 September 1993.

145. *18th Report of the Royal Commission on Environmental Pollution, Transport and the Environment*, HMSO, London, 1994.

146. Roger Stokes and Bridget Taylor, `Where next for transport policy?' in Roger Jowell, John Curtice, Lindsay Brook and Daphne Ahrendt (Eds), *British Social Attitudes the 11th Report 1994/95*, Social and Community Planning Research, London, 1994.

147. *European Attitudes towards Urban Traffic Problems and Public Transport*, Eurobarometer, Commission of the European Communities, Brussels, July 1991.

148. Tony Bush, `Motorways are not free', *Financial Times*, London, 31 January 1995.

149. Ian Rodger, `Trucks headed off at the pass', *Financial Times*, London, 26 February 1994.

150. Chris Gossop and Adrian Webb, `Getting around: public and private transport' in Andrew Blowers (Ed), *Planning for a Sustainable Environment*, Town and Country Planning Association, Earthscan, London, 1993.

151. *The Future Development of the Common Transport Policy: a Global Approach to the Construction of a Community Framework for Sustainable Mobility*, Bulletin of the European Communities, Supplement 3/93, Brussels, 1993.

152. Nicholas Schoon, `Strict lead limits in water to cost £8.5bn', *Independent*, 20 October 1994.

153. Richard North, `Britain will end dumping in North Sea by 1998', *Independent*, London, 6 March 1990.

154. `Britain's beaches left to wait for sewage clean-up', *Independent*, London, 11 February 1995.

155. Polly Ghazi, `UK loses North Sea war on pollution', *Observer*, London, 26 March 1995.

156. Nicholas Schoon, `Extra spending has led to cleaner rivers', *Independent*, London, 1 June 1994.

157. *Toxic Waste: Second Report of the Environment Committee, 1988-89*, House of Commons Paper 22-1, HMSO, London, 1989.

158. John Ardill, `Tory MP leads attack over near disaster on waste', *Guardian*, London, 9 March 1989.

159. *Packaging and Packaging Waste*, House of Lords Committee on the European Communities, HMSO, London, 1993.

160. Neil Buckley, `EU ministers wrap up agreement on packaging', *Financial Times*, London, 29 December 1993.

161. Bronwen Maddox, `Recycling target seen as a load of rubbish', *Financial Times*, London, 28 April 1994.

162. Michael Lindemann, `Green light begins to flash for recyclable cars in Germany', *Financial Times*, London, 3 August 1994.

163. Christopher Brown-Humes, `Running on rubbish', *Financial Times*, London, 4 May 1994.

164. M.Sandnes, *Country to Country Deposition Budget Matrices for the Years 1985, 1987, 1989, 1990 and 1991*, EMEP/MSC-W Report 1/92, 1992.

165. *Environmental Data Report 1993-94*, United Nations Environment Programme, Blackwell, Oxford, 1994.

166. *World Development Report 1992: Development and the Environment*, The International Bank for Reconstruction and Development, Washington DC, Oxford University Press, Oxford, 1992.

167. World Resources Institute, Washington DC quoted in `Disappearing forests fan fears over tropical action plan' *New Scientist*, London, 23 January 1990.

168. Greta Nilsson, *The Endangered Species Handbook*, Animal Welfare Institute, Washington DC, 1990.

169. Norman Myers, *Biodiversity and Biodepletion*, Green College Centre for Environmental Policy and Understanding, Oxford University, Oxford, 1993.

170. Paul Ehrlich and Edward Wilson, `Biodiversity studies: science and policy', *Science*, 16 August 1991.

171. Sir Crispin Tickell, *The Diversity of Life*, lecture to the Oxford Scientific Society, 12 November, Green College, Oxford University, Oxford, 1993.

172. *Vital Signs 1994*, Worldwatch Institute, Washington DC, 1994.

173. Peter Knight, `Climate cools to CFCs', *Financial Times*, London, 23 February 1994.

174. Leonie J. Archer, *Aircraft Emissions and the Environment: $CO_2$, $SO_2$, $HO_2$, $NO_2$*, Oxford Institute for Energy Studies, Oxford, 1993.

175. *Report of the Intergovernmental Panel on Climate Change*, United Nations Environment Programme and World Meteorological Organisation, 1990.

176. `Busy bacteria may reduce the risk of a runaway greenhouse', *New Scientist*, London, 26 May 1990.

177. John Sinclair, `Global warming may distort carbon cycle', *New Scientist*, London, 26 May 1990.

178. Peter Kilworth, Hook Institute of Atmosphere Research, Oxford, quoted by William Brown in `Flipping Oceans could turn up the heat', *New Scientist*, London, 25 August 1990.

179. Peter Wadhams, Scott Polar Research Institute director, quoted by Robin McKie in `Warmer world skates on even thinner ice', *Observer*, London, 22 July 1990.

180. John Gribbin, `Methane may amplify climate change', *New Scientist*, London, 2 June 1990.

181. Martin Parry, senior agricultural advisor on IPCC report team, quoted by Tom Wilkie in `Danger to bread-baskets from global warming spelt out', *Independent*, London, 25 October 1990.

182. Tim Radford, `Iceberg linked to global warming', *Guardian*, London, 1 March 1995.

183. Paul Brown, Minister pledges war on warming', *Guardian*, London, 9 March 1995.

184. *Annual Abstract of Statistics 1995,* Central Statistical Office, HMSO, London, 1995.

185. Walt Patterson, `Energy issues another challenge', *New Scientist*, London, 28 January 1989.

186. *Renewable Energy Sources Statistics 1989-91*, Eurostat, Commission of the European Communities, Brussels, 1995.

187. Nicholas Schoon, `Number of windfarms set to double by 2000', *Independent*, London, 21 December 1994.

188. Paul Brown, `Wave power undercuts nuclear cost', *Guardian*, London, 19 March 1990.

189. Russell Buxton, `Gas turbine systems', in Michael Grubb and John Walker (Eds), *Emerging Energy Technologies: Impacts and Policy Implications*, Royal Institute of International Affairs, London, 1992.

190. Michael Grubb, `Wind energy', in Michael Grubb and John Walker (Eds), *Emerging Energy Technologies: Impacts and Policy Implications*, Royal Institute of International Affairs, London, 1992.

191. Bob Hill, `Solar electricity from photovoltaics', in Michael Grubb and John Walker (Eds), *Emerging Energy Technologies: Impacts and Policy Implications*, Royal Institute of International Affairs, London, 1992.

192. Keith Rouse, `Building energy management' in Michael Grubb and John Walker (Eds), *Emerging Energy Technologies: Impacts and Policy Implications*, Royal Institute of International Affairs, London, 1992.

193. Association for the Conservation of Energy, memorandum to Energy Committee of the House of Commons, memoranda of Evidence, Volume II, *Energy Implications of the Greenhouse Effect, Sixth Report, Energy Committee of the House of Commons*, HMSO, London, 1989.

194. George Graham, `Wonder lightbulb saves energy', *Financial Times*, London, 22 October 1994.

195. March Consulting Group, *Energy Efficiency in Domestic Electric Appliances*, report for the Energy Efficiency Office , Department of Energy, HMSO, London, 1990.

196. `Most and least efficient appliances', *Which?*, Consumers' Association, London, August 1994.

197. J.Goldenberg, T.Johansson, A Reddy and R.Williams, *Energy for a Sustainable World*, World Resources Institute, Washington DC, 1987.

198. John Carvel, `Britain halts new EU plan to tax energy, *Guardian*, London, 6 October 1994.

199. `Rules for EU tax on energy', *Financial Times*, London, 11 May 1995.

200. Terry Barker, *Taxing Pollution instead of Jobs*, paper at conference on Full Employment in Europe, at Robinson College, Cambridge University, 7-8 July 1994, Cambridge Econometrics, Cambridge, 1994.

201. Ian Christie and Heather Rolfe with Robin Legrand, *Cleaner Production in Industry: integrating business goals and environmental management*, Policy Studies Institute, London, 1995.

202. ECOTEC, *The UK Environmental Industry: succeeding in the changing global market*, Department of Trade and Industry/Department of the Environment, HMSO, London, 1994.

203. Sharon Witherspoon, `The greening of Britain: romance and rationality', Roger Jowell, John Curtice, Lindsay Brook and Daphne Ahrendt, *British Social Attitudes: the 11th report, 1994/95*, Social and Community Planning Research, London, 1994.

204. *Eurobarometer 41*, Commission of the European Communities, Brussels, July 1994.

# 6 Employment

205. OECD, *The OECD Jobs Study: Facts, Analysis, Strategies*, Organisation for Economic Cooperation and Development, Paris, 1994.

206. Eurostat figures quoted by Robert Taylor in `Clocking up the overtime', *Financial Times*, London, 25 January 1995.

207. `Labour market survey among employees', *European Economy*, Commission of the European Communities, Brussels, October 1994.

208. *Employment Outlook*, Organisation for Economic Cooperation and Development, Paris, July 1994.

209. *Employment in Europe*, Commission of the European Communities, Brussels 1994.

210. *European Social Policy: a way forward for the Union*, White Paper, Commission of the European Communities, Brussels 1994.

211. Caroline Southey, `Opt-out Britain tops EU league table on social laws', *Financial Times*, 13 May 1995.

212. David Gardner, `Historic EU accord on works councils', *Financial Times*, London, 23 June 1994.

213. Jim Northcott and Petra Rodgers, *Microelectronics in British Industry: what's happening in Britain*, PSI, London, 1982.

214. Jim Northcott and Petra Rodgers, *Microelectronics in British Industry: the pattern of change*, PSI, London, 1984.

215. Jim Northcott, *Microelectronics in British Industry: promise and performance*, PSI, London, 1986.

216. Jim Northcott and Annette Walling, *The Impact of Microelectronics: diffusion, benefits and problems in British industry*, PSI, London, 1988.

217. Jim Northcott, Petra Rodgers, Werner Knetsch and Bérengère de Lestapis, *Microelectronics in Industry: an international comparison: Britain, France and Germany*, PSI, London, 1990.

218. Ian Christie, Jim Northcott and Annette Walling, *Employment Effects of New Technology in Manufacturing*, PSI, London, 1990.

219. Jim Northcott, Colin Brown, Ian Christie, Michael Sweeney and Annette Walling, *Robots in British Industry: expectations and experience*, PSI, London, 1986.

220. Jim Northcott, Colin Fogarty and Malcolm Trevor, *Chips and Jobs: acceptance of new technology at work*, PSI, London, 1985.

221. W.W.Daniel, *Workplace Industrial Relations and Technical Change*, PSI, London, 1986.

222. M.Rigg, I.Christie and M.White, *Advanced Polymers and Composites: creating key skills*, PSI for Training Agency, Sheffield, 1989.

223. Werner Knetsch and Mario Kliche, *Die Industrielle Mikroelektronik-Anwsendung in Verarbeitenden Gewerbe der Bundesrepublik Deutschland*, VDI-VDE, Technologiezentrum, Berlin, 1986.

224. Bérengère de Lestapis, *Diffusion de la Micro-Electronique dans l'Industrie*, Bureau d'Informations et de Prévisions Economiques (BIPE), Paris, 1985.

225. Olof Löfgren, *Microelectronics in Swedish Industry*, National Industrial Board, Stockholm, 1988.

226. Ulrik Jrgensen and K.S.Vilstrup, *Spredning af Informatiionsteknologi i Dansk Industri 1987*, Institut for Forbrugs-og-Hondningsanalyser, Copenhagen, 1988.

227. Robert Bowie and Alan Bollard, *The Diffusion of Microelectronics through New Zealand Manufacturing*, New Zealand Institute of Economic Research, Wellington, 1987.

228. S.Prais and K.Wagner, `Productivity and management: the training of foremen in Britain and Germany', *National Institute Economic Review*, no.123, London, February 1988.

229. M.Rigg, *Training in Britain: individuals' perspectives*, PSI, HMSO, London, 1989.

230. John Authors and Lisa Wood, `Little knowledge is a dangerous thing', *Financial Times, London, 15 December 1993.*

231. Education Statistics for the UK 1994, *Department of Education, HMSO, London,1995.*

232. *Education at a Glance: OECD indicators*, Organisation for Economic Cooperation and Development, Paris, 1995.

233. Alan Smithers and Pamela Robinson, *Post-18 Education: growth, change, prospect*, Council for Industry and Higher Education, London, 1995.

234. Eurostat figures quoted in *Social Trends 1994*, HMSO, London, 1994.

235. Robert Chote, `Dole count should be replaced' *Financial Times*, London, 5 April 1995.

236. Emma Tucker, `Measures which obscured the extent of joblessness', *Financial Times*, London, 20 May 1994.

237. Larry Elliott and Ruth Kelly, `Unemployment and figures of speech', *Guardian*, London, 10 January 1994.

238. James Nicholson, `Dole queue drop masks inactivity', `*Guardian*, London, 20 June 1994.

239. *Economic Trends*, Central Statistical Office, HMSO, London, April 1995.

240. Michael White, *Against Unemployment*, PSI, London, 1991.

241. Council of Mortgage Lenders, press release, London, February 1991.

242. Margaret Whitehead, *The Health Divide*, 1987.

243. Michaela Benzeval, Ken Judge and Margaret Whitehead, *Tackling Inequalities in Health*, King's Fund, London, 1995.

244. Ruth Kelly and Larry Elliott, `Study links crime to jobless rise', *Guardian*, 7 January 1994.

245. Terry Kirby, `70 per cent of convicted offenders are found to be unemployed', *Independent*, London, 9 April 1994.

246. Cambridge Econometrics, `Industry and the British Economy', quoted by Alan Pike, `Services seen as major job creators', *Financial Times*, London, 4 January 1994.

247. Paul Ormerod, `The Western employment policy is going round in circles', *Demos Quarterly*, Demos London, 2, 1994.

248. Andrew Glyn, `The assessment: unemployment and equality', *Oxford Review of Economic Policy*, Oxford University Press, Oxford, spring 1995.

249. Robert Rowthorn, `Capital formation and Unemployment', *Oxford Review of Economic Policy*, Oxford University Press, Oxford, spring 1995.

250. Barrie Stevens and Wolfgang Michalski, *Long-term Prospects for Work and Social Cohesion in OECD Countries*, Organisation for Economic Cooperation and Development, Paris, 1994.

251. Geoff Mulgan and Helen Wilkinson, `Well-being and time, *Demos*, London, 5, 1995.

252. *White Paper: Growth, Competitiveness, Employment: the challenges and ways forward into the 21st century*, White Paper, Commission of the European Communities, Brussels, 1993.

253. Terry Barker, *Taxing Pollution instead of Jobs*, paper at Cambridge Econometrics conference on `Full employment in Europe', at Robinson College, Cambridge, 7-8 July 1994.

## 7 The Economy

254. *Human Development Report 1994*, United Nations Developntent Programme, New York, 1994.

255. *Main Economic Development Indicators*, Organisation for Economic Cooperation and Development, Paris, May 1995.

256. *Annual Abstract of Statistics 1995*, HMSO, London, 1995, and earlier.

257. *European Economy: 1994 Broad Economic Policy Guidelines*, Commission of the European Communities, Brussels, 1994.

258. N.Crafts and G.Toniolo, *Post-war Growth: an overview*, Centre for Economic Policy Research, London, 1995.

259. Cambridge Econometrics projections in Jim Northcott, *Britain in 2010*, PSI, London, 1991.

260. ERECO and IFO projections quoted by Kurt Vogler-Ludwig, `Effects on industries and regions', paper at Cambridge Econometrics conference on *Full Employment in Europe*, at Robinson College, Cambridge, 7-8 July 1994.

261. OECD figures quoted in *Financial Times*, London, 25 February 1994.

262. A.D.Cosh, A.Hughes and R.E.Rowthorn, `The competitive role of UK manufacturing industry 1979-2003', Kirsty Hughes (Ed), *The Future of UK Competitiveness and the Role of Industrial Policy*, PSI, London, 1993.

263. *Economic Trends*, Central Statistical Office, HMSO, London, April 1995, and earlier.

264. Guy de Jonquières, `Can Europe compete? Service Industries', *Financial Times*, London, 1 March 1994.

265. John Gapper and Tracy Corrigan, `Can Europe compete? Financial Services', *Financial Times*, 4 March 1994.

266. Robert Rowthorn, `Capital formation and unemployment', *Oxford Review of Economic Policy*, Oxford University Press, Oxford, spring 1995.

267. *Competitiveness and Cohesion: trends in the regions*, Commission of the European Communities, Brussels, 1994.

268. *Eurobarometer*, no. 41, Commission of the European Communities, Brussels, July 1994.

269. CBI survey figures quoted by Gillian Tett in `CBI fuels short-termism debate', *Financial Times*, London, 25 July 1994.

270. *STI Database*, Organisation for Economic Cooperation and Development, Paris, February 1995.

271. `Research after Maastricht: an assessment, a strategy', *Bulletin of the European Communities*, supplement 2/92, Commission of the European Communities, Brussels, 1992.

272. `An industrial competitiveness policy for the European Union', *Bulletin of the European Union*, supplement 3/94, Commission of the European Communities, Brussels, 1994.

273. `The GATT deal', *Financial Times*, London, 16 December 1993.

274. *World Investment Report 1993: transnational corporations and international production*, United Nations, New York, 1995.

275. *The State of World Population 1994*, United Nations Population Fund, New York, 1994.

276. Alexander Nicoll, `China fingers crossed for safe landing' in `IMF World Economy and Finance', *Financial Times*, London, 24 September 1993.

277. Figures from IMF and central banks quoted in `Foreign Exchange Survey', *Financial Times*, London, 26 May 1993.

278. *World Development Report 1993*, International Bank for Reconstruction and Development, Washington DC, 1993.

279. *Foreign Exchange Management*, Touche Ross, London, 1993.

280. *Monthly Digest of Statistics*, Central Statistical Office, HMSO, London, June 1995, and earlier.

281. Martin Wolf, `Doing good, despite ourselves', *Financial Times*, London, 16 December 1993.

282. J.Howells, M.Wood, *The Globalisation of Production and Technology*, Centre for Urban and Regional Studies, University of Newcastle upon Tyne, for FAST MONITOR Programme, Forecasting and Assessment in Science and Technology, Commission of the European Communities, Brussels, 1991.

283. P.Cecchini, *The European Challenge 1992: the benefits of a single market*, Wildwood House, London, 1988.

284. Andrew Hill, `Balloon struggles to get airborne', *Financial Times*, London, 5 January 1994.

285. GATT Secretariat Background Paper, *An Analysis of the Proposed Uruguay Round Agreement with Particular Emphasis on Aspects of Interest to Developing Countries*, GATT, Geneva, 1993.

286. Samuel Brittan, `Where GATT's $200bn really comes from', *Financial Times*, London, 4 October 1993.

287. *Assessing the Effects of the Uruguay Round*, Trade Policy Issues 2, Organisation for Economic Cooperation and Development, Paris, February, 1995.

288. Matthew Crabbe, `Cashing in on the cash', *Sunday Times*, London, 27 September 1992.

289. James Blitz and Emma Tucker, `Pointing a finger is pure speculation', *Financial Times*, London, 25 September 1992.

290. Matthew Lynn, `Traders get a warm glow from hot money', *Sunday Times*, London, 20 September 1992.

291. Dan Atkinson, `Crisis fuelled by hot money', *Guardian*, London, 18 September 1992.

292. `Sterling is being sold like water running out of a tap', in `ERM and Maastricht', *Financial Times*, London, 20 September 1992.

## 9 Monetary Union

294 `One money one market', *European Economy*, no. 44, Commission of the European Communities, Brussels, 1992.

294. Geoffrey Denton, *Federalism and the European Union after Maastricht*, Wilton Park Paper 67, Wilton Park, Steyning, 1993.

295. Opinion polls by MORI in Britain and by Emnid in Germany in November 1994, reported in *Financial Times*, London, 5 December 1994.

296. *Survey on the Introduction of the Single Currency: a First Contribution on the Practical Aspects*, European Banking Federation, Brussels, 1995.

297. *Main Economic Indicators*, Organisation for Economic Cooperation and Development, Paris, May 1995.

298. Lionel Barber and David Buchan, `EU leaders plan 1999 launch for Euro-currency', *Financial Times*, London, 27 June 1995.

299. John Gapper and Lionel Barber, `European banks issue EMU warning', *Financial Times*, London, 20 September 1994.

300. Peter Ludlow with Niels Ersbll and Raymond Barre, *Preparing for 1996 and a Larger European Union: principles and priorities*, Centre for European Policy Studies, Brussels, 1995.

301. Philip Gawith, `Tietmeyer sets out tough line on EMU convergence criteria', *Financial Times*, London, 5 November 1994.

302. Karl Lamers, `Compelling case for monetary union', *Financial Times*, London, 7 November 1994.

303. Tichard Portes (Ed), *The Making of Monetary Union*, Centre for Economic Policy Research, London, 1991.

304. Donald Sassoon, `A new political order?', in David Marquand (Ed), *A More Perfect Union?*, Institute for Public Policy Research, London, 1992.

305. Michael Shackleton, `Democratic accountability in the European Union', in Frank Brouwer, Valerio Linter and Michael Newman (Eds), *Economic Policy Making in the European Union*, Federal Trust, London, 1994.

306. *Towards the Single Currency*, Federal Trust Papers for the Intergovernmental Conference of the European Union, Federal Trust, London, 1995.

307. Stuart Holland, *The European Imperative*, Spokesman, Nottingham, 1993.

308. Christopher Johnson, `Fiscal and monetary policy in the Economic and Monetary Union', in Frank Brouwer, Valerio Linter and Michael Newman (Eds), *Economic Policy Making in the European Union*, Federal Trust, London, 1994.

309. *Competitiveness and Cohesion: trends in the regions*, Commission of the European Communities, Brussels, 1994.

310. José Vinals, *Building a Monetary Union in Europe: is it worthwhile, where do we stand, and where are we going?*, Centre for Economic Policy Research, London, 1994.

311 P. De Grauwe and W.Vanhaverbeke, `Labour markets and European monetary unification', in P.R.Masson and M.P.Taylor (Eds), *Policy Issues in the European Community*, Cambridge University Press, Cambridge, 1993.

312. J.Sachs and X.Sala-i-Martin, `Fiscal federalism and optimum currency areas: evidence for Europe and the United States', in M.Canzonieri, V.Grilli and P.R.Masson (Eds), *Establishing a Central Bank: Issues in Europe and Lessons from the US*, Cambridge University Press, Cambridge, 1992.

313. MacDougall, *Report of the Study Group on the Role of Public Finance in European Integration*, Commission of the European Communities, Brussels, 1977.

314. Dieter Biehl, `The public finances of the Union', in Andrew Duff, John Pinder and Roy Price (Eds), *Maastricht and beyond: building the European Union*, Federal Trust, London, 1994.

## 10 Enlargement

315. *PHARE, Assistance for Economic Restructuring in the Countries of Central and Eastern Europe*, Commission of the European Communities, Brussels, 1992.

316. *Europinion*, Commission of the European Communities, Brussels, January 1995.

317. *Europinion*, Commission of the European Communities, Brussels, May 1994.

318. *The Enlargement of the European Union*, Background Report, Commission of the European Communities, London, 1994.

319. *The Challenge of Enlargement: Commission opinion on the application of the Republic of Cyprus for membership*, Commission of the European Communities, Brussels, 1993.

320. Ian Rodger, `Swiss seek EU deals', *Financial Times*, London, 24 January 1995.

321. *Transition Report*, European Bank for Reconstruction and Development, London, 1994.

322. UN/ECE figures quoted by Frances Williams in `West urged to step up aid to Eastern Europe', *Financial Times*, London, 6 December 1994.

323. Damien Neven, `Trade liberalisation in Eastern Europe' in Riccardo Faini and Richard Portes (Eds), *European Trade with Eastern Europe: adjustment and opportunities*, Centre for Economic Policy Research, London, 1995.

324. Nicholas Hopkinson, *Enlarging the European Union in Northern, Central and Eastern Europe*, Wilton Park Paper 81, Wilton Park, Steyning, 1994.

325. *Central and Eastern Eurobarometer*, Commission of the European Communities, Brussels, March, 1995.

326. *European Economy no. 58, 1994, Broad Economic Policy Guidelines*, Commission of the European Communities, Brussels, 1994.

327. K.Anderson and R.Tyers, *Implications of EC Expansion for European Agricultural Policies*, Centre for Economic Policy Research, London, 1993.

328. T.Coucherne and others, `Stable money - sound finances', *European Economy no.53*, Commission of the European Communities, Brussels, 1993.

329. John Morrison, `Pereyaslav and after: the Russian-Ukrainian relationship', *International Affairs*, the Royal Institute of International Affairs, London, October, 1993.

330. *The State of World Population 1993*, United Nations Population Fund, United Nations, New York, 1993.

331. David Gardner, `Brussels urges wider trade zone', *Financial Times*, London, 20 October 1994.

332. Richard Baldwin, *Towards an Integrated Europe*, Centre for Economic Policy Research, London, 1994.

333. *The World in 1995*, The Economist, London, 1994.

334. Kirsty Hughes, `European enlargement, competitiveness and integration', in P.Devine, Y.Katsoulacos and R.Sugden, *Competitiveness, Subsidiarity and Objectives: issues for European industrial strategy*, 1995.

335. *World Development Report 1995: workers in an integrating world*, International Bank for Reconstruction and Development, Washington DC, 1995.

336. Anna Michalski and Helen Wallace, *The European Community: the challenge of enlargement*, Royal Institute of International Affairs, London, 1992.

337. Richard Porter (Ed), *Is Bigger Better? the economics of EC enlargement*, Centre for Economic Policy Research, London, 1993.

338. Peter Ludlow with Niels Ersbll and Raymond Barre, *Preparing for 1996 and a Larger European Union: principles and priorities*, Centre for European Policy Studies, Brussels, 1995.

## 11 The Future of Europe

339. *Eurobarometer no. 41*, Commission of the European Communities, Brussels, July 1994.

340. *Central and Eastern Eurobarometer*, Commission of the European Communities, Brussels, March 1995.

341. Richard Baldwin, *Towards an Integrated Europe*, Centre for Economic Policy Research, London, 1994.

342. Jonathan Ockenden and Michael Franklin, *European Agriculture: making the CAP fit the future*, Royal Institute of International Affairs, London, 1992.

343. Court of Auditors, *Annual Report concerning the Financial Year 1993*, Commission of the European Communities, Brussels, 24 November 1994.

344. Michael Franklin, *The EC Budget: realism, redistribution and radical reform*, Royal Institute of International Affairs, London, 1992.

345. *European Economy no. 58, broad economic policy guidelines*, Commission of the European Communities, Brussels, 1994.

346 John Fitzmaurice, `The European Commission', in Andrew Duff, John Pinder and Tony Price (Eds), *Maastricht and beyond: building the European Union*, Federal Trust, London, 1994.

347. Peter Ludlow with Niels Ersbll and Raymond Barre, *Preparing for 1996 and a Larger European Union: principles and priorities*, Centre for European Policy Studies, Brussels, 1995.

348. *Eurobarometer no. 38*, Commission of the European Communities, Brussels, December 1992.

## 12 The Future of Britain and Europe

349. *Eurobarometer no. 41*, Commission of the European Communities, Brussels, July 1994.

350. Eurobarometer no. 38, Commission of the European Communities, Brussels, December 1992.

351. Harris Research, European Opinion Poll, *Financial Times*, 1 June 1994.

352. *Annual Abstract of Statistics 1995*, Central Statistical Office, HMSO, London, 1995.

353. *European Economy no. 58, broad economic policy guidelines*, Commission of the European Communities, Brussels, 1994.

354. N.Crafts and G.Toniolo, *Post-war Growth: an overview*, Centre for Economic Policy Research, London, 1995.